Cooking Healthy

with the

Kids in
Mind

Cooking Healthy

with the

Kids in Mind

A Healthy Exchanges® Cookbook

JoAnna M. Lund

with Barbara Alpert

G. P. Putnam's Sons
New York

Before using the recipes and advice in this book, consult your physician or health-care provider to be sure they are appropriate for you. The information in this book is not intended to take the place of any medical advice. It reflects the author's experiences, studies, research, and opinions regarding a healthy lifestyle. All material included in this publication is believed to be accurate. The publisher assumes no responsibility for any health, welfare, or subsequent damage that might be incurred from use of these materials.

G. P. Putnam's Sons
Publishers Since 1838
a member of
Penguin Putnam Inc.
200 Madison Avenue
New York, NY 10016

For more information about Healthy Exchanges products, contact:
Healthy Exchanges, Inc.
P.O. Box 124
DeWitt, Iowa 52742-0124
(319) 659-8234

Published simultaneously in Canada

Diabetic exchanges calculated by Rose Hoenig, R.D., L.D.

ISBN 0-399-14358-0

Printed in the United States of America

BOOK DESIGN BY AMANDA DEWEY

This book is dedicated in loving memory to my parents, Jerome and Agnes McAndrews, who taught me the true meaning of the word "family." Family isn't about *where* people live, it's about *how* they live. Our house was modest, but the love and loyalty within our home were immense.

This book is also dedicated to families everywhere who share that same love and loyalty. Family can mean many things—from households headed by single mothers to homes where a widowed father is "doing his best," from houses where three generations happily coexist to *all* the other definitions of family, regardless of race, color, or creed.

As usual, my mother had an appropriate poem in her vast collection for helping us find the beauty in how God created all of us as brothers and sisters in the family of mankind.

God's Paint Brush

I watched God's paint brush sweep across a winter sky
One early morning, as the brightening sunrise came into
      view.
No artist could ever duplicate its splendor or even try
To blend the gorgeous colors of every shade and hue.
Because no one but the Master has the paints and touch
To paint a perfect sunrise amid the drop of majestic sky,
Likewise, only He can create the world and such
And in His infinite greatness, creatures like you and I.

—*Agnes Carrington McAndrews*

Acknowledgments

As a mother and grandmother whose children have "flown the coop," nothing gives me more pleasure than those precious times when my entire family gathers together at my dinner table to enjoy foods I've stirred up for them with love. Give me my mixing bowl, my wire whisk, and my family—and I have a successful recipe for celebration!

For helping me share my "successful recipe" with others, I want to publicly express my love and thanks to:

Cliff Lund, my husband and the stepfather of my children "by law," but according to them, their father in every sense of the word "by love." Cliff makes sure all the boring necessary work is done so that I can do all the exciting fun things. He is, as the song says, "the wind beneath my wings."

Becky and John Taylor, James and Pam Dierickx, and Tom and Angie Dierickx, my children. I must have taught my kids well, because they all chose spouses whom I couldn't love and respect more! Best of all, my kids pitch in to help with whatever needs doing at Healthy Exchanges. The growth of my business brought us closer together instead of driving us further apart.

Zachary and Joshua Dierickx, my precious grandchildren and the sparkle of my eyes. Their hugs and kisses mean more to me than all the gold stored in Fort Knox.

Mary Benischek and Regina Reyes, my sisters. How proud our parents in Heaven must be, knowing that we are working together and using our talents we inherited from them as I spread my message of HELP to others. Mary's bluegrass band provides the theme music for both my radio and public television programs, and Regina makes sure that my words are spelled correctly in my books and newsletters.

Loretta Rothbart, Juanita Dithmart, and Dale Lund, my sisters- and brother-in law. What a great group of cheerleaders!

Loretta is our office manager, Juanita works in our café, and Dale helps move "whatever" whenever "whatever" needs moving.

Cleland and Marjorie Lund, my parents-in-law. It's been almost twenty years now since they opened their arms wide and lovingly brought me and my children into the Lund fold.

John Duff, my editor. When I chose to work with a "New York publisher," I never dreamed that not only would I get a top-notch editor, but that I would gain a friend as well.

Angela Miller and Coleen O'Shea, my agents. If family means those people you can both trust and depend on, then they most certainly qualify!

Barbara Alpert, my writing partner. We've grown so close over the few years we've worked together, I consider her not only a friend, but a sister-in-spirit.

Rose Hoenig, R.D., L.D., my dietetic consultant. We met by "chance" six years ago, and have been happily working together as a team ever since.

Phyllis Grann, Susan Petersen, Liz Perl, Barbara O'Shea, and everyone at Putnam who has become part of my "publishing family." A better team can't be found!

John McEwen, John McLean, Pattye O'Connor, Chris Rylko, Jenny Steinle, and everyone at West 175, the producers of my public television program. With their help, I've been able to visit so many families all over America on a weekly basis, which otherwise I never could have done.

Karen Foner, Paula Percy, and everyone at QVC who realized that what I have to share is just what their audience wanted. I'm both proud and honored that they've accepted me into the QVC family, and I'm grateful for the opportunities they've given me.

The men, women, and children all over America who've chosen to break bread with my "common folk" healthy dishes at their dinner tables. No greater honor will ever be given me than knowing that my recipes are being enjoyed in so many households.

And God, my Creator, through Whom all my blessings flow, from the love of my family to the food on our table.

Contents

■ ■ ■ ■ ■ ■ ■ ■

The Recipes

Introduction

■ ■ ■ ■ ■ ■ ■ ■ ■

Why Raising a Healthy Family Is a Great Goal, and How to Make It Happen

Family has always been part of Healthy Exchanges since the very first day I decided to stop dieting and start living healthy. I wanted to be healthy so I wouldn't be a burden to my children; I wanted to find recipes that were tasty enough to feed my husband and my son still living at home; I wanted to live long enough to be a grandmother and watch those beautiful babies grow up. Because I cared so much about my family, I found the courage to change my path for the better.

Family is also at the heart of who I am. Every one of my books is dedicated to my parents, who gave their children so much, no matter how little they had. My sisters help me in my work, and we've found real satisfaction in working together. Most of all, my children, now all grown-up, give me the greatest joy in my life, no matter how much pleasure I take in the success of Healthy Exchanges.

That's why this book is especially dear to my heart, and why I hope it will bring families everywhere together around the dinner table—and together in good health. With Healthy Exchanges recipes on the menu, family members can enjoy eating together again—no dull diet meals for Mom, no special dishes for Dad who's watching his blood pressure, and because everything is so tasty and fun to eat, even your kids will relish dining at home instead of at the local fast-food joint. Everything is here, from delicious but quick hot breakfasts, lunches to eat at home or at school, dinners so filling everyone will be satisfied—plus irresistible desserts, great snacks, and terrific party foods—all of them healthy and with the exchanges already figured out for you.

I wrote this book because I wanted to share with others what I wish I'd known when I was raising my own children, and what I now share with my grandkids. So often, parents come home exhausted, especially now that they have to work harder and companies have cut their staffs. Hearing the hungry voices of children wondering what's for dinner is enough to drive any Mama bird crazy trying to figure out what to feed all those little birds in her nest.

Every child has personal tastes, and those tastes change often during childhood. (Onions might be "yecch" at age three and "yum" by age six.) Only by trying a variety of foods can you determine what your child is willing and happy to eat, but when you've got an abundance of *healthy* possibilities, you can feel confident about whatever they choose. (One of the reasons kids are such good taste testers is that they will tell you what they really think, and what they like, and you'll know they mean it because either they'll clean their plates and ask for more, or they'll push something aside and head for the toy pile!)

How can you help your children develop a healthy attitude about food? First, by setting an example for them. Kids watch everything, and they learn from what they see you do. If you always eat until you're so full you can't move, they may start to do the same.

There's a time and a place for everything, and as long as you make Healthy Exchanges eating the anchor of your kids' nutrition, it's okay for them to indulge occasionally in pizza or fast-food burgers when they're out with friends. If you don't make them feel guilty for enjoying themselves, a couple of pieces will be a satisfying treat, but if you get upset about the slightest unhealthy item, they're likely to start bingeing on "forbidden" foods whenever they're out of your sight.

Nutrition and Your Children

The physicians and nutrition professionals I've consulted over the years suggest that offering your children a variety of nourishing foods is best. They're generally not in favor of harsh restrictions when it comes to fat and protein, for instance, even if the Food Pyramid encourages adults to cut back on these food groups.

Many parents want to know what kind of milk their children should drink. Most pediatricians feel that up to age two, whole milk is best because children need the fat in it for optimum growth. But after age two, switching over to one percent milk or nonfat (skim) milk is a good idea.

Another concern of parents I meet is the use of sugar substitutes. I get my information from the American Dietetic Association, and its position at the present time is that, used in moderation, sugar substitutes are safe for children to consume. Besides, the amounts are tiny (just divide a recipe quantity by the number of servings and you'll see that). If you're still concerned, you can choose to substitute sugar for sugar substitute in my recipes.

How much should children eat? Again, it varies from child to child and depends on age, energy expended, and appetite. The Healthy Exchanges program was created primarily for adults (see the chapter "Food Exchanges and Weight Loss Choices™"), but current government guidelines suggest the following daily exchanges for children:

Fruits	2 or more, including one with vitamin C
Vegetables	3 or more servings
Grains	6 or more servings
Milk, Cheese, Yogurt	4 servings (low fat or nonfat)
Meat, Fish, Poultry, Beans, Eggs, Nuts	2 to 3 servings (where a serving is 2 to 4 ounces lean meat, fish, or chicken; or 1 egg; or 2 tablespoons peanut butter)
Fats, Oils, and Added Sugars	Limit to a minimum where possible

Your children may not always want or need to eat on a schedule, and it's great if you can try to be flexible about when and what they eat. I usually recommend that adults eat three meals and two snacks each day, but children may need even more "mealtimes" than that. I find that most young children eat more often but eat less at each little meal or snack. That's just fine—it helps their digestion and gives them energy for all their activities. (If you've ever tried to follow a six-year-old around for an hour or two, you know how much energy they expend!)

Even though most nutritionists don't recommend restricting fat in a diet for very young children, it's a good idea to offer reduced-fat items when you can. Peanut butter and carrot sticks makes a great snack, especially if the peanut butter is the reduced-fat kind, but that doesn't mean you should hand over the jar!

Helping Your Children Eat Healthy

What can you do to help your children make healthy choices? Moderation is my best suggestion. At a pizza place, limit the number of toppings, but choose your favorites. (Veggie isn't the only possibility here! And a small amount of pepperoni can be better than piling on extra cheese.) It's good practice because in every part of your life, you have to learn to make choices. At a fast-food restaurant, don't supersize your portions just because it's a great value. You'll pay the price eventually—if not at the register, further down the road in health problems. Just think of it this way: there's nothing wrong with enjoying French fries occasionally, but you don't want to eat them every single day.

I always say that I don't do plate patrol, not around my friends, and especially not with my family. When someone watches what you eat, it makes you feel as if you're not trusted, and that ends up encouraging a feeling of rebellion as soon as you're out from under the "eagle eye" of a parent. This book offers so many possibilities, you'll be able to offer lots of good-tasting choices that don't make your kids feel as if they're being deprived of foods they like. And when they're getting to eat what they like at home, they're less likely to gobble down every high-fat snack food when they're out of the house.

What About Snacking?

Most children can only store enough energy for a few hours, so snacking is a vital part of their daily menu plans. For fussy eaters, snacking is an opportunity to get more nutrients. For kids who tend to overeat at meals and then feel too full to move, snacking is a technique to help them eat less at each meal and still be satisfied throughout the day.

I've got a whole chapter of recipes devoted to healthy snacks, but it's not always possible to give your child a homemade treat. Some good snacks include fresh fruits and vegetables, low-fat cookies, popcorn or pretzels, small boxes of cereal, and juice.

Sometimes, though, your choices are tougher. What are your options when the family heads for the local movie theater? There's always a big counterful of candy and huge tubs of buttery popcorn, and it can be hard to resist even if you're an adult and *know* it's not good for you. Again, choose moderation, and let your children have what they enjoy. Give them a couple of pieces of licorice instead of the entire bag. Order a small popcorn and don't get the squirt of butter on top—most movie popcorn has plenty of flavor without it. If they beg for a box of gummy bears, divide it up among them. They may complain a little at first, but they'll soon learn to enjoy what they have and focus on the movie, which is why you're there in the first place!

School Lunches—Can You Be Sure They're Eating Healthy Away from Home?

Many parents worry a lot about school lunches. They hope their kids are getting good nutrition but they also know that even if they send lunch along with their kids, some kids eat it, some trade it, and some just trash it. Once they're out of your sight, they're out of your control, so you just have to try to set a good example and help them make the right choices most of the time. If your local paper publishes the school lunch menu, discuss it briefly with your children. Maybe you'll decide they can bring their lunches on a couple of days, and buy lunch on days when the menu looks good to both of you.

Some children want to buy lunch every day because that's "what everyone else does" and they want to fit in. You may want to make a "contract" with your kids: you'll let them buy lunch, but you'd like them to promise to include at least a container of milk and a piece of fruit with whatever else they choose. Yes, you're trusting that they'll do what they say, but it's good practice for your children. By giving them responsibility and showing them you think they can handle it, you help them grow into mature people who understand why making healthy choices is important.

How Family History Can Teach
Good Health Habits

The best way to help your children choose a healthy lifestyle is to live one yourself, to teach by example. But it's also a great idea to talk to your children about good health habits. Once they're old enough to understand, you may want to discuss family health concerns as a way of bringing up the subject. Suppose Grandma developed diabetes late in her life, or perhaps Grandpa is being treated for heart disease or high cholesterol. You might want to explain that bad eating habits or a failure to exercise can contribute to developing such illnesses. "We know more now than we did when Grandma and Grandpa were young, and that's why we're cutting back on red meat," you might say. Your goal is not to scare your kids into better behavior. You want to encourage them to make healthy choices because it'll make them feel good all over! (You also never want to say, "You're sitting at this table until you clean your plate." That kind of talk just reinforces bad habits and turns mealtime into wartime.)

Cooking with Kids

I've always welcomed my children into the kitchen, figuring it was a great time for us to be together. When you're working full-time *and* raising a family, as so many people are, any chance you find to visit with your kids is precious. Most children will want to join in when you're preparing a meal or trying a new recipe, but only you can decide what tasks they're best suited to, especially when it comes to using a knife or the stove.

At least until your kids hit their teens, I believe some kitchen supervision is necessary. Control their access to your sharp knives, and explain to them repeatedly the procedure for using things like the microwave (no metal dishes, for instance, and covering liquids you're heating). Let them work with you in the ways you judge are safe, and explain what you're doing as you go along. They'll enjoy learning new words, not to mention some of the mysteries of where the food on the table comes from! Once your children are teenagers, and you're confident they'll be careful, start allowing them to use the kitchen on their own. Resist the urge to hang around and watch what they do. They need to feel you trust them; when they do, they're more likely to act trustworthy.

My daughter, Becky, was fourteen when she decided to prepare a banana bread to enter in the 4-H County Fair. It was summer, and she was watching her younger brothers that day while I was at work. She baked the bread and left it to cool on the kitchen table. A little while later, her brother James came in, and it smelled so good and he didn't know it was for the fair, so he and his friends gobbled down a big chunk of it. She couldn't believe it. So she stirred up another one and set it out to cool. This time, her brother Tommy came through with a group of friends and ate a big chunk of that one. Well, by now, Becky was frantic. She'd baked two beautiful breads and had nothing to show for it. She had to go to the store for more ingredients, and I had to tell my sons by phone that they'd had their fill and they were to leave her banana bread alone! By the time she made her third banana bread of the day, her technique had improved so much that she won a blue ribbon at the fair!

Even here at the "House That Recipes Built," we sometimes get some extra help when we're testing recipes. There was one time recently when all three daughters of Lori Hansen, who helps me with my catering business and lots of other projects, came into the kitchen and asked if they could help. We put them to work immediately. Abigail spooned the chopped pears on top of one dessert, while her older sister Amanda learned the best way to measure liquids and then whisked up all the pudding blends for several pies for our taste-testing buffet. And Allison supervised and helped decorate, picking out the perfectly shaped slivered almonds for the flowers on top of one cake!

Recently, I was at a speaking engagement where a lady told me that her three-year-old niece had made my Pumpkin Chiffon Pie from beginning to end with no help from her aunt—and only a little supervision! So when I say my pies are easy to fix, you'd better believe it. If a three-year-old can do it, then anyone can!

Should Kids Help Plan the Menu?

I think it's great to involve your children as much as possible in meal and menu planning, but that doesn't necessarily mean always taking your kids to the store with you. Often they can be a tremendous distraction; you may find you're spending more on groceries than you intended, or discover it's so hard to concentrate, you forget some items on your list. But once you're home, get their help in unloading the car and putting things away, if they're able, and use that time to talk about what you'll be cooking this week. You might talk about the choices: "Should I fix the lemon cheesecake or the chocolate pie?" By giving your children a voice in the food you serve, you're involving them in the process and showing them that healthy eating can also be fun! I do this with my grandkids when we're making breakfast, and they love helping to choose what I'm going to make.

''But, Mommy, Somebody Called Me Fat!''

Children can be terribly sensitive when it comes to issues of weight and appearance. And if your child comes home crying that someone called him or her "fat," it hurts you to see that child upset. Nothing hurts children more than being "different." They so desperately want to fit in, but if they happen to be chubbier than many in their class (or taller, or smaller, or different in some other way), they may come running to you for comfort.

What can you do? Well, if the child is actually overweight, don't offer a cookie as a comfort! More important, don't try to smooth over the situation if the concern is real. But also don't overdo it. Think about what you can do to help in a very real way. Are you part of the problem? Do you have a sedentary lifestyle, are you also overweight, and do you overfeed your family? If so, then resolve to work at living a healthier life that includes your children. Go through this book together and choose some recipes that sound yummy to your children. That'll give them a personal interest in helping you prepare a healthy meal, and they'll come to the table with more excitement.

Another way to encourage your kids in a healthy lifestyle is to make changes in *when* you eat. If you're a late-night muncher in front of the television, you're sending a message that it's okay to eat the evening away as you watch your favorite shows. By planning an after-dinner snack, perhaps even saving "dessert" for later if they're full from dinner, you don't deprive your children but you show them how to make better choices. Kids who don't eat late at night usually sleep better, wake up less often during the night, and generally get up in the morning feeling energetic and refreshed.

Helping your child cope with unpleasant words is harder. I think it's best to explain that sometimes good people say things that aren't nice, but that you mustn't let what they say hurt you. (Remember "sticks and stones"? It's still true.) You might add that some people, whether they're six or sixty-six, would rather be mean than be friends, and isn't that sad? By showing your children that you actually feel sorry for people who are nasty, you teach them how to build their own self-esteem.

How you handle your child's concern about being overweight is very important. If your daughter wants to go on a strict diet because someone called her fat, encourage her to make healthy eating her goal instead, and help her find ways to increase activity rather than targeting food as the "enemy."

Avoid using expressions like "Eating that will make you fat" or "No more dessert for you, then"—they create a diet mentality, an atmosphere of deprivation that can launch your child on a cycle of failure that may last into adulthood. Instead, remind your child that he or she is growing all the time, and what might seem like chubbiness now will often be outgrown in a few months or years. Set a good example by preparing healthy foods as often as you can and ordering healthy selections when you eat out. Most of all, take a positive attitude when it comes to your children's weight concerns, and teach them to focus on their successes instead of their slip-ups!

Making Exercise a Family Affair

I wasn't surprised to read that the National Center for Health Statistics estimates that nearly 5 million children ages six to seventeen are overweight. That's about 10 percent of the current school-age population, and it's more than double what was recorded in 1965. Pediatricians blame everything from video games and long hours in front of the computer to the frequent visits of many families to fast-food restaurants. Whatever the cause, the cure can be as simple as getting your child to exercise—and enjoy it.

But how do you decide what exercise is best? It's important that any fitness activity make your child feel good, not clumsy. If your child wants to take ballet, she should be encouraged, whether or not she looks great in a leotard. But encouraging her to take up gymnastics when she gazes with fear at the balance beam makes no sense. (Not only that, but gymnastics, while good for flexibility, doesn't deliver the kind of aerobic exercise your child really needs.)

Show your child how to live a more active lifestyle by increasing the activity in your own life. Ride your bikes to the grocery store together. Go for a walk after dinner or early in the morning before the rest of the family is awake. Make going up and down stairs into a kind of game—you may even want to keep a chart that tracks the number of up-and-down laps he covers!

Are there other ways you can sneak a little more exercise into your child's life? Could she walk to school with a neighbor instead of getting a ride from her dad? What about assigning your children some active chores? Raking leaves, washing the car, running with your family dog, helping you bring in packages from the car—anything you can think of that requires motion will burn a few more calories!

If your son or daughter shows interest in a team sport, try to find a way you can support their interest. Coach a Little League team, or offer to lead warm-up exercises if you can't throw a ball very well. Build an obstacle course in your yard and encourage your kids to bring their friends over to practice working out like the pros. It's amazing what you can do with a few old tires and your old jungle gym.

Dancing is another great way for kids to let off steam. Let them crank up the CD player a little loud as long as they twist and jump and hop to the music until they flop, exhausted, on the rug.

Whatever you can do to increase the amount of activity in your child's life, do it! Put the emphasis on health and feeling good, not on losing weight, and you're likely to help your child establish a lifetime love of fitness.

Your Family and Food: The Role It Plays

It's easy to get caught up in trying to be a good parent. You worry when your kids don't clean their plates or when they fill their tummies with junk food. You're concerned about what your parents might think of how you're raising your children, never suspecting that Grandma and Grandpa are just so happy to see the kids, they don't care if all they eat is hugs and kisses!

Once I became a grandparent, I didn't worry so much since I now know that if the kids don't eat everything I might want them to at this meal, eventually they'll get hungry and make up for it at the next. And I learned that the world won't end if they don't *always* eat their vegetables.

Sometimes your children are the ones who show you the power of food to nourish a family. I will never forget—in fact, it makes me cry to think of it—a night shortly after my children's father and I were divorced. Becky was in the sixth grade and James in the fourth grade. I was driving home from work after stopping to pick up Tommy from day care. I was feeling so very, very sad, thinking that we weren't a family anymore.

As I drove up to the house, I saw two sets of eyes peeking out from the curtains. My kids had been waiting for Mommy to come home. And as I walked through the back door and headed for the kitchen, I realized that James and Becky had already fixed supper. They knew I was tired and worn-out, they just sensed it—and so they did it all. They'd made minute steaks and green beans, and Becky had stirred up a Jell-O salad. I cried and smiled all through that meal. My kids and the food we shared that night made us feel like a family again.

JoAnna M. Lund
and Healthy
Exchanges

■ ■ ■ ■ ■ ■ ■ ■

Food is the first invited guest to every special occasion in every family's memory scrapbook. From baptism to graduation, from weddings to wakes, food brings us together.

It wasn't always that way at our house. I used to eat alone, even when my family was there, because while they were dining on real food, I was nibbling at whatever my newest diet called for. In fact, for twenty-eight years, I called myself the diet queen of DeWitt, Iowa.

I tried every diet I came across, every one I could afford, and every one that found its way to my small town in eastern Iowa. I was willing to try anything that promised to "melt off the pounds," determined to deprive my body in every possible way in order to become thin at last.

I sent away for expensive "miracle" diet pills. I starved

myself on the Cambridge Diet and the Bahama Diet. I gobbled diet candies, took thyroid pills, fiber pills, prescription and over-the-counter diet pills. I went to endless weight-loss support group meetings—but I somehow managed to turn healthy programs such as Overeaters Anonymous, Weight Watchers, and TOPS into unhealthy diets . . . diets I could never follow for more than a few months.

I was determined to discover something that worked long-term, but each new failure increased my desperation that I'd never find it.

I ate strange concoctions and rubbed on even stranger potions. I tried liquid diets. I agreed to be hypnotized. I tried reflexology and even had an acupressure device stuck in my ear!

Does my story sound a lot like yours? I'm not surprised. No wonder the weight-loss business is a billion-dollar industry!

Every new thing I tried seemed to work—at least at first. And losing that first five or ten pounds would get me so excited, I'd believe that this new miracle diet would, finally, get my weight off for keeps.

Inevitably, though, the initial excitement wore off. The diet's routine and boredom set in, and I quit. I shoved the pills to the back of the medicine chest; pushed the cans of powdered shake mix to the rear of the kitchen cabinets; slid all the program materials out of sight under my bed; and once more I felt like a failure.

Like most dieters, I quickly gained back the weight I'd lost each time, along with a few extra "souvenir" pounds that seemed always to settle around my hips. I'd done the diet-lose-weight-gain-it-all-back "yo-yo" on the average of once a year. It's no exaggeration to say that over the years I've lost 1,000 pounds—and gained back 1,150 pounds.

Finally, at the age of forty-six I weighed more than I'd ever imagined possible. I'd stopped believing that any diet could work for me. I drowned my sorrows in sacks of cake donuts and wondered if I'd live long enough to watch my grandchildren grow up.

Something had to change.

I had to change.

Finally, I did.

I'm just over fifty now—and I'm 130 pounds less than my all-time high of close to 300 pounds. I've kept the weight off for more than six years. I'd like to lose another ten pounds, but I'm not obsessed about it. If it takes me two or three years to accomplish it, that's okay.

What I *do* care about is never saying hello again to any of those unwanted pounds I said good-bye to!

How did I jump off the roller coaster I was on? For one thing, I finally stopped looking to food to solve my emotional problems. But what really shook me up—and got me started on the path that changed my life—was Operation Desert Storm in early 1991. I sent three children off to the Persian Gulf war— my son-in-law, Matt, a medic in Special Forces; my daughter, Becky, a full-time college student and member of a medical unit in the Army Reserve; and my son James, a member of the Inactive Army Reserve reactivated as a chemicals expert.

Somehow, knowing that my children were putting their lives on the line got me thinking about my own mortality—and I knew in my heart the last thing they needed while they were overseas was to get a letter from home saying that their mother was ill because of a food-related problem.

The day I drove the third child to the airport to leave for Saudi Arabia, something happened to me that would change my life for the better—and forever. I stopped praying my constant prayer as a professional dieter, which was simply "Please, God, let me lose ten pounds by Friday." Instead, I began praying, "God, please help me not to be a burden to my kids and my family." I quit praying for what I wanted and started praying for what I needed—and in the process my prayers were answered. I couldn't keep the kids safe—that was out of my hands—but I could try to get healthier to better handle the stress of it. It was the least I could do on the homefront.

That quiet prayer was the beginning of the new JoAnna Lund. My initial goal was not to lose weight or create healthy recipes. I only wanted to become healthier for my kids, my husband, and myself.

Each of my children returned safely from the Persian Gulf war. But something didn't come back—the 130 extra pounds I'd been lugging around for far too long. I'd finally accepted the truth after all those agonizing years of suffering through on-again, off-again dieting.

There are no "magic" cures in life.

No miracle potion, pill, or diet will make unwanted pounds disappear.

I found something better than magic, if you can believe it. When I turned my weight and health dilemma over to God for guidance, a new JoAnna Lund and Healthy Exchanges were born.

I discovered a new way to live my life—and uncovered an unexpected talent for creating easy "common folk" healthy recipes, and sharing my commonsense approach to healthy living. I learned that I could motivate others to change their lives and adopt a positive outlook. I began publishing cookbooks and a monthly food newsletter, and speaking to groups all over the country.

I like to say, "*When life handed me a lemon, not only did I make healthy, tasty lemonade, I wrote the recipe down!*"

What I finally found was not a quick fix or a short-term diet, but a great way to live well for a lifetime.

I want to share it with you.

Food Exchanges and Weight Loss Choices™

■ ■ ■ ■ ■ ■ ■ ■

Healthy Exchanges® Weight Loss Choices™/Exchanges

If you've ever been on one of the national weight-loss programs like Weight Watchers or Diet Center, you've already been introduced to the concept of measured portions of different food groups that make up your daily food plan. If you are not familiar with such a system of weight-loss choices or exchanges, here's a brief explanation. (If you want or need more detailed information, you can write to the American Dietetic Association or the American Diabetes Association for comprehensive explanations.)

The idea of food exchanges is to divide foods into basic food groups. The foods in each group are measured in servings that have comparable values. These groups include Proteins/Meats, Breads/Starches, Vegetables, Fats, Fruits, Skim Milk, Free Foods, and Optional Calories.

Each choice or exchange included in a particular group has

about the same number of calories and a similar carbohydrate, protein, and fat content as the other foods in that group. Because any food on a particular list can be "exchanged" for any other food in that group, it makes sense to call the food groups *exchanges* or *choices*.

I like to think we are also "exchanging" bad habits and food choices for good ones!

By using Weight Loss Choices or exchanges you can choose from a variety of foods without having to calculate the nutrient value of each one. This makes it easier to include a wide variety of foods in your daily menus and gives you the opportunity to tailor your choices to your unique appetite.

If you want to lose weight, you should consult your physician or other weight-control expert regarding the number of servings that would be best for you from each food group. Since men generally require more calories than women, and since the requirements for growing children and teenagers differ from adults, the right number of exchanges for any one person is a personal decision.

I have included a suggested plan of weight-loss choices in the pages following the exchange lists. It's a program I used to lose 130 pounds, and it's the one I still follow today.

(If you are a diabetic or have been diagnosed with heart problems, it is best to meet with your physician before using this or any other food program or recipe collection.)

Food Group Weight Loss Choices™ Exchanges

Not all food group exchanges are alike. The ones that follow are for anyone who's interested in weight loss or maintenance. If you are a diabetic, you should check with your health-care provider or dietitian to get the information you need to help you plan your diet. Diabetic exchanges are determined by the American Diabetic Association, and information about them is provided in *The Diabetic's Healthy Exchanges Cookbook* (Perigee).

Every Healthy Exchanges recipe provides calculations in three ways:

- Weight Loss Choices/Exchanges
- Calories, Fat, Protein, Carbohydrates, and Fiber Grams, and Sodium in milligrams
- Diabetic Exchanges calculated for me by a registered dietitian

Healthy Exchanges recipes can help you eat well and recover your health, whatever your health concerns may be. Please take a few minutes to review the exchange lists and the suggestions that follow on how to count them. You have lots of great eating in store for you!

Proteins

Meat, poultry, seafood, eggs, cheese, and legumes.

One exchange of Protein is approximately 60 calories. Examples of one Protein choice or exchange:

1 ounce cooked weight of lean meat, poultry, or seafood
2 ounces white fish
1½ ounces 97% fat-free ham
1 egg (limit to no more than 4 per week)
¼ cup egg substitute
3 egg whites
¾ ounce reduced-fat cheese
½ cup fat-free cottage cheese
2 ounces cooked or ¾ ounces uncooked dry beans
1 tablespoon peanut butter (also count 1 Fat exchange)

Breads

Breads, crackers, cereals, grains, and starchy vegetables. One exchange of Bread is approximately 80 calories. Examples of one Bread choice or exchange:

1 slice bread or 2 slices reduced-calorie bread (40 calories or less)
1 roll, any type (1 ounce)
½ cup cooked pasta or ¾ ounce uncooked (scant ½ cup)
½ cup cooked rice or 1 ounce uncooked (⅓ cup)
3 tablespoons flour
¾ ounce cold cereal
½ cup cooked hot cereal or ¾ ounce uncooked (2 tablespoons)
½ cup corn (kernels or cream-style) or peas
4 ounces white potato, cooked, or 5 ounces uncooked
3 ounces sweet potato, cooked, or 4 ounces uncooked
3 cups air-popped popcorn
7 fat-free crackers (¾ ounce)
3 (2½-inch squares) graham crackers
2 (¾-ounce) rice cakes or 6 mini
1 tortilla, any type (6-inch diameter)

Fruits

All fruits and fruit juices. One exchange of Fruit is approximately 60 calories. Examples of one Fruit choice or exchange:

1 small apple or ½ cup slices
1 small orange
½ medium banana
¾ cup berries (except strawberries and cranberries)
1 cup strawberries or cranberries
½ cup canned fruit, packed in fruit juice or rinsed well
2 tablespoons raisins
1 tablespoon spreadable fruit spread

½ cup apple juice (4 fluid ounces)
½ cup orange juice (4 fluid ounces)
½ cup applesauce

Skim Milk

Milk, buttermilk, and yogurt. One exchange of Skim Milk is approximately 90 calories. Examples of one Skim Milk choice or exchange:

1 cup skim milk
½ cup evaporated skim milk
1 cup low-fat buttermilk
¾ cup plain fat-free yogurt
⅓ cup nonfat dry milk powder

Vegetables

All fresh, canned, or frozen vegetables other than the starchy vegetables. One exchange of Vegetable is approximately 30 calories. Examples of one Vegetable choice or exchange:

½ cup vegetable
¼ cup tomato sauce
1 medium fresh tomato
½ cup vegetable juice

Fats

Margarine, mayonnaise, vegetable oils, salad dressings, olives, and nuts. One exchange of Fat is approximately 40 calories. Examples of one Fat choice or exchange:

1 teaspoon margarine or 2 teaspoons reduced-calorie margarine

1 teaspoon butter
1 teaspoon vegetable oil
1 teaspoon mayonnaise or 2 teaspoons reduced-calorie mayonnaise
1 teaspoon peanut butter
1 ounce olives
¼ ounce pecans or walnuts

Free Foods

Foods that do not provide nutritional value but are used to enhance the taste of foods are included in the Free Foods group. Examples of these are spices, herbs, extracts, vinegar, lemon juice, mustard, Worcestershire sauce, and soy sauce. Cooking sprays and artificial sweeteners used in moderation are also included in this group. However, you'll see that I include the caloric value of artificial sweeteners in the Optional Calories of the recipes.

You may occasionally see a recipe that lists "free food" as part of the portion. According to the published exchange lists, a free food contains fewer than 20 calories per serving. Two or three servings per day of free foods/drinks are usually allowed in a meal plan.

Optional Calories

Foods that do not fit into any other group but are used in moderation in recipes are included in Optional Calories. Foods that are counted in this way include sugar-free gelatin and puddings, fat-free mayonnaise and dressings, reduced-calorie whipped toppings, reduced-calorie syrups and jams, chocolate chips, coconut, and canned broth.

Sliders™

These are 80 Optional Calorie increments that do not fit into any particular category. You can choose which food group to *slide* these into. It is wise to limit this selection to approximately three to four per day to ensure the best possible nutrition for your body while still enjoying an occasional treat.

Sliders™ may be used in either of the following ways:

1. If you have consumed all your Protein, Bread, Fruit, or Skim Milk Weight Loss Choices for the day, and you want to eat additional foods from those food groups, you simply use a Slider. It's what I call "healthy horse-trading." Remember that Sliders may not be traded for choices in the Vegetables or Fats food groups.

2. Sliders may also be deducted from your Optional Calories for the day or week. ¼ Slider equals 20 Optional Calories; ½ Slider equals 40 Optional Calories; ¾ Slider equals 60 Optional Calories; and 1 Slider equals 80 Optional Calories.

Healthy Exchanges®
Weight Loss Choices™

My original Healthy Exchanges program of Weight Loss Choices™ was based on an average daily total of 1,400 to 1,600 calories per day. That was what I determined was right for my needs, and for those of most women. Because men require additional calories (about 1,600 to 1,900), here are my suggested plans for women and men. (*If you require more or fewer calories, please revise this plan to meet your individual needs.*)

Each day, women should plan to eat:

2 Skim Milk servings, 90 calories each
2 Fat servings, 40 calories each
3 Fruit servings, 60 calories each
4 Vegetable servings or more, 30 calories each
5 Protein servings, 60 calories each
5 Bread servings, 80 calories each

Each day, men should plan to eat:

2 Skim Milk servings, 90 calories each
4 Fat servings, 40 calories each
3 Fruit servings, 60 calories each
4 Vegetable servings or more, 30 calories each
6 Protein servings, 60 calories each
7 Bread servings, 80 calories each

Young people should follow the program for Men but add 1 Skim Milk serving for a total of 3 servings. (Suggested exchanges for Children are listed in the introduction.)

You may also choose to add up to 100 Optional Calories per day, and up to 21 to 28 Sliders per week at 80 calories each. If you choose to include more Sliders in your daily or weekly totals, deduct those 80 calories from your Optional Calorie "bank."

A word about Sliders. These are to be counted toward your totals after you have used your allotment of choices of Skim Milk, Protein, Bread, and Fruit for the day. By "sliding" an additional choice into one of these groups, you can meet your individual needs for that day. Sliders are especially helpful when traveling, stressed-out, eating out, or for special events. I often use mine so I can enjoy my favorite Healthy Exchanges desserts. Vegetables are not to be counted as Sliders. Enjoy as many Vegetable Choices as you need to feel satisfied. Because we want to limit our fat intake to moderate amounts, additional Fat Choices should not be counted as Sliders. If you choose to include more fat on an *occasional* basis, count the extra choices as Optional Calories.

Keep a daily food diary of your Weight Loss Choices, checking off what you eat as you go. If, at the end of the day, your required selections are not 100 percent accounted for, but you have done the best you can, go to bed with a clear conscience. There will be days when you have ¼ Fruit or ½ Bread left over. What are you going to do—eat two slices of an orange or half a slice of bread and throw the rest out? I always say, "Nothing in life comes out exact." Just do the best you can . . . *the best you can.*

Try to drink at least eight 8-ounce glasses of water a day. Water truly is the "nectar" of good health.

As a little added insurance, I take a multivitamin each day. It's not essential, but if my day's worth of well-planned meals "bites the dust" when unexpected events intrude on my regular routine, my body still gets its vital nutrients.

The calories listed in each group of choices are averages. Some choices within each group may be higher or lower, so it's important to select a variety of different foods instead of eating the same three or four all the time.

Use your Optional Calories! They are what I call "life's little extras." They make all the difference in how you enjoy your food and appreciate the variety available to you. Yes, we can get by without them, but do you really want to? Keep in mind that you should be using all your daily Weight Loss Choices first to ensure you are getting the basics of good nutrition. But I guarantee that Optional Calories will keep you from feeling deprived—and help you reach your weight-loss goals.

Sodium, Fat, Cholesterol, and Processed Foods

■ ■ ■ ■ ■ ■ ■ ■

*A*re Healthy Exchanges ingredients really healthy?

When I first created Healthy Exchanges, many people asked about sodium, about whether it was necessary to calculate the percentage of fat, saturated fat, and cholesterol in a healthy diet, and about my use of processed foods in many recipes. I researched these questions as I was developing my program, so you can feel confident about using the recipes and food plan.

Sodium

Most people consume more sodium than their bodies need. The American Heart Association and the American Diabetes

Association recommend limiting daily sodium intake to no more than 3,000 milligrams per day. If your doctor suggests you limit your sodium even more, then *you really must read labels.*

Sodium is an essential nutrient and should not be completely eliminated. It helps to regulate blood volume and is needed for normal daily muscle and nerve functions. Most of us, however, have no trouble getting "all we need" and then some.

As with everything else, moderation is my approach. I rarely ever have salt on my list as an added ingredient. But if you're especially sodium-sensitive, make the right choices for you—and save high-sodium foods such as sauerkraut for an occasional treat.

I use lots of spices to enhance flavors, so you won't notice the absence of salt. In the few cases where it is used, salt is vital for the success of the recipe, so please don't omit it.

When I do use an ingredient high in sodium, I try to compensate by using low-sodium products in the remainder of the recipe. Many fat-free products are a little higher in sodium to make up for any loss of flavor that disappeared along with the fat. But when I take advantage of these fat-free, higher-sodium products, I stretch that ingredient within the recipe, lowering the amount of sodium per serving. A good example is my use of fat-free and reduced-sodium canned soups. While the suggested number of servings per can is two, I make sure my final creation serves at least four and sometimes six. So the soup's sodium has been "watered down" from one-third to one-half of the original amount.

Even if you don't have to watch your sodium intake for medical reasons, using moderation is another "healthy exchange" to make on your own journey to good health.

Fat Percentages

We've been told that 30 percent is the magic number—that we should limit fat intake to 30 percent or less of our total calories. It's good advice, and I try to have a weekly average of 15 percent to 25 percent myself. I believe any less than 15 percent is really just another restrictive diet that won't last. And more than 25 percent on a regular basis is too much of a good thing.

When I started listing fat grams along with calories in my recipes, I was tempted to include the percentage of calories from fat. After all, in the vast majority of my recipes, that percentage is well below 30 percent. This even includes my pie recipes that allow you a realistic serving instead of many "diet" recipes that tell you a serving is one-twelfth of a pie.

Figuring fat grams is easy enough. Each gram of fat equals 9 calories. Multiply fat grams by 9, then divide that number by the total calories to get the percentage of calories from fat.

So why don't I do it? After consulting four registered dietitians for advice, I decided to omit this information. They felt that it's too easy for people to become obsessed by that 30 percent figure, which is after all supposed to be a percentage of total calories over the course of a day or a week. We mustn't feel we can't include a healthy ingredient such as pecans or olives in one recipe just because, on its own, it has more than 30 percent of its calories from fat.

An example of this would be a casserole made with 90 percent lean red meat. Most of us benefit from eating red meat in moderation, as it provides iron and niacin in our diets, and it also makes life more enjoyable for us and those who eat with us. If we *only* look at the percentage of calories from fat in a serving of this one dish, which might be as high as 40 to 45 percent, we might choose not to include this recipe in our weekly food plan.

The dietitians suggested that it's important to consider the total picture when making such decisions. As long as your overall food plan keeps fat calories to 30 percent, it's all right to enjoy an occasional dish that is somewhat higher in fat content. Healthy foods I include in **MODERATION** include 90 percent lean red meat, olives, and nuts. I don't eat these foods every day, and you may not either. But occasionally, in a good recipe, they make all the difference in the world between just getting by (deprivation) and truly enjoying your food.

Remember, the goal is eating in a healthy way so you can enjoy and live well the rest of your life.

Saturated Fats and Cholesterol

You'll see that I don't provide calculations for saturated fats or cholesterol amounts in my recipes. It's for the simple and yet not so simple reason that accurate, up-to-date, brand-specific information can be difficult to obtain from food manufacturers, especially since the way in which they produce food keeps changing rapidly. But once more I've consulted with registered dietitians and other professionals and found that, because I use only a few products that are high in saturated fat, and use them in such limited quantities, my recipes are suitable for patients concerned about controlling or lowering cholesterol. You'll also find that whenever I do use one of these ingredients *in moderation*, everything else in the recipe, and in the meals my family and I enjoy, is low in fat.

Processed Foods

Just what *is* processed food, anyway? What do I mean by the term "processed food," and why do I use them, when the "purest" recipe developers in Recipe Land consider them "pedestrian" and won't ever use something from a box, container, or can? A letter I received and a passing statement from a stranger made me reflect on what I mean when I refer to processed foods, and helped me reaffirm why I use them in my "common folk" healthy recipes.

If you are like the vast millions who agree with me, then I'm not sharing anything new with you. And if you happen to disagree, that's okay, too. After all, this is America, the Land of the Free. We are blessed to live in a great nation where we can all believe what we want about anything.

A few months ago, a woman sent me several articles from various "whole food" publications and wrote that she was wary of processed foods, and wondered why I used them in my recipes. She then scribbled on the bottom of her note, "Just how healthy *is* Healthy Exchanges?" Then, a few weeks later, during a chance visit at a public food event with a very pleasant woman, I was struck by how we all have our own definitions of what processed foods are. She shared with me, in a somewhat self-righteous manner, that she *never* uses processed foods. She only cooked with fresh fruits and vegetables, she told me. Then later she said that she used canned reduced-fat soups all the time! Was her definition different than mine? I wondered. Soup in a can, whether it's reduced in fat or not, still meets my definition of a processed food.

So I got out a copy of my book *HELP: Healthy Exchanges Lifetime Plan* and reread what I had written back then about processed foods. Nothing in my definition had changed since I wrote that section. I still believe that healthy processed foods, such as canned soups, prepared piecrusts, sugar-free instant puddings, nonfat sour cream, and frozen whipped topping, when used properly, all have a place as ingredients in healthy recipes.

I never use an ingredient that hasn't been approved by either the American Diabetic Association, the American Dietetic Association, or the American Heart Association. Whenever I'm in doubt, I send for their position papers, then ask knowledgeable registered dietitians to explain those papers to me in layman's language. I've been assured by all of them that the sugar- and fat-free products I use in my recipes are indeed safe.

If you don't agree, nothing I can say or write will convince you otherwise. But, if you've been using the healthy processed foods and have been concerned about the almost daily hoopla you hear about yet another product that's going to be the doom of all of us, then just stick with reason. For every product on the grocery shelves, there are those who want you to buy it and there are those who don't, *because they want you to buy their products instead.* So we have to learn to sift the fact from the fiction. Let's take sugar substitutes, for example. In making your own evaluations, you should be skeptical about any information provided by the sugar substitute manufacturers, because they have a vested interest in our buying their products. Likewise, ignore any information provided by the sugar industry, because they have a vested interest in our *not* buying sugar substitutes. Then, if you aren't sure if you can really trust the government or any of its agencies, toss out their data, too. That leaves the three associations I mentioned above. Do you think any of them would say a product is safe if it isn't? Or say a product isn't safe when it is? They have nothing to gain or lose, *other than their integrity,* if they intentionally try to mislead us. That's why I only go to these associations for information concerning healthy processed foods.

I certainly don't recommend that everything we eat should come from a can, box, or jar. I think the best of all possible worlds is to start with the basics: grains such as rice, pasta, or corn. Then, for example, add some raw vegetables and extra-lean meat such as poultry, fish, beef, or pork. Stir in some healthy canned soup or tomato sauce, and you'll end up with something that is not only healthy but tastes so good, everyone from toddlers to great-grandparents will want to eat it!

I've never been in favor of spraying everything we eat with chemicals, and I don't believe that all our foods should come out of packages. But I do think we should use the best available healthy processed foods to make cooking easier and food taste better. I take advantage of the good-tasting low-fat and low-sugar products found in any grocery store. My recipes are created for busy people like me, people who want to eat healthily and economically but who still want the food to satisfy their taste buds. I don't expect anyone to visit out-of-the-way health food stores or find the time to cook beans from scratch— *because I don't!* Most of you can't grow fresh food in the backyard and many of you may not have access to farmers' markets or large supermarkets. I want to help you figure out realistic ways to make healthy eating a reality *wherever you live,* or you will not stick to a healthy lifestyle for long.

So if you've been swayed (by individuals or companies with vested interests or hidden agendas) into thinking that all processed foods are bad for you, you may want to reconsider your position. Or if you've been fooling yourself into believing that you *never* use processed foods but regularly reach for that healthy canned soup, stop playing games with yourself—you are using processed foods in a healthy way. And, if you're like me and use healthy processed foods in *moderation,* don't let anyone make you feel ashamed about including these products in your healthy lifestyle. Only *you* can decide what's best for *you* and your family's needs.

Part of living a healthy lifestyle is making those decisions and then getting on with life. Congratulations on choosing to live a healthy lifestyle, and let's celebrate together by sharing a piece of Healthy Exchanges pie that I've garnished with Cool Whip Lite!

JoAnna's Ten Commandments of Successful Cooking

■ ■ ■ ■ ■ ■ ■ ■

A very important part of any journey is knowing where you are going and the best way to get there. If you plan and prepare before you start to cook, you should reach mealtime with foods to write home about!

1. **Read the entire recipe from start to finish** and be sure you understand the process involved. Check that you have all the equipment you will need *before* you begin.

2. **Check the ingredient list** and be sure you have *everything* and in the amounts required. Keep cooking sprays handy—while they're not listed as ingredients, I use them all the time (just a quick squirt!).

3. **Set out *all* the ingredients and equipment needed** to

prepare the recipe on the counter near you *before* you start. Remember that old saying, *A stitch in time saves nine?* It applies in the kitchen, too.

4. **Do as much advance preparation as possible** before actually cooking. Chop, cut, grate, or whatever is needed to prepare the ingredients and have them ready before you start to mix. Turn the oven on at least ten minutes before putting food in to bake, to allow the oven to preheat to the proper temperature.

5. **Use a kitchen timer** to tell you when the cooking or baking time is up. Because stove temperatures vary slightly by manufacturer, you may want to set your timer for five minutes less than the suggested time just to prevent over-cooking. Check the progress of your dish at that time, then decide if you need the additional minutes or not.

6. **Measure carefully.** Use glass measures for liquids and metal or plastic cups for dry ingredients. My recipes are based on standard measurements. Unless I tell you it's a scant or full cup, measure the cup level.

7. **For best results, follow the recipe instructions exactly.** Feel free to substitute ingredients that *don't tamper* with the basic chemistry of the recipe, but be sure to leave key ingredients alone. For example, you could substitute sugar-free instant chocolate pudding for sugar-free instant butterscotch pudding, but if you use a six-serving package when a four-serving package is listed in the ingredients, or you use instant when cook-and-serve is required, you won't get the right result.

8. **Clean up as you go.** It is much easier to wash a few items at a time than to face a whole counter of dirty dishes later. The same is true for spills on the counter or floor.

9. **Be careful about doubling or halving a recipe.** Though many recipes can be altered successfully to serve more or fewer people, *many cannot.* This is especially true when it comes to spices and liquids. If you try to double a recipe that calls for 1 teaspoon pumpkin-pie spice, for example, and you double the spice, you may end up with a too-spicy taste. I usually suggest increasing spices or liquid by 1½ times when doubling a recipe. If it tastes a little bland to you, you can increase the spice to 1¾ times the original amount the next time you prepare the dish. Remember: You can always add more, but you can't take it out after it's stirred in.

The same is true with liquid ingredients. If you wanted to **triple** a recipe like my Rio Grande Rice because you were planning to serve a crowd, you might think you should use three times as much of every ingredient. Don't, or you could end up with Rio Grande Rice Soup! The original recipe calls for 1¾ cups of chunky tomato sauce, so I'd suggest using 3½ cups when you **triple** the recipe (or 2¾ cups if you **double** it). You'll still have a good-tasting dish that won't run all over the plate.

10. **Write your reactions next to each recipe once you've served it.**
Yes, that's right, I'm giving you permission to write in this book. It's yours, after all. Ask yourself: Did everyone like it? Did you have to add another half teaspoon of chili seasoning to please your family, who like to live on the spicier side of the street? You may even want to rate the recipe on a scale of 1★ to 4★, depending on what you thought of it. (Four stars would be the top rating—and I hope you'll feel that way about many of my recipes.) Jotting down your comments while they are fresh in your mind will help you personalize the recipe to your own taste the next time you prepare it.

My Best Healthy Exchanges Tips and Tidbits

■ ■ ■ ■ ■ ■ ■ ■

Measurements, General Cooking Tips, and Basic Ingredients

The word *moderation* best describes **my use of fats, sugar substitutes,** and **sodium** in these recipes. Wherever possible, I've used cooking spray for sautéing and for browning meats and vegetables. I also use reduced-calorie margarine and no-fat mayonnaise and salad dressings. Lean ground turkey *or* ground beef can be used in the recipes. Just be sure whatever you choose is at least *90 percent lean.*

I've also included **small amounts of sugar and brown sugar substitutes as the sweetening agent** in many of the recipes. I don't drink a hundred cans of soda a day or eat enough artificially sweetened foods in a 24-hour time period to be troubled by sugar substitutes. But if this is a concern of yours and you *do not* need to watch your sugar intake, you can always replace the sugar substitutes with processed sugar and the sugar-free products with regular ones.

I created my recipes knowing they would also be used by hypoglycemics, diabetics, and those concerned about triglycerides. If you choose to use sugar instead, be sure to count the additional calories.

A word of caution when cooking with **sugar substitutes**: Use **saccharin**-based sweeteners when **heating or baking**. In recipes that **don't require heat, Aspartame** (known as Nutrasweet) works well in uncooked dishes but leaves an aftertaste in baked products.

I'm often asked why I use an **8-by-8-inch baking dish** in my recipes. It's for portion control. If the recipe says it serves 4, just cut down the center, turn the dish, and cut again. Like magic, there's your serving. Also, if this is the only recipe you are preparing requiring an oven, the square dish fits into a tabletop toaster oven easily and energy can be conserved.

To make life even easier, **whenever a recipe calls for ounce measurements** (other than raw meats) I've included the closest cup equivalent. I need to use my scale daily when creating recipes, so I've measured for you at the same time. Most of the recipes are for **4 to 6 servings**. If you don't have that many to feed, do what I do: freeze individual portions. Then all you have to do is choose something from the freezer and take it to work for lunch or have your evening meals prepared in advance for the week. In this way, I always have something on hand that is both good to eat and good for me.

Unless a recipe includes hard-boiled eggs, cream cheese, mayonnaise, or a raw vegetable or fruit, **the leftovers should freeze well**. (I've marked recipes that freeze well with the symbol of a **snowflake**.) This includes most of the cream pies. Divide any recipe up into individual servings and freeze for your own "TV" dinners.

Another good idea is **cutting leftover pie into individual pieces and freezing each one separately** in a small Ziploc freezer bag. Then the next time you want to thaw a piece of pie for yourself, you don't have to thaw the whole pie. It's great this way for brown-bag lunches, too. Just pull a piece out of the freezer on your way to work and by lunchtime you will have a wonderful dessert waiting for you.

Unless I specify **"covered" for simmering or baking**, prepare my recipes **uncovered**. Occasionally you will read a recipe that asks you to cover a dish for a time, then to uncover, so read the directions carefully to avoid confusion—and to get the best results.

Low-fat cooking spray is another blessing in a Healthy Exchanges kitchen. It's currently available in three flavors . . .

- **Olive oil–flavored** when cooking Mexican, Italian, or Greek dishes
- **Butter-flavored** when the hint of butter is desired
- **Regular** for everything else.

A quick spray of butter flavored makes air-popped popcorn a low-fat taste treat, or try it as a butter substitute on steaming hot corn on the cob. One light spray of the skillet when browning meat will convince you that you're using "old-fashioned fat," and a quick coating of the casserole dish before you add the ingredients will make serving easier and cleanup quicker.

I use reduced-sodium **canned chicken broth** in place of dry bouillon to lower the sodium content. The intended flavor is still present in the prepared dish. As a reduced-sodium beef broth is not currently available (at least not in DeWitt, Iowa), I use the canned regular beef broth. The sodium content is still lower than regular dry bouillon.

Whenever **cooked rice or pasta** is an ingredient, follow the package directions, but eliminate the salt and/or margarine called for. This helps lower the sodium and fat content. It tastes just fine; trust me on this.

Here's another tip: When **cooking rice or noodles**, why not cook extra "for the pot"? After you use what you need, store leftover rice in a covered container (where it will keep for a couple of days). With noodles like spaghetti or macaroni, first rinse and drain as usual, then measure out what you need. Put the leftovers in a bowl covered with water, then store in the refrigerator, covered, until they're needed. Then, measure out what you need, rinse and drain them, and they're ready to go.

Does your **pita bread** often tear before you can make a sandwich? Here's my tip to make them open easily: cut the bread in half, put the halves in the microwave for about 15 seconds, and they will open up by themselves. *Voilà!*

When **chunky salsa** is listed as an ingredient, I leave the degree of "heat" up to your personal taste. In our house, I'm considered a wimp. I go for the "mild" while Cliff prefers "extra-hot." How do we compromise? I prepare the recipe with mild salsa because he can always add a spoonful or two of the hotter version to his serving, but I can't enjoy the dish if it's too spicy for me.

Milk and Yogurt

Take it from me—nonfat dry milk powder is great! I *do not* use it for drinking, but I *do* use it for cooking. Three good reasons why:

1. It is very **inexpensive**.
2. It does not **sour** because you use it only as needed. Store the box in your refrigerator or freezer and it will keep almost forever.
3. You can easily **add extra calcium** to just about any recipe without added liquid. I consider nonfat dry milk powder one of Mother Nature's modern-day miracles of convenience. But do purchase a good national name brand (I like Carnation), and keep it fresh by proper storage.

In many of my pies and puddings, I use nonfat dry milk powder and water instead of skim milk. Usually I call for ⅔ cup nonfat dry milk powder and 1¼ to 1½ cups water or liquid. This way I can get the nutrients of two cups of milk, but much less liquid, and the end result is much creamier. Also, the recipe sets up quicker, usually in 5 minutes or less. So if someone knocks at your door unexpectedly at mealtime, you can quickly throw a pie together and enjoy it minutes later.

You can make your own **"sour cream"** by combining ¾ cup plain fat-free yogurt with ⅓ cup nonfat dry milk powder. There are four benefits in doing this: (1) The dry milk stabilizes the yogurt and keeps the whey from separating. (2) The dry milk slightly helps to cut the tartness of the yogurt. (3) It's still virtually fat-free. (4) The calcium has been increased by 100 percent. Isn't it great how we can make that distant relative of sour cream a first kissin' cousin by adding the nonfat dry milk powder? Or, if you place 1 cup of plain fat-free yogurt in a sieve lined with a coffee filter, and place the sieve over a small bowl and refrigerate for about 6 hours, you will end up with a very good alternative for sour cream. To **stabilize yogurt** when cooking or baking with it, just add 1 teaspoon cornstarch to every ¾ cup yogurt.

If a recipe calls for **evaporated skim milk** and you don't have any in the cupboard, make your own. For every ½ cup evaporated skim milk needed, combine ⅓ cup nonfat dry milk powder and ½ cup water. Use as you would evaporated skim milk.

You can also make your own **sugar-free and fat-free sweetened condensed milk** at home. Combine 1⅓ cups nonfat dry milk powder and ½ cup cold water in a 2-cup glass measure. Cover and microwave on HIGH until mixture is hot but *not* boiling. Stir in ½ cup Sprinkle Sweet or Sugar Twin. Cover and refrigerate at least 4 hours. This mixture will keep for up to two weeks in the refrigerator. Use in just about any recipe that calls for sweetened condensed milk.

For any recipe that calls for **buttermilk**, you might want to try JO's Buttermilk: Blend one cup of water and ⅔ cup dry milk powder (the nutrients of two cups of skim milk). It'll be thicker than this mixed-up milk usually is, because it's doubled. Add 1 teaspoon white vinegar and stir, then let it sit for at least 10 minutes.

One of my subscribers was looking for a way to further

restrict salt intake and needed a substitute for **cream of mushroom soup**. For many of my recipes, I use Healthy Request Cream of Mushroom Soup, as it is a reduced-sodium product. The label suggests two servings per can, but I usually incorporate the soup into a recipe serving at least four. By doing this, I've reduced the sodium in the soup by half again.

But if you must restrict your sodium even more, try making my Healthy Exchanges **Creamy Mushroom Sauce**. Place 1½ cups evaporated skim milk and 3 tablespoons flour in a covered jar. Shake well and pour mixture into a medium saucepan sprayed with butter-flavored cooking spray. Add ½ cup canned sliced mushrooms, rinsed and drained. Cook over medium heat, stirring often, until mixture thickens. Add any seasonings of your choice. You can use this sauce in any recipe that calls for one 10¾-ounce can of cream of mushroom soup.

Why did I choose these proportions and ingredients?

- 1½ cups evaporated skim milk is the amount in one can.
- It's equal to three Milk choices or exchanges.
- It's the perfect amount of liquid and flour for a medium cream sauce.
- 3 tablespoons flour is equal to one Bread/Starch choice or exchange.
- Any leftovers will reheat beautifully with a flour-based sauce, but not with a cornstarch base.
- The mushrooms are one Vegetable choice or exchange.
- This sauce is virtually fat-free, sugar-free, and sodium-free.

Proteins

I use eggs in moderation. I enjoy the real thing on an average of three to four times a week. So, my recipes are calculated on using whole eggs. However, if you choose to use egg substitute in place of the egg, the finished product will turn out just fine and the fat grams per serving will be even lower than those listed.

If you like the look, taste, and feel of **hard-boiled eggs** in salads but haven't been using them because of the cholesterol in the yolk, I have a couple of alternatives for you. (1) Pour an 8-ounce carton of egg substitute into a medium skillet sprayed with cooking spray. Cover skillet tightly and cook over low heat until substitute is just set, about 10 minutes. Remove from heat and let set, still covered, for 10 minutes more. Uncover and cool completely. Chop set mixture. This will make about 1 cup of chopped egg. (2) Even easier is to hard-boil "real eggs," toss the yolk away, and chop the white. Either way, you don't deprive yourself of the pleasure of egg in your salad.

In most recipes calling for **egg substitutes**, you can use 2 egg whites in place of the equivalent of 1 egg substitute. Just break the eggs open and toss the yolks away. I can hear some of you already saying, "But that's wasteful!" Well, take a look at the price on the egg substitute package (which usually has the equivalent of 4 eggs in it), then look at the price of a dozen eggs, from which you'd get the equivalent of 6 egg substitutes. Now, what's wasteful about that?

Whenever I include **cooked chicken** in a recipe, I use roasted white meat without skin. Whenever I include **roast beef or pork** in a recipe, I use the loin cuts because they are much leaner. However, most of the time, I do my roasting of all these meats at the local deli. I just ask for a chunk of their lean roasted meat, 6 or 8 ounces, and ask them not to slice it. When I get home, I cube or dice the meat and am ready to use it in my recipe. The reason I do this is threefold: (1) I'm getting just the amount I need without leftovers; (2) I don't have the expense of heating the oven; and (3) I'm not throwing away the bone, gristle, and fat I'd be cutting away from the meat. Overall, it is probably cheaper to "roast" it the way I do.

Did you know that you can make an acceptable meat loaf without using egg for the binding? Just replace every egg with ¼ cup of liquid. You could use beef broth, tomato sauce, even applesauce, to name just a few. For a meat loaf to serve 6, I always use 1 pound of extra-lean ground beef or turkey, 6 tablespoons of dried fine bread crumbs, and ¼ cup of the liquid, plus anything else healthy that strikes my fancy at the time. I mix well and place the mixture in an 8-by-8-inch baking dish or 9-by-5-inch loaf pan sprayed with cooking spray. Bake uncovered at 350 degrees for 35 to 50 minutes (depending on the added ingredients). You will never miss the egg.

Any time you are **browning ground meat** for a casserole and want to get rid of almost all the excess fat, just place the uncooked meat loosely in a plastic colander. Set the colander in a glass pie plate. Place in microwave and cook on HIGH for 3 to 6 minutes (depending on the amount being browned), stirring often. Use as you would for any casserole. You can also chop up onions and brown them with the meat if you want.

Fruits and Vegetables

If you want to enjoy a **"fruit shake"** with some pizazz, just combine soda water and unsweetened fruit juice in a blender. Add crushed ice. Blend on HIGH until thick. Refreshment without guilt.

You'll see that many recipes use ordinary **canned vegetables**. They're much cheaper than reduced-sodium versions, and once you rinse and drain them, the sodium is reduced anyway. I believe in saving money wherever possible so we can afford the best fat-free and sugar-free products as they come onto the market.

All three kinds of **vegetables—fresh, frozen, and canned**—have their place in a healthy diet. My husband, Cliff, hates the taste of frozen or fresh green beans, thinks the texture is all wrong, so I use canned green beans instead. In this case, canned vegetables have their proper place when I'm feeding my husband. If someone in your family has a similar concern, it's important to respond to it so everyone can be happy and enjoy the meal.

When I use **fruits or vegetables** like apples, cucumbers, and zucchini, I wash them really well and **leave the skin on**. It provides added color, fiber, and attractiveness to any dish. And, because I use processed flour in my cooking, I like to increase the fiber in my diet by eating my fruits and vegetables in their closest-to-natural state.

To help keep **fresh fruits and veggies fresh**, just give them a quick "shower" with lemon juice. The easiest way to do this is to pour purchased lemon juice into a kitchen spray bottle and store in the refrigerator. Then, every time you use fresh fruits or vegetables in a salad or dessert, simply give them a quick spray with your "lemon spritzer." You just might be amazed by how this little trick keeps your produce from turning brown so fast.

The next time you warm canned vegetables such as carrots or green beans, drain and heat the vegetables in ¼ cup beef or chicken broth. It gives a nice variation to an old standby. Here's a simple **white sauce** for vegetables and casseroles without using added fat that can be made by spraying a medium saucepan with butter-flavored cooking spray. Place 1½ cups evaporated skim milk and 3 tablespoons flour in a covered jar. Shake well. Pour into sprayed saucepan and cook over medium heat until thick, stirring constantly. Add salt and pepper to taste. You can also add ½ cup canned drained mushrooms and/ or 3 ounces (¾ cup) shredded reduced-fat cheese. Continue cooking until cheese melts.

Zip up canned or frozen green beans with **chunky salsa**: ½ cup to 2 cups beans. Heat thoroughly. Chunky salsa also makes a wonderful dressing on lettuce salads. It only counts as a vegetable, so enjoy.

Another wonderful **South-of-the-Border** dressing can be stirred up by using ½ cup of chunky salsa and ¼ cup fat-free Ranch dressing. Cover and store in your refrigerator. Use as a dressing for salads or as a topping for baked potatoes.

For **gravy** with all the "old time" flavor but without the extra fat, try this almost effortless way to prepare it. (It's almost as easy as opening up a store-bought jar.) Pour the juice off your roasted meat, then set the roast aside to "rest" for about 20 minutes. Place the juice in an uncovered cake pan or other large flat pan (we want the large air surface to speed up the cooling process) and put in the freezer until the fat congeals on top and you can skim it off. Or, if you prefer, use a skimming pitcher purchased at your kitchen gadget store. Either way, measure about 1½ cups skimmed broth and pour into a medium saucepan. Cook over medium heat until heated through, about 5 minutes. In a covered jar, combine ½ cup water or cooled potato broth with 3 tablespoons flour. Shake well. Pour flour mixture into warmed juice. Combine well using a wire whisk. Continue cooking until gravy thickens, about 5 minutes. Season with salt and pepper to taste.

Why did I use flour instead of cornstarch? Because any leftovers will reheat nicely with the flour base and would not with a cornstarch base. Also, 3 tablespoons of flour works out to 1 Bread/Starch exchange. This virtually fat-free gravy makes about 2 cups, so you could spoon about ½ cup gravy on your low-fat mashed potatoes and only have to count your gravy as ¼ Bread/Starch exchange.

Desserts

Thaw **lite whipped topping** in the refrigerator overnight. Never try to force the thawing by stirring or using a microwave to soften. Stirring it will remove the air from the topping that gives it the lightness and texture we want, and there's not enough fat in it to survive being heated.

How can I **frost an entire pie with just ½ cup of whipped topping?** First, don't use an inexpensive brand. I use Cool Whip Lite or La Creme Lite. Make sure the topping is fully thawed. Always spread from the center to the sides using a rubber spatula. This way, ½ cup topping will literally cover an entire pie. Remember, the operative word is *frost*, not pile the entire container on top of the pie!

For a special treat that tastes anything but "diet," try placing **spreadable fruit** in a container and microwave for about 15 seconds. Then pour the melted fruit spread over a serving of nonfat ice cream or frozen yogurt. One tablespoon of spreadable fruit is equal to 1 fruit serving. Some combinations to get you started are apricot over chocolate ice cream, strawberry over strawberry ice cream, or any flavor over vanilla.

Another way I use spreadable fruit is to make a delicious **topping for a cheesecake or angel food cake**. I take ½ cup of fruit and ½ cup Cool Whip Lite and blend the two together with a teaspoon of coconut extract.

Here's a really **good topping** for the fall of the year. Place 1½ cups unsweetened applesauce in a medium saucepan or 4-cup glass measure. Stir in 2 tablespoons raisins, 1 teaspoon apple pie spice, and 2 tablespoons Cary's Sugar Free Maple Syrup. Cook over medium heat on stove or process on HIGH in microwave until warm. Then spoon about ½ cup warm mixture over pancakes, French toast, or fat-free and sugar-free vanilla ice cream. It's as close as you will get to guilt-free apple pie!

A quick yet tasty way to prepare **strawberries for shortcake** is to place about ¾ cup sliced strawberries, 2 tablespoons Diet Mountain Dew, and sugar substitute to equal ¼ cup sugar in a blender container. Process on BLEND until mixture is smooth. Pour mixture into bowl. Add 1¼ cups sliced strawberries and mix well. Cover and refrigerate until ready to serve with shortcake.

The next time you are making treats for the family, try using **unsweetened applesauce** for some or all of the required oil in the recipe. For instance, if the recipe calls for ½ cup cooking oil, use up to the ½ cup in applesauce. It works and most people will not even notice the difference. It's great in purchased cake mixes, but so far I haven't been able to figure out a way to deep-fat fry with it!

Another trick I often use is to include tiny amounts of "real people" food, such as coconut, but extend the flavor by using extracts. Try it—you will be surprised by how little of the real thing you can use and still feel you are not being deprived.

If you are preparing a pie filling that has ample moisture, just line **graham crackers** in the bottom of a 9-by-9-inch cake pan. Pour the filling over the top of the crackers. Cover and refrigerate until the moisture has enough time to soften the crackers. Overnight is best. This eliminates the added **fats and sugars of a piecrust.**

When **stirring fat-free cream cheese to soften it**, use only a sturdy spoon, never an electric mixer. The speed of a mixer can cause the cream cheese to lose its texture and become watery.

Did you know you can make your own **fruit-flavored yogurt?** Mix 1 tablespoon of any flavor of spreadable fruit spread with ¾ cup plain yogurt. It's every bit as tasty and much cheaper. You can also make your own **lemon yogurt** by combining 3 cups plain fat-free yogurt with 1 tub Crystal Light lemonade powder. Mix well, cover, and store in refrigerator. I think you will be pleasantly surprised by the ease, cost, and flavor of this "made from scratch" calcium-rich treat. P.S. You can make any flavor you like by using any of the Crystal Light mixes—Cranberry? Iced tea? You decide.

Sugar-free puddings and gelatins are important to many of my recipes, but if you prefer to avoid sugar substitutes, you could still prepare the recipes with regular puddings or gelatins. The calories would be higher, but you would still be cooking low-fat.

When a recipe calls for **chopped nuts** (and you only have whole ones), who wants to dirty the food processor just for a couple of tablespoons? You could try to chop them using your cutting board, but be prepared for bits and pieces to fly all over the kitchen. I use "Grandma's food processor." I use the biggest nuts I can find, put them in a small glass bowl, and chop them into chunks just the right size using a metal biscuit cutter.

If you have a **leftover muffin** and are looking for something a little different for breakfast, you can make a **"breakfast sundae."** Crumble the muffin into a cereal bowl. Sprinkle a serving of fresh fruit over it and top with a couple of tablespoons of nonfat plain yogurt sweetened with sugar substitute and your choice of extract. The thought of it just might make you jump out of bed with a smile on your face. (Speaking of muffins, did you know that if you fill the unused muffin wells with water when baking muffins, you help ensure more even baking and protect the muffin pan at the same time?) Another muffin hint: Lightly spray the inside of paper baking cups with butter-flavored cooking spray before spooning the muffin batter into them. Then you won't end up with paper clinging to your fresh-baked muffins.

The secret of making **good meringues** without sugar is to use 1 tablespoon of Sprinkle Sweet or Sugar Twin for every egg white, and a small amount of extract. Use ½ to 1 teaspoon for the batch. Almond, vanilla, and coconut are all good choices. Use the same amount of cream of tartar you usually do. Bake the meringue in the same old way. Don't think you can't have meringue pies because you can't eat sugar. You can, if you do it my way. (Remember that egg whites whip up best at room temperature.)

Homemade or Store-Bought?

I've been asked which is better for you: homemade from scratch, or purchased foods. My answer is *both!* They each have a place in a healthy lifestyle, and what that place is has everything to do with you.

Take **piecrusts**, for instance. If you love spending your spare time in the kitchen preparing foods, and you're using low-fat, low-sugar, and reasonably low sodium ingredients, go for it! But if, like so many people, your time is limited and you've learned to read labels, you could be better off using purchased foods.

I know that when I prepare a pie (and I experiment with a couple of pies each week, because this is Cliff's favorite dessert) I use a purchased crust. Why? Mainly because I can't make a good-tasting piecrust that is lower in fat than the brands I use.

Also, purchased piecrusts fit my rule of "If it takes longer to fix than to eat, forget it!"

I've checked the nutrient information for the purchased piecrusts against recipes for traditional and "diet" piecrusts, using my computer software program. The purchased crust calculated lower in both fat and calories! I have tried some low-fat and low-sugar recipes, but they just didn't spark my taste buds, or were so complicated you needed an engineering degree just to get the crust in the pie plate.

I'm very happy with the purchased piecrusts in my recipes, because the finished product rarely, if ever, has more than 30 percent of total calories coming from fats. I also believe that we have to prepare foods our families and friends will eat with us on a regular basis and not feel deprived, or we've wasted time, energy, and money.

I could use a purchased "lite" **pie filling**, but instead I make my own. Here I can save both fat and sugar, and still make the filling almost as fast as opening a can. The bottom line: Know what you have to spend when it comes to both time and fat/sugar calories, then make the best decision you can for you and your family. And don't go without an occasional piece of pie because you think it isn't *necessary*. A delicious pie prepared in a healthy way is one of the simple pleasures of life. It's a little thing, but it can make all the difference between just getting by with the bare minimum and living a full and healthy lifestyle.

Many people have experimented with my tip about **substituting applesauce and artificial sweetener for butter and sugar**, but what if you aren't satisfied with the result? One woman wrote to me about a recipe for her grandmother's cookies that called for 1 cup butter and 1½ cups sugar. Well, any recipe that depends on as much butter and sugar as this one does is generally not a good candidate for "healthy exchanges." The original recipe needed a large quantity of fat to produce a crisp cookie just like Grandma made.

Unsweetened applesauce can be used to substitute for vegetable oil with various degrees of success, but not to replace butter, lard, or margarine. If your recipe calls for ½ cup oil or less, and it's a quick bread, muffin, or bar cookie, it should work to replace the oil with applesauce. If the recipe calls for more than ½ cup oil, then experiment with half oil, half applesauce. You've still made the recipe healthier, even if you haven't removed all the oil from it.

Another rule for healthy substitution: Up to ½ cup sugar or less can be replaced by *an artificial sweetener that can withstand the heat of baking*, like Sugar Twin or Sprinkle Sweet. If it requires more than ½ cup sugar, cut the amount needed by 75 percent and use ½ cup sugar substitute and sugar for the rest. Other options: Reduce the butter and sugar by 25 percent and see if the finished product still satisfies you in taste and appearance. Or, make the cookies just like Grandma did, realizing they are part of your family's holiday tradition. Enjoy a moderate serving of a couple of cookies once or twice during the season, and just forget about them the rest of the year.

I'm sure you'll add to this list of cooking tips as you begin preparing Healthy Exchanges recipes and discover how easy it can be to adapt your own favorite recipes using these ideas and your own common sense.

A Peek into My Pantry and My Favorite Brands

■ ■ ■ ■ ■ ■ ■ ■

Everyone asks me what foods I keep on hand and what brands I use. There are lots of good products on the grocery shelves today—many more than we dreamed about even a year or two ago. And I can't wait to see what's out there twelve months from now. The following are my staples and, where appropriate, my favorites *at this time*. I feel these products are healthier, tastier, easy to get—and deliver the most flavor for the least amount of fat, sugar, or calories. If you find others you like as well *or better,* please use them. This is only a guide to make your grocery shopping and cooking easier.

Fat-free plain yogurt *(Yoplait or Dannon)*
Nonfat dry skim milk powder *(Carnation)*
Evaporated skim milk *(Carnation)*

Skim milk
Fat-free cottage cheese
Fat-free cream cheese *(Philadelphia)*
Fat-free mayonnaise *(Kraft)*
Fat-free salad dressings *(Kraft)*
Fat-free sour cream *(Land O Lakes)*
Reduced-calorie margarine *(Weight Watchers, Promise, or Smart Beat)*
Cooking spray
   Olive oil–flavored and regular *(Pam)*
   Butter-flavored for sautéing *(Weight Watchers)*
   Butter-flavored for spritzing *after* cooking *(I Can't Believe It's Not Butter!)*
Vegetable oil *(Puritan canola oil)*
Reduced-calorie whipped topping *(Cool Whip Lite or Cool Whip Free)*
Sugar substitute
   if no heating is involved *(Equal)*
   if heating is required
      white *(Sugar Twin or Sprinkle Sweet)*
      brown *(Brown Sugar Twin)*
Sugar-free gelatin and pudding mixes *(JELL-O)*
Baking mix *(Bisquick Reduced Fat)*
Pancake mix *(Aunt Jemima Reduced-Calorie)*
Reduced-calorie maple syrup *(Cary's Sugar Free)*
Parmesan cheese *(Kraft fat-free)*
Reduced-fat cheese *(Kraft ⅓ Less Fat)*
Shredded frozen potatoes *(Mr. Dell's)*
Spreadable fruit spread *(Smucker's, Welch's, or Knott's Berry Farm)*
Peanut butter *(Peter Pan reduced-fat, Jif reduced-fat, or Skippy reduced-fat)*
Chicken broth *(Healthy Request)*
Beef broth *(Swanson)*
Tomato sauce *(Hunt's—Chunky and Regular)*
Canned soups *(Healthy Request)*
Tomato juice *(Campbell's Reduced-Sodium)*

Ketchup *(Heinz Light Harvest or Healthy Choice)*
Purchased piecrust
  unbaked *(Pillsbury—from dairy case)*
  graham cracker, butter-flavored, or chocolate-flavored
    (Keebler)
Crescent rolls *(Pillsbury Reduced Fat)*
Pastrami and corned beef *(Carl Buddig Lean)*
Luncheon meats *(Healthy Choice or Oscar Mayer)*
Ham *(Dubuque 97% fat-free and reduced-sodium or Healthy
    Choice)*
Frankfurters and Kielbasa sausage *(Healthy Choice)*
Canned white chicken, packed in water *(Swanson)*
Canned tuna, packed in water *(Chicken of the Sea)*
90-95 percent lean ground turkey and beef
Soda crackers *(Nabisco Fat-Free)*
Reduced-calorie bread—40 calories per slice or less
Hamburger buns—80 calories each or less
Rice—instant, regular, brown, and wild
Instant potato flakes *(Betty Crocker Potato Buds)*
Noodles, spaghetti, and macaroni
Salsa *(Chi Chi's Mild Chunky)*
Pickle relish—dill, sweet, and hot dog
Mustard—Dijon, prepared, and spicy
Unsweetened apple juice
Unsweetened applesauce
Fruit—fresh, frozen (no sugar added), or canned in juice
Vegetables—fresh, frozen, or canned
Spices—JO's Spices
Lemon and lime juice (in small plastic fruit-shaped bottles
    found in produce section)
Instant fruit beverage mixes *(Crystal Light)*
Dry dairy beverage mixes *(Nestlé Quik and Swiss Miss)*
"Ice Cream"—*(Wells' Blue Bunny sugar- and fat-free)*

The items on my shopping list are everyday foods found in
just about any grocery store in America. But all are as low in
fat, sugar, calories, and sodium that I can find—and that still

taste good! I can make any recipe in my cookbooks and news-letters as long as I have my cupboards and refrigerator stocked with these items. Whenever I use the last of any one item, I just make sure I pick up another supply the next time I'm at the store.

If your grocer does not stock these items, why not ask if they can be ordered on a trial basis? If the store agrees to do so, be sure to tell your friends to stop by, so that sales are good enough to warrant restocking the new products. Competition for shelf space is fierce, so only products that sell well stay around.

Shopping the
Healthy Exchanges
Way

■ ■ ■ ■ ■ ■ ■ ■

$\mathcal{S}$ometimes, as part of a cooking demonstration, I take the group on a field trip to the nearest supermarket. There's no better place to share my discoveries about which healthy products taste best, which are best for you, and which healthy products don't deliver enough taste to include in my recipes.

While I'd certainly enjoy accompanying you to your neighborhood store, we'll have to settle for a field trip *on paper*. I've tasted and tried just about every fat- and sugar-free product on the market, but so many new ones keep coming all the time, you're going to have to learn to play detective on your own. I've turned label reading into an art, but often the label doesn't tell me everything I need to know.

Sometimes you'll find, as I have, that the product with *no* fat doesn't provide the taste satisfaction you require; other times, a no-fat or low-fat product just doesn't cook up the same way as the original product. And some foods, including even the leanest meats, can't eliminate *all* the fat. That's okay, though—a healthy diet should include anywhere from 15 to 25 percent of total calories from fat on any given day.

Take my word for it—your supermarket is filled with lots of delicious foods that can and should be part of your healthy diet for life. Come, join me as we check it out on the way to the checkout!

First stop, the **salad dressing** aisle. Salad dressing is usually a high-fat food, but there are great alternatives available. Let's look first at the regular Ranch dressing—2 tablespoons have 170 calories and 18 grams of fat—and who can eat just 2 tablespoons? Already, that's about half the fat grams most people should consume in a day. Of course, it's the most flavorful too. Now let's look at the low-fat version. Two tablespoons have 110 calories and 11 grams of fat; they took about half of the fat out, but there's still a lot of sugar there. The fat-free version has 50 calories and zero grams of fat, but they also took most of the flavor out. Here's what you do to get it back: add a tablespoon of fat-free mayonnaise, a few parsley flakes, and about a half teaspoon of sugar substitute to your 2-tablespoon serving. That trick, with the fat-free mayo and sugar substitute, will work with just about any fat-free dressing and give it more of that full-bodied flavor of the high-fat version. Be careful not to add too much sugar substitute—you don't want it to become sickeningly sweet.

I use Kraft fat-free **mayonnaise** at 10 calories per tablespoon to make scalloped potatoes, too. The Smart Beat brand is also a good one.

Before I buy anything at the store, I read the label carefully: the total fat plus the saturated fat; I look to see how many calories are in a realistic serving, and I say to myself, Would I eat that much—or would I eat more? I look at the sodium and I look at the total carbohydrates. I like to check those ingredients because I'm cooking for diabetics and heart patients, too. And I check the total calories from fat.

Remember that 1 fat gram equals 9 calories, while 1 protein or 1 carbohydrate gram equals 4 calories.

A wonderful new product is I Can't Believe It's Not Butter! spray, with zero calories and zero grams of fat in four squirts. It's great for your air-popped popcorn. As for **light margarine spread**, beware—most of the fat-free brands don't melt on toast, and they don't taste very good either, so I just leave them on the shelf. For the few times I do use a light margarine I tend to buy Smart Beat Ultra, Promise Ultra, or Weight Watchers Light Ultra. The number-one ingredient in them is water. I occasionally use the light margarine in cooking, but I don't really put margarine on my toast anymore. I use apple butter or make a spread with fat-free cream cheese mixed with a little spreadable fruit instead.

So far, Pillsbury hasn't released a reduced-fat **crescent roll**, so you'll only get one crescent roll per serving from me. I usually make eight of the rolls serve twelve by using them for a crust. The house brands may be lower in fat, but they're usually not as good flavorwise—and don't quite cover the pan when you use them to make a crust. If you're going to use crescent rolls with lots of other stuff on top, then a house brand might be fine.

The Pillsbury French Loaf makes a wonderful **pizza crust** and fills a giant jelly roll pan. One-fifth of this package "costs" you only 1 gram of fat (and I don't even let you have that much!). Once you use this for your pizza crust, you will never go back to anything else instead. I use it to make calzones, too.

I only use Philadelphia fat-free **cream cheese** because it has the best consistency. I've tried other brands, but I wasn't happy with them. Healthy Choice makes lots of great products, but their cream cheese just doesn't work as well with my recipes.

Let's move to the **cheese** aisle. My preferred brand is Kraft ⅓ Less Fat Shredded Cheeses. I will not use the fat-free versions because *they don't melt.* I would gladly give up sugar and fat, but I will not give up flavor. This is a happy compromise. I use the reduced-fat version, I use less, and I use it where your eyes "eat" it, on top of the recipe. So you walk away satisfied and with a finished product that's very low in fat. If you want to make grilled cheese sandwiches for your kids, use the Kraft ⅓ Less Fat cheese slices, and it'll taste exactly like the one they're used to. The fat-free will not.

Some brands have come out with a fat-free **hot dog**, but the ones we've tasted haven't been very good. So far, among the low-fat brands, I think Healthy Choice tastes the best. Did you know that regular hot dogs have as many as 15 grams of fat?

Dubuque's Extra-Lean Reduced-Sodium **ham** tastes wonderful, reduces the sodium as well as the fat, and gives you a larger serving. Don't be fooled by products called turkey ham; they may *not* be lower in fat than a very lean pork product. Here's one label as an example: I checked a brand of turkey ham called Genoa. It gives you a 2-ounce serving for 70 calories and 3½ grams of fat. The Dubuque extra-lean ham, made from pork, gives you a 3-ounce serving for 90 calories, but only 2½ grams of fat. *You get more food and less fat.*

The same can be true for packaged **ground turkey**; if you're not buying *fresh* ground turkey, you may be getting a product with turkey skin and a lot of fat ground up in it. Look to be sure the package is labeled with the fat content; if it isn't, run the other way!

Your best bets in **snack foods** are pretzels, which are always low in fat, as well as the chips from the Guiltless Gourmet, which taste especially good with one of my dips.

Frozen dinners can be expensive and high in sodium, but it's smart to have two or three in the freezer as a backup when your best-laid plans go awry and you need to grab something on the run. It's not a good idea to rely on them too much— what if you can't get to the store to get them, or you're short on cash? The sodium can be high on some of them because they often replace the fat with salt, so do read the labels. Also ask yourself if the serving is enough to satisfy you; for many of us, it's not.

Egg substitute is expensive, and probably not necessary unless you're cooking for someone who has to worry about every bit of cholesterol in his or her diet. If you occasionally have a fried egg or an omelet, *use the real egg.* For cooking, you can usually substitute two egg whites for one whole egg. Most of the time it won't make any difference, but check your recipe carefully.

Frozen pizzas aren't particularly healthy, but used occasionally, in moderation, they're okay. Your best bet is to make your own using the Pillsbury French Loaf. Take a look at the frozen pizza package of your choice, though, because you may find that plain cheese pizza, which you might think would be the healthiest, might actually have the most fat. Since there's nothing else on there, they have to cover the crust with a heavy layer of high-fat cheese. A veggie pizza generally uses less cheese and more healthy, crunchy vegetables.

Healthy frozen desserts are hard to find except for the Weight Watchers brands. I've always felt that their portions are so small, and for their size still pretty high in fat and sugar. (This is one of the reasons I think I'll be successful marketing my frozen desserts someday. After Cliff tasted one of my earliest healthy pies—and licked the plate clean—he remarked that if I ever opened a restaurant, people would keep coming back for my desserts alone!) Keep an eye out for fat-free or very low-fat frozen yogurt or sorbet products. Even Häagen-Dazs, which makes some of the highest-fat-content ice cream, now has a fat-free fruit sorbet pop out that's pretty good. I'm sure there will be more before too long.

You have to be realistic: What are you willing to do, and what are you *not* willing to do? Let's take bread, for example. Some people just have to have the real thing—rye bread with caraway seeds or a whole-wheat version with bits of bran in it.

I prefer to use reduced-calorie **bread** because I like a *real* sandwich. This way, I can have two slices of bread and it counts as only one Bread/Starch exchange.

Do you love **croutons?** Forget the ones from the grocery store—they're extremely high in fat. Instead, take reduced-calorie bread, toast it, give it a quick spray of I Can't Believe It's Not Butter! Spray, and let it dry a bit. Cut the bread in cubes.

Then, for an extra-good flavor, put the pieces in a plastic bag with a couple of tablespoons of Kraft House Italian (a reduced-fat Parmesan/Romano cheese blend) and shake them up. You might be surprised at just how good they are! Another product that's really good for a crouton—Corn Chex cereal. Sprinkle a few Chex on top of your salad, and I think you'll be pleasantly surprised. I've also found that Rice Chex, crushed up, with parsley flakes and a little bit of Parmesan cheese, make a great topping for casseroles that you used to put potato chips on.

Salad toppers can make a lot of difference in how content you feel after you've eaten. Some low-fat cheese, some home-made croutons, and even some bacon bits on top of your greens deliver an abundance of tasty satisfaction. I always use the real Hormel **bacon bits** instead of the imitation bacon-flavored bits. I only use a small amount, but you get that real bacon flavor—and less fat too.

How I Shop for Myself

I always keep my kitchen stocked with my basic staples; that way, I can go to the cupboard and create new recipes any time I'm inspired. I hope you will take the time (and allot the money) to stock your cupboards with items from the staples list, so you can enjoy developing your own healthy versions of family favorites without making extra trips to the market.

I'm always on the lookout for new products sitting on the grocery shelf. When I spot something I haven't seen before, I'll usually grab it, glance at the front, then turn it around and read the label carefully. I call it looking at the promises (the "come-on" on the front of the package) and then at the warranty (the ingredients list and the label on the back).

If it looks as good on the back as it does on the front, I'll say okay and either create a recipe on the spot or take it home for when I do think of something to do with it. Picking up a new product is just about the only time I buy something not on my list.

The items on my shopping list are normal, everyday foods, but as low-fat and low-sugar (*while still tasting good*) as I can find. I can make any recipe in this book as long as these staples are on my shelves. After using these products for a couple of weeks, you will find it becomes routine to have them on hand. And I promise you, I really don't spend any more at the store now than I did a few years ago when I told myself I couldn't afford some of these items. Back then, of course, plenty of unhealthy, high-priced snacks I really didn't need somehow made the magic leap from the grocery shelves into my cart. Who was I kidding?

Yes, you often have to pay a little more for fat-free or low-fat products, including meats. But since I frequently use a half pound of meat to serve four to six people, your cost per serving will be much lower.

Try adding up what you were spending before on chips and cookies, premium brand ice cream and fatty cuts of meat, and you'll soon see that we've *streamlined* your shopping cart, and taken the weight off your pocketbook as well as your hips!

Remember, your good health is *your* business—but it's big business too. Write to the manufacturers of products you and your family enjoy but feel are just too high in fat, sugar, or sodium to be part of your new healthy lifestyle. Companies are spending millions of dollars to respond to consumers' concerns about food products, and I bet that in the next few years, you'll discover fat-free and low-fat versions of nearly every product piled high on your supermarket shelves!

The
Family-Friendly
+
Healthy Exchanges
Kitchen

■ ■ ■ ■ ■ ■ ■ ■ ■

You might be surprised to discover I still don't have a massive test kitchen stocked with every modern appliance and handy gadget ever made. The tiny galley kitchen where I first launched Healthy Exchanges has room for only one person at a time, but it never stopped me from feeling the sky's the limit when it comes to seeking out great healthy taste!

Because storage is at such a premium in my kitchen, I don't waste space with equipment I don't really need. Here's a list of what I consider worth having. If you notice serious gaps in your equipment, you can probably find most of what you need at a local discount store or garage sale. If your kitchen is equipped with more sophisticated appliances, don't feel guilty about using them. Enjoy every appliance you can find room for or that you can afford. Just be assured that healthy, quick, and delicious food can be prepared with the "basics."

A Healthy Exchanges Kitchen Equipment List

Good-quality nonstick skillets (medium, large)

Good-quality saucepans (small, medium, large)

Glass mixing bowls (small, medium, large)

Glass measures (1-cup, 2-cup, 4-cup, 8-cup)

Sharp knives (paring, chef, butcher)

Rubber spatulas

Wire whisks

Measuring spoons

Measuring cups

Large mixing spoons

Egg separator

Covered jar

Vegetable parer

Grater

Potato masher

Electric mixer

Electric blender

Electric skillet

Cooking timer

Slow cooker

Air popper for popcorn

Kitchen scales (unless you *always* use my recipes)

Wire racks for cooling baked goods

Electric toaster oven (to conserve energy when only one item is being baked or for recipes with short baking times)

4-inch round custard dishes

Glass pie plates

8-by-8-inch glass baking dishes

Cake pans (9-by-9-, 9-by-13-inch)

10¾-by-7-by-1½-inch biscuit pan

Cookie sheets (good nonstick ones)

Jelly-roll pan

Muffin tins

5-by-9-inch bread pan

Plastic colander

Cutting board

Pie wedge server

Square-shaped server

Can opener (I prefer manual)

Rolling pin

How to Read a
Healthy Exchanges®
Recipe

■ ■ ■ ■ ■ ■ ■

The Healthy Exchanges
Nutritional Analysis

Before using these recipes you may wish to consult your physician or health-care provider to be sure they are appropriate for you. The information in this book is not intended to take the place of any medical advice. It reflects my experiences, studies, research, and opinions regarding healthy eating.

Each recipe includes nutritional information calculated in three ways:

Healthy Exchanges Weight Loss Choices™ or Exchanges
Calories, fiber, and fat grams
Diabetic exchanges

In every Healthy Exchanges recipe, the diabetic exchanges have been calculated by a registered dietitian. All the other calculations were done by computer, using the Food Processor

II software. When the ingredient listing gives more than one choice, the first ingredient listed is the one used in the recipe analysis. Due to inevitable variations in the ingredients you choose to use, the nutritional values should be considered approximate.

The annotation "(limited)" following Protein counts in some recipes indicates that consumption of whole eggs should be limited to four per week.

Please note the following symbols:

☆ This means you should read the recipe's directions carefully for special instructions about **division** of ingredients.

❋ This symbol indicates **freezes well.**

A Few Cooking Terms to Ease the Way

■■■■■■■■

Everyone can learn to cook *The Healthy Exchanges Way*. It's simple, it's quick, and the results are delicious! If you've tended to avoid the kitchen because you find recipe instructions confusing or complicated, I hope I can help you feel more confident. I'm not offering a full cooking course here, just some terms I use often that I know you'll want to understand.

Bake	To cook food in the oven; sometimes called roasting
Beat	To mix very fast with a spoon, wire whisk, or electric mixer
Blend	To mix two or more ingredients together thoroughly so that the mixture is smooth
Boil	To cook in liquid until bubbles form

Brown	To cook at low to medium-low heat until ingredients turn brown
Chop	To cut food into small pieces with a knife, blender, or food processor
Cool	To let stand at room temperature until food is no longer hot to the touch
Combine	To mix ingredients together with a spoon
Dice	To chop into small, even-sized pieces
Drain	To pour off liquid; sometimes you will need to reserve the liquid to use in the recipe, so please read carefully.
Drizzle	To sprinkle drops of liquid (for example, chocolate syrup) lightly over top of food
Fold in	To combine delicate ingredients with other foods by using a gentle, circular motion. Example: adding Cool Whip Lite to an already stirred-up bowl of pudding.
Preheat	To heat your oven to the desired temperature, usually about 10 minutes before you put your food in to bake
Sauté	To cook in skillet or frying pan until food is soft
Simmer	To cook in a small amount of liquid over low heat; this lets the flavors blend without too much liquid evaporating.
Whisk	To beat with a wire whisk until mixture is well mixed; don't worry about finesse here, just use some elbow grease!

How to Measure

I try to make it as easy as possible by providing more than one measurement for many ingredients in my recipes—both the weight in ounces and the amount measured by a measuring cup, for example. Just remember:

- You measure **solids** (flour, Cool Whip Lite, yogurt, macaroni, nonfat dry milk powder) in your set of separate measuring cups (¼, ⅓, ½, 1 cup)
- You measure **liquids** (Diet Mountain Dew, water, tomato juice) in the clear glass or plastic cups that measure ounces, cups, and pints. Set the cup on a level surface and pour the liquid into it, or you may get too much.
- You can use your measuring spoon set for liquids or solids. **Note:** Don't pour a liquid like an extract into a measuring spoon held over the bowl, because you might overpour; instead, do it over the sink.

Here are a few handy equivalents:

3 teaspoons	equals	1 tablespoon
4 tablespoons	equals	¼ cup
5⅓ tablespoons	equals	⅓ cup
8 tablespoons	equals	½ cup
10⅔ tablespoons	equals	⅔ cup
12 tablespoons	equals	¾ cup
16 tablespoons	equals	1 cup
2 cups	equals	1 pint
4 cups	equals	1 quart
8 ounces liquid	equals	1 fluid cup

That's it. Now, ready, set, cook!

The Recipes

Get-Out-of-Bed Breakfasts

■■■■■■■■

My grandbaby Josh is an early riser like his Grandma Jo. (His brother, Zach, is more like Grandpa Cliff—they like to stay up late at night together and then sleep in!) When they stay with us, the boys sleep in their sleeping bags on the family room rug, and little Josh wakes up when I do, around 5:00 or 5:30. As I begin preparing breakfast, he always comes into the kitchen to see what's happening. He loves to hang around while I cook. He's so small standing next to the counter, so I usually pile up a couple of thick catalogs on a dining room chair. Morning is a great time for Josh. He just seems to wake up happy, and when he's happy, he smiles from ear to ear. (He's only two so the preparation doesn't interest him much, just what's piled on his little plate.) And oh, how he smiles when he has scrambled eggs (like my **Creamy Scrambled Eggs with Franks**), or one of my healthy breakfast recipes that deliver sunshine and warmth in every bite!

☙

Must children eat a full breakfast in order to succeed in school and have sufficient energy for the day? It's a good idea, but sitting down to a big meal doesn't always fit into your family schedule. The recipes in this section offer a range of possibilities, from substantial hot dishes perfect for a relaxed weekend morning (**Ham Breakfast Casserole**) to my own versions of breakfast-on-the-run (**Island Breakfast Muffins**) when your son or daughter is racing for the bus! If mornings are always stressful and rushed in your house, you may want to help your kids prepare for the next day the night before, laying out clothes and packing school bags. That way, there will be a bit more time for a sit-down breakfast to start off the day.

Get-Out-of-Bed Breakfasts

Scrambled Egg Hash

Creamy Scrambled Eggs
with Franks

Ham Breakfast Casserole

All-American Pancakes

Cheese-Corn Griddle
Cakes

Sunshine Pancake
Sandwiches

Island Breakfast Muffins

Breakfast Drop Scones

Quick-n-Easy Sticky Rolls

Peanut Butter and Jelly
French Toast

Pineapple Upside-Down
French Toast

Apple Breakfast Strata

Breakfast Tarts

Peanut Butter and Jelly
Wraps

Scrambled Egg Hash

■ ■ ■ ■ ■ ■ ■ ■

If you've ever felt like a short-order cook, trying to please everyone and never getting to sit down and enjoy your own breakfast, here's a diner-type delight that combines your family's favorites in one tummy-pleasing dish! *Serves 4 (1 cup)*

3 cups (10 ounces) shredded loose packed frozen potatoes, thawed
1 full cup (6 ounces) diced Dubuque 97% fat-free ham or any extra-lean ham

6 eggs, beaten, or equivalent in egg substitute
¼ teaspoon lemon pepper
¼ cup Land O Lakes no-fat sour cream

In a large skillet sprayed with butter-flavored cooking spray, brown potatoes and ham for about 10 minutes, stirring occasionally. Add eggs and lemon pepper. Mix well to combine. Stir in sour cream. Lower heat and continue cooking until eggs are set, stirring occasionally.

HINT: Mr. Dell's frozen shredded potatoes are a good choice *or* raw shredded potatoes may be used in place of frozen potatoes.

Each serving equals:
HE: 2½ Protein (1½ limited), ½ Bread, 15 Optional Calories

225 Calories, 9 gm Fat, 18 gm Protein, 18 gm Carbohydrate, 475 mg Sodium, 61 mg Calcium, 2 gm Fiber

DIABETIC: 2½ Meat, 1 Starch

Creamy Scrambled Eggs with Franks

This unusual skillet dish is sure to win you cheers from children who could eat hot dogs at every meal! Maybe you've never considered healthy franks a breakfast meat, but they provide good taste and healthy protein in this flavorful combo.

Serves 4 (¾ cup)

8 ounces Healthy Choice 97% fat-free frankfurters, diced

6 eggs or equivalent in egg substitute

½ teaspoon lemon pepper

1 teaspoon dried parsley flakes

¼ cup Land O Lakes no-fat sour cream

In a large skillet sprayed with butter-flavored cooking spray, sauté frankfurters for 3 to 4 minutes. Lower heat. In a medium bowl, combine eggs, lemon pepper, and parsley flakes. Pour egg mixture into skillet. Add sour cream. Mix well to combine. Continue cooking until eggs are set, stirring occasionally.

Each serving equals:
HE: 2¾ Protein (1½ limited), ¼ Slider

152 Calories, 8 gm Fat, 14 gm Protein, 6 gm Carbohydrate, 460 mg Sodium, 54 mg Calcium, 0 gm Fiber

DIABETIC: 2 Meat, ½ Starch

Ham Breakfast Casserole

■ ■ ■ ■ ■ ■ ■ ■

Start your busy weekend off with this hearty baked entree packed with enough goodness and flavor to fuel the entire family's activity-filled day! Soccer practice, errands all over town, or just a few delightful hours in the garden—you'll all enjoy endless energy along with great nutrition.   *Serves 4*

8 slices reduced-calorie
   white bread☆
1 full cup (6 ounces) finely
   diced Dubuque 97% fat-
   free ham or any extra-
   lean ham
½ cup (one 2.5-ounce jar)
   sliced mushrooms,
   drained
¾ cup (3 ounces) shredded
   Kraft reduced-fat
   Cheddar cheese

4 eggs, beaten, or
   equivalent in egg
   substitute
1⅓ cups skim milk
1 teaspoon dried onion
   flakes
1 teaspoon dried parsley
   flakes
½ teaspoon lemon pepper

Spray an 8-by-8-inch baking dish with butter-flavored cooking spray. Place 4 slices of bread in prepared baking dish. Sprinkle ham, mushrooms, and Cheddar cheese over top. Cover with remaining 4 slices of bread. In a medium bowl, combine eggs and skim milk. Add onion flakes, parsley flakes, and lemon pepper. Mix well to combine. Evenly pour egg mixture over bread. Cover and refrigerate for at least 1 hour or up to overnight. Uncover and bake at 350 degrees for 1 hour. Place baking dish on a wire rack and let set for 5 minutes. Cut into 4 servings.

Each serving equals:
HE: 3 Protein (1 limited), 1 Bread, ⅓ Skim Milk, ¼ Vegetable

289 Calories, 9 gm Fat, 27 gm Protein, 25 gm Carbohydrate, 873 mg Sodium, 317 mg Calcium, 5 gm Fiber

DIABETIC: 3 Meat, 1½ Starch/Carbohydrate

All-American Pancakes

■ ■ ■ ■ ■ ■ ■ ■ ■

*A*pple pie for breakfast? You bet, when it's my party-in-a-pancake that delivers such good-for-you goodness! The cozy aroma of this dish is simply mouthwatering.   *Serves 4*

1 cup Cary's Sugar Free Maple Syrup
1 cup (2 small) cored, unpeeled, and chopped cooking apples
1½ cups Aunt Jemima Reduced Calorie Pancake Mix

1½ cups water
⅓ cup (1½ ounces) shredded Kraft reduced-fat Cheddar cheese
2 tablespoons Hormel Bacon Bits

In a medium saucepan, combine maple syrup and apples. Simmer over medium-low heat while preparing pancakes, stirring occasionally. In a medium bowl, combine pancake mix and water. Stir in Cheddar cheese and bacon bits. Using a ¼-cup measuring cup as a guide, pour batter onto a hot griddle or skillet sprayed with butter-flavored cooking spray to form 8 pancakes. Lightly brown on both sides. For each serving, place 2 pancakes on a plate and spoon about ⅓ cup syrup mixture over top.

Each serving equals:

HE: 2 Bread, ½ Fruit, ¼ Protein, ½ Slider, 12 Optional Calories

252 Calories, 4 gm Fat, 13 gm Protein, 41 gm Carbohydrate, 925 mg Sodium, 342 mg Calcium, 6 gm Fiber

DIABETIC: 2 Starch, ½ Fruit, ½ Meat

Cheese-Corn Griddle Cakes

■ ■ ■ ■ ■ ■ ■ ■

Instead of the same old pancakes you've been serving for years, ignite those teen taste buds with this luscious breakfast option. Aren't we lucky it's so easy to make healthy versions of old-time goodies?   *Serves 6*

½ cup yellow cornmeal
¾ cup Bisquick Reduced
   Fat Baking Mix
2 tablespoons Sugar Twin
   or Sprinkle Sweet
1 egg or equivalent in egg
   substitute

1 tablespoon vegetable oil
⅔ cup skim milk
Full ½ cup (2¼ ounces)
   shredded Kraft reduced-
   fat Cheddar cheese

In a medium bowl, combine cornmeal, baking mix, and Sugar Twin. Add egg, oil, and skim milk. Mix gently just until combined. Fold in Cheddar cheese. Using a ¼-cup measuring cup as a guide, pour batter onto a hot griddle or skillet sprayed with butter-flavored cooking spray. Lightly brown on both sides. Serve at once.

HINT: Good served with Cary's Sugar Free Maple Syrup.

Each serving equals:
HE: 1⅓ Bread, ⅔ Protein, ¼ Fat, 12 Optional Calories

166 Calories, 6 gm Fat, 7 gm Protein, 21 gm Carbohydrate, 286 mg Sodium, 118 mg Calcium, 1 gm Fiber

DIABETIC: 1½ Starch/Carbohydrate, ½ Meat, ½ Fat

Sunshine Pancake Sandwiches

▪ ▪ ▪ ▪ ▪ ▪ ▪ ▪

Some recipes are inspired by the children you're cooking for—how about this delectable and fun dish I created to charm my grandbabies, Zach and Josh? They both love pancakes, so that's what I most often fix when they come to visit! *Serves 4*

1 (8-ounce) package
    Philadelphia fat-free
    cream cheese
¼ cup + 2 tablespoons
    Sugar Twin or Sprinkle
    Sweet ☆
1 cup unsweetened orange
    juice ☆
1 teaspoon coconut extract
1 (4-serving) package
    JELL-O sugar-free

vanilla cook-and-serve
    pudding mix
⅔ cup Carnation Nonfat
    Dry Milk Powder
½ cup water
1½ cups Bisquick Reduced
    Fat Baking Mix
1 cup skim milk
2 tablespoons flaked
    coconut

In a small bowl, stir cream cheese with a spoon until soft. Add ¼ cup Sugar Twin, 1 tablespoon orange juice, and coconut extract. Mix gently to combine. Set aside. In a medium sauce-pan, combine dry pudding mix, dry milk powder, remaining orange juice, and water. Cook over medium-low heat until mixture thickens, stirring often. Meanwhile, in a large bowl, combine baking mix, remaining 2 tablespoons Sugar Twin, and skim milk. Using a ¼-cup measuring cup as a guide, pour batter onto a hot griddle or skillet sprayed with butter-flavored cooking spray to form 8 pancakes. Lightly brown on both sides. For each serving, place 1 pancake on a serving plate, spread about ¼ cup cream cheese mixture over top, arrange another pancake over cream cheese mixture, spoon about ⅓ cup orange sauce over top, and garnish with 1½ teaspoons coconut. Serve at once.

Each serving equals:
HE: 2 Bread, 1 Protein, ¾ Skim Milk, ½ Fruit, ¼ Slider, 17 Optional
Calories

---

328 Calories, 4 gm Fat, 18 gm Protein, 55 gm Carbohydrate,
978 mg Sodium, 255 mg Calcium, 1 gm Fiber

DIABETIC: 2½ Starch, 1 Meat, ½ Fruit, ½ Skim Milk *or* 3½ Starch/
Carbohydrate, 1 Meat

Island Breakfast Muffins

■ ■ ■ ■ ■ ■ ■ ■

$\mathcal{S}$ure, a teaspoon of diet margarine on your English muffin will keep your calories and fat grams low, but who wants to settle for just okay? Here's a terrific topping rich with sweet and tangy temptation! *Serves 4*

1 (8-ounce) package
   Philadelphia fat-free
   cream cheese
Sugar substitute to equal 1
   tablespoon sugar
1 teaspoon rum extract
⅛ teaspoon ground
   cinnamon

1 cup (one 8-ounce can)
   crushed pineapple,
   packed in fruit juice,
   drained
¼ cup raisins
2 English muffins, split
   and toasted

In a medium bowl, stir cream cheese with a spoon until soft. Add sugar substitute, rum extract, and cinnamon. Mix well to combine. Stir in drained pineapple and raisins. Evenly spoon about ½ cup mixture on each muffin half.

HINT: To plump up raisins without "cooking," place in a glass measuring cup and microwave on HIGH for 20 seconds.

Each serving equals:
HE: 1 Bread, 1 Protein, 1 Fruit, 2 Optional Calories

172 Calories, 0 gm Fat, 11 gm Protein, 32 gm Carbohydrate, 481 mg Sodium, 46 mg Calcium, 2 gm Fiber

DIABETIC: 1 Starch, 1 Meat, 1 Fruit

Breakfast Drop Scones

■ ■ ■ ■ ■ ■ ■ ■

Scones are one scrumptious reason why the sun never set on the British Empire! They're a delightful morning treat for the whole family served fresh, fruity, and oh-so-hot from the oven. Save a few minutes by mixing the dry ingredients the night before if you like.

Serves 8

1½ cups Bisquick Reduced
  Fat Baking Mix
2 tablespoons Sugar Twin
  or Sprinkle Sweet
½ cup raisins

½ cup (3 ounces) chopped
  dried apricots
⅔ cup Carnation Nonfat
  Dry Milk Powder
⅔ cup water

Preheat oven to 425 degrees. Spray a baking sheet with butter-flavored cooking spray. In a large bowl, combine baking mix, Sugar Twin, raisins, and apricots. In a small bowl, combine dry milk powder and water. Add milk mixture to baking mix mixture. Mix just until dry ingredients are moistened. Drop by heaping tablespoon onto prepared baking sheet to form 8 scones. Bake for 10 to 12 minutes. Place baking sheet on a wire rack. Lightly spray tops with butter-flavored cooking spray. Serve warm or cold.

Each serving equals:

HE: 1 Bread, 1 Fruit, ¼ Skim Milk, 2 Optional Calories

149 Calories, 1 gm Fat, 4 gm Protein, 31 gm Carbohydrate, 294 mg Sodium, 95 mg Calcium, 2 gm Fiber

DIABETIC: 1 Starch, 1 Fruit

Quick-n-Easy Sticky Rolls

■ ■ ■ ■ ■ ■ ■ ■ ■

Homemade sticky buns are better than a dozen alarm clocks to make your family rise and shine! Easy and quick, these make an everyday breakfast taste like a holiday.　　　**Serves 6**

2 tablespoons Brown
　Sugar Twin
¼ cup Cary's Sugar Free
　Maple Syrup
½ teaspoon apple pie spice
3 tablespoons (¾ ounce)
　chopped pecans

¼ cup raisins
1 (7.5-ounce) can Pillsbury
　refrigerated buttermilk
　biscuits

Preheat oven to 350 degrees. Spray a 9-inch pie plate with butter-flavored cooking spray. In prepared pie plate, combine Brown Sugar Twin, maple syrup, and apple pie spice. Stir in pecans and raisins. Separate biscuits and cut each biscuit into 4 pieces. Drop biscuit pieces evenly over syrup mixture. Lightly spray top of biscuit pieces with butter-flavored cooking spray. Bake for 12 to 15 minutes or until golden brown. Cut into 6 wedges. Serve hot.

Each serving equals:
HE: 1¼ Bread, ½ Fat, ⅓ Fruit, 8 Optional Calories

135 Calories, 3 gm Fat, 3 gm Protein, 24 gm Carbohydrate,
327 mg Sodium, 4 mg Calcium, 2 gm Fiber

DIABETIC: 1½ Starch/Carbohydrate, ½ Fat

Peanut Butter and Jelly French Toast

■ ■ ■ ■ ■ ■ ■ ■

It takes just a bit of peanut butter to persuade your mouth there's something wonderful going on! When you add some spreadable fruit, everyone will be glad they got up in time for breakfast! **Serves 4**

⅓ cup Carnation Nonfat
    Dry Milk Powder
½ cup water
1 teaspoon vanilla extract
1 egg or equivalent in egg
    substitute

¼ cup Peter Pan reduced-
    fat peanut butter
¼ cup grape spreadable
    fruit spread
8 slices reduced-calorie
    bread

In a shallow bowl, combine dry milk powder, water, and vanilla extract. Add egg. Mix well to combine. Spread 1 tablespoon peanut butter and 1 tablespoon grape fruit spread over the tops of 4 slices of bread. Top each with another slice of bread. Dip each "sandwich" into milk mixture, coating both sides. Place on hot griddle or large skillet sprayed with butter-flavored cooking spray. Brown on both sides.

Each serving equals:
HE: 1¼ Protein (¼ limited), 1 Bread, 1 Fruit, 1 Fat, ¼ Skim Milk

247 Calories, 7 gm Fat, 12 gm Protein, 34 gm Carbohydrate,
352 mg Sodium, 110 mg Calcium, 6 gm Fiber

DIABETIC: 1½ Starch/Carbohydrate, 1 Meat, 1 Fruit, 1 Fat

Pineapple Upside-Down French Toast

■ ■ ■ ■ ■ ■ ■ ■

This breakfast version of a beloved dessert will make every member of the family smile! I've been known to offer this quick and pretty dish as the centerpiece of a birthday morning meal, but you don't have to save it for special occasions.

Serves 4 (2 pieces)

2 cups (two 8-ounce cans) pineapple slices, packed in fruit juice, drained and ¼ cup liquid reserved
4 maraschino cherries, halved
¼ cup Brown Sugar Twin

1⅓ cups skim milk
2 eggs or equivalent in egg substitute
1 teaspoon ground cinnamon
½ teaspoon vanilla extract
8 slices reduced-calorie bread

Preheat oven to 375 degrees. In a rimmed 9-by-13-inch cookie sheet sprayed with butter-flavored cooking spray, evenly arrange pineapple slices. Place ½ cherry in center of each ring. Evenly sprinkle Brown Sugar Twin over pineapple slices. In a shallow bowl, combine skim milk, reserved pineapple juice, eggs, cinnamon, and vanilla extract. Dip bread slices into milk mixture, coating both sides. Evenly place bread slices over pineapple. Evenly pour any remaining milk mixture over bread. Bake for 20 to 25 minutes.

Each serving equals:
HE: 1 Bread, 1 Fruit, ½ Protein (limited), ⅓ Skim Milk, 15 Optional Calories

235 Calories, 3 gm Fat, 11 gm Protein, 41 gm Carbohydrate, 305 mg Sodium, 172 mg Calcium, 6 gm Fiber

DIABETIC: 1½ Starch, 1 Fruit, ½ Meat

Apple Breakfast Strata

■ ■ ■ ■ ■ ■ ■ ■

Planning a family brunch that calls for something a little extra-special? Why not stir up this fragrant, oven-baked egg dish that puffs up golden and fills your kitchen with the irresistible scent of baked apples? It's a winner!　　*Serves 6*

8 slices reduced-calorie
　French or Italian
　bread, cut into 1-inch
　cubes ☆
1 (8-ounce) package
　Philadelphia fat-free
　cream cheese
1¼ cups Cary's Sugar Free
　Maple Syrup ☆

2 cups (4 small) cored,
　peeled, and chopped
　cooking apples
⅔ cup Carnation Nonfat
　Dry Milk Powder
1 cup water
6 eggs or equivalent in egg
　substitute
1 teaspoon apple pie spice

Place half of bread cubes in an ungreased 11-by-7-inch loaf pan. In a large bowl, stir cream cheese with a spoon until soft. Add ½ cup maple syrup. Mix gently to combine. Drop cream cheese mixture by spoonful evenly over top of bread cubes. Evenly sprinkle chopped apples over cream cheese mixture. Top with remaining bread cubes. In a large bowl, combine dry milk powder and water. Add eggs and apple pie spice. Mix well to combine using a wire whisk. Pour milk mixture evenly over top. Cover and refrigerate for at least 2 hours or up to overnight. Bake at 375 degrees for 30 to 35 minutes or until strata is set. Drizzle remaining ¾ cup maple syrup evenly over top. Cut into 6 servings. Serve at once.

Each serving equals:
HE: 1⅔ Protein (1 limited), ⅔ Bread, ⅔ Fruit, ⅓ Skim Milk, ¼ Slider, 13 Optional Calories

291 Calories, 7 gm Fat, 18 gm Protein, 39 gm Carbohydrate, 676 mg Sodium, 150 mg Calcium, 2 gm Fiber

DIABETIC: 2 Starch/Carbohydrate, 1½ Meat, ½ Fruit

Breakfast Tarts

■ ■ ■ ■ ■ ■ ■ ■

These are fast and fun, my own homemade version of those classic fast-food breakfast sandwiches enjoyed by families everywhere. And you get to enjoy two, so it's double the pleasure and double the taste!   *Serves 5 (2 each)*

1 (7.5-ounce) can Pillsbury refrigerated buttermilk biscuits
1 full cup (6 ounces) finely diced Dubuque 97% fat-free ham or any extra-lean ham
⅓ cup (1½ ounces)

shredded Kraft reduced-fat Cheddar cheese
4 eggs or equivalent in egg substitute
2 tablespoons skim milk
½ teaspoon lemon pepper
1 teaspoon dried parsley flakes

Preheat oven to 400 degrees. Spray 10 wells of a 12-hole muffin pan with butter-flavored cooking spray. Separate biscuits and place each biscuit into a muffin cup, pressing dough up sides to edge of cup. Evenly divide ham and Cheddar cheese among biscuit cups. In a medium bowl, combine eggs, skim milk, lemon pepper, and parsley flakes. Spoon mixture evenly over top. Bake for 10 to 15 minutes or until centers are firm. Place muffin pan on a wire rack and let set for 2 to 3 minutes. Serve at once.

HINT: Fill unused muffin wells with water. It protects the muffin tin and ensures even baking.

Each serving equals:
HE: 2 Protein (¾ limited), 1½ Bread, 3 Optional Calories

224 Calories, 8 gm Fat, 16 gm Protein, 22 gm Carbohydrate, 775 mg Sodium, 82 mg Calcium, 2 gm Fiber

DIABETIC: 2 Meat, 1½ Starch

Peanut Butter and Jelly Wraps

■ ■ ■ ■ ■ ■ ■ ■ ■

*W*hen everyone is racing for the bus or the carpool, insisting there's no time to eat a healthy breakfast, hand them a napkin and one of these swirly sandwiches that are just perfect for gobbling on the run!   *Serves 4*

1 (8-ounce) package Philadelphia fat-free cream cheese
¼ cup Peter Pan reduced-fat peanut butter

4 (6-inch) flour tortillas
6 tablespoons spreadable fruit spread (any flavor)

In a small bowl, stir cream cheese with a spoon until soft. Add peanut butter. Mix well to combine. Spread about ⅓ cup mixture over each tortilla. Evenly spread 1½ tablespoons fruit spread over top of each. Roll up tortillas. Serve at once or cover and refrigerate until ready to serve.

Each serving equals:
HE: 2 Protein, 1½ Fruit, 1 Fat, 1 Bread

284 Calories, 8 gm Fat, 14 gm Protein, 39 gm Carbohydrate, 570 mg Sodium, 10 mg Calcium, 1 gm Fiber

DIABETIC: 1½ Meat, 1 Fruit, 1 Fat, 1 Starch

Super-Duper Soups (and Sandwiches, Too)

■ ■ ■ ■ ■ ■ ■ ■

Hot soup on cold days is one of my fondest childhood memories, and when I create a soup like **Chicken Pot Pie Chowder**, I know it's in part because I want my kids to remember the cozy goodness of this soothing dish. Soup is a working mom's best friend sometimes, and from the very early years of raising my children, I always liked serving soup. It's economical, it's a kind of "make-do" meal that suits my thrifty upbringing, and you can fix it on the weekend, then warm it up during the week. My kids' favorites were any kind of potato soup (I've included a couple of those in this section). And like childen everywhere, they loved chicken soup, with noodles or with rice. What more cozy warm feeling could there be than stirring up soup for your family?

◎

But what would soup be without its delightful partner, the sandwich? If you're tired of serving the same old sandwiches to your family, I just know you'll find some fresh new ideas in this group of recipes. The ingredients are familiar, but the combinations offer some original ways to nourish your children without destroying your budget or taking up your limited free time. Whether lunch is a picnic on the patio (try **Creamy Tomato**

Chowder) or a quick bite nibbled on the way to soccer practice (**Veggie Egg Salad Pitas**), here are a bundle of tasty dishes your family is sure to enjoy!

𝒮𝑜𝓊𝓅𝓈

■ ■ ■ ■ ■ ■ ■ ■

Pea and Potato Soup

Minestrone in Minutes

Easy Alphabet Vegetable
   Soup

Creamy Tomato Chowder

Chicken Carrot Chowder

Chicken Pot Pie Chowder

Cream of Chicken Corn
   Chowder

Chicken Vegetable Rice
   Soup

Frankly Corn Chowder

Frankfurter Noodle Soup

Green Bean and Ham
   Chowder

Hamburger Milk Gravy
   Potato Chowder

Meatball Soup

Tommy's Chili

Pea and Potato Soup

■ ■ ■ ■ ■ ■ ■ ■

My son Tommy really loves potatoes, and unlike James, he also loves peas. So I created this rich, thick, and creamy soup to satisfy growing boys (and men!).   *Serves 4 (1⅓ cups)*

2 cups (10 ounces) diced
    raw potatoes
¾ cup chopped celery
¼ cup chopped onion
1½ cups hot water
1 cup frozen peas, thawed
1 (10¾-ounce) can

Healthy Request Cream of
    Mushroom Soup
1⅓ cups skim milk
1 teaspoon dried parsley
    flakes
¼ teaspoon black pepper

In a large saucepan, combine potatoes, celery, onion, and water. Cover and cook over medium heat for 15 minutes or until vegetables are tender. Stir in peas. DO NOT DRAIN. Add mushroom soup, skim milk, parsley flakes, and black pepper. Mix well to combine. Lower heat and simmer until mixture is heated through, stirring often.

HINT: Thaw peas by placing in a colander and rinsing under hot water for one minute.

Each serving equals:
HE: 1 Bread, ½ Vegetable, ⅓ Skim Milk, ½ Slider, 1 Optional Calorie

154 Calories, 2 gm Fat, 7 gm Protein, 27 gm Carbohydrate, 367 mg Sodium, 177 mg Calcium, 3 gm Fiber

DIABETIC: 2 Starch

Minestrone in Minutes

▪ ▪ ▪ ▪ ▪ ▪ ▪ ▪

Here's a traditional Italian classic reinvented for busy families who relish a substantial vegetable soup enriched with a little pasta. The seasonings will fill your kitchen with a wonderful aroma in no time at all!　　　*Serves 4 (1½ cups)*

1¾ cups (one 14½-ounce can) Swanson Beef Broth
1¾ cups water
1 cup shredded cabbage
½ cup chopped onion
1¾ cups (one 15-ounce can) Hunt's Chunky Tomato Sauce
½ cup frozen cut green beans

½ cup frozen cut carrots
1 teaspoon Italian seasoning
1 teaspoon dried parsley flakes
¼ teaspoon dried minced garlic
Scant ½ cup (1½ ounces) uncooked elbow macaroni

In a large saucepan, combine beef broth, water, cabbage, onion, tomato sauce, green beans, carrots, Italian seasoning, parsley flakes, and garlic. Bring mixture to a boil. Add uncooked macaroni. Mix well to combine. Lower heat, cover, and simmer for 15 minutes or until vegetables and macaroni are tender, stirring occasionally.

Each serving equals:
HE: 3 Vegetable, ½ Bread, 8 Optional Calories

105 Calories, 1 gm Fat, 4 gm Protein, 20 gm Carbohydrate, 872 mg Sodium, 25 mg Calcium, 3 gm Fiber

DIABETIC: 2½ Vegetable, ½ Starch *or* 1½ Starch/Carbohydrate

Easy Alphabet Vegetable Soup

■ ■ ■ ■ ■ ■ ■ ■

Ever since childhood, we've loved "playing" with our food—especially when it's my easy version of alphabet soup! Can you spell out "healthy" and "easy" in little noodles before you gobble them down?   *Serves 4 (1 full cup)*

2 cups (one 16-ounce can)
   Healthy Request
   Chicken Broth
2 cups Healthy Request
   tomato juice or any
   reduced-sodium tomato
   juice
½ cup water
1 teaspoon Worcestershire
   sauce
½ cup chopped celery

¼ cup chopped onion
½ cup frozen cut carrots
¾ cup frozen cut green
   beans
¼ cup frozen peas
¼ cup frozen whole kernel
   corn
⅔ cup (1½ ounces)
   uncooked alphabet or
   tiny shell macaroni

In a large saucepan, combine chicken broth, tomato juice, water, and Worcestershire sauce. Add celery, onion, carrots, and green beans. Mix well to combine. Bring mixture to a boil. Stir in peas, corn, and uncooked macaroni. Lower heat and simmer for 15 minutes or until vegetables and macaroni are tender, stirring occasionally.

Each serving equals:
HE: 2 Vegetable, ¾ Bread, 8 Optional Calories

128 Calories, 0 gm Fat, 6 gm Protein, 26 gm Carbohydrate, 348 mg Sodium, 35 mg Calcium, 3 gm Fiber

DIABETIC: 2 Vegetable, 1 Starch

Creamy Tomato Chowder

■ ■ ■ ■ ■ ■ ■ ■

Do you find it hard to ensure your family gets all the calcium it needs every day? Here's a tasty dish that delivers the nutrition of almost a full cup of skim milk in every serving—but they'll just think it's yummy!   *Serves 4 (1½ cups)*

¾ cup finely chopped celery
1 (10¾-ounce) can Healthy Request Tomato Soup
1½ cups (one 12-fluid-ounce can) Carnation Evaporated Skim Milk
1¾ cups (one 14½-ounce can) stewed tomatoes, coarsely chopped and undrained
1½ cups (8 ounces) diced cooked potatoes
¾ cup (3 ounces) shredded Kraft reduced-fat Cheddar cheese
1 teaspoon dried parsley flakes

In a large saucepan sprayed with butter-flavored cooking spray, sauté celery for 6 to 8 minutes, or just until tender. Stir in tomato soup, evaporated skim milk, and undrained stewed tomatoes. Add potatoes, Cheddar cheese, and parsley flakes. Mix well to combine. Lower heat and simmer for 5 minutes, or until mixture is heated through and cheese melts, stirring occasionally.

Each serving equals:
HE: 1¼ Vegetable, 1 Protein, ¾ Skim Milk, ½ Bread, ½ Slider, 5 Optional Calories

253 Calories, 5 gm Fat, 16 gm Protein, 36 gm Carbohydrate, 841 mg Sodium, 490 mg Calcium, 3 gm Fiber

DIABETIC: 1 Vegetable, 1 Meat, 1 Skim Milk, 1 Starch

Chicken Carrot Chowder

■ ■ ■ ■ ■ ■ ■ ■

$\mathcal{S}$o much chicken flavor (the two kinds of soup and the chicken meat too!) and all those carrots combine in this marvelous microwave meal in a bowl. It couldn't be easier, and it couldn't be tastier, either! *Serves 4 (1¼ cups)*

2 cups (one 16-ounce can)
   Healthy Request
   Chicken Broth
¾ cup finely chopped
   celery
¼ cup finely chopped onion
1 (10¾-ounce) can
   Healthy Request Cream
   of Chicken Soup

2 cups (one 16-ounce can)
   diced carrots, rinsed and
   drained
1 cup (5 ounces) chopped
   cooked chicken breast
¼ cup chopped fresh
   parsley

In an 8-cup glass measuring bowl, combine chicken broth, celery, and onion. Microwave on HIGH (100% power) for 1 minute. Stir in chicken soup, carrots, and chicken. Continue microwaving on HIGH for 3 minutes or until mixture is hot. When serving, sprinkle 1 tablespoon parsley over top of each bowl.

HINT: If you don't have leftovers, purchase a chunk of cooked chicken breast from your local deli.

Each serving equals:
HE: 1½ Vegetable, 1¼ Protein, ½ Slider, 13 Optional Calories

143 Calories, 3 gm Fat, 15 gm Protein, 14 gm Carbohydrate, 622 mg Sodium, 54 mg Calcium, 2 gm Fiber

DIABETIC: 1 Vegetable, 1 Meat, ½ Starch

Chicken Pot Pie Chowder

■ ■ ■ ■ ■ ■ ■

There's no more beloved main dish than old-fashioned chicken pot pie, so why not enjoy those luscious ingredients in a cozy and oh-so-substantial soup? My daughter, Becky, told me that few dishes bring back happy childhood memories as well as this one does! *Serves 4 (1⅓ cups)*

2 cups (one 16-ounce can) Healthy Request Chicken Broth
½ cup diced onion
1½ cups (8 ounces) diced cooked chicken breast
1 cup frozen whole kernel corn, thawed
½ cup frozen peas, thawed
1 cup (one 8-ounce can) sliced carrots, rinsed and drained

1 (10¾-ounce) can Healthy Request Cream of Celery Soup
⅔ cup Carnation Nonfat Dry Milk Powder
¾ cup (3 ounces) shredded Kraft reduced-fat Cheddar cheese
1 teaspoon dried parsley flakes

In a large saucepan, combine chicken broth and onion. Bring mixture to a boil. Stir in chicken, corn, peas, and carrots. In a small bowl, combine celery soup, dry milk powder, Cheddar cheese, and parsley flakes. Add soup mixture to chicken mixture. Mix well to combine. Lower heat and simmer for 10 minutes, stirring occasionally.

HINTS:
1. If you don't have leftovers, purchase a chunk of cooked chicken breast from your local deli.
2. Thaw corn and peas by placing in a colander and rinsing under hot water for one minute.

Each serving equals:

HE: 3 Protein, ¾ Bread, ¾ Vegetable, ½ Skim Milk, 8 Optional Calories

---

303 Calories, 7 gm Fat, 32 gm Protein, 28 gm Carbohydrate, 858 mg Sodium, 370 mg Calcium, 3 gm Fiber

---

DIABETIC: 3 Meat, 1 Starch, ½ Vegetable, ½ Skim Milk

Cream of Chicken Corn Chowder

■ ■ ■ ■ ■ ■ ■ ■ ■

*C*orn and chicken go so well together, just like love and marriage in the song! Add some noodles to thicken this soup even more, and you've got a culinary partnership whose flavor goes on forever! *Serves 4 (1 cup)*

1 (10¾-ounce) can
Healthy Request Cream
of Chicken Soup
2 cups skim milk
1 cup frozen whole kernel
corn, thawed
Scant 1 cup (1½ ounces)
uncooked noodles

1 teaspoon dried parsley
flakes
1 teaspoon dried onion
flakes
1 cup (5 ounces) diced
cooked chicken breast

In a medium saucepan, combine chicken soup, skim milk, corn, uncooked noodles, parsley flakes, and onion flakes. Bring mixture to a boil. Stir in chicken. Lower heat and simmer for 15 minutes, or until noodles are tender, stirring occasionally.

HINTS:
1. Thaw corn by placing in a colander and rinsing under hot water for one minute.
2. If you don't have leftovers, purchase a chunk of cooked chicken breast from your local deli.

Each serving equals:
HE: 1¼ Protein, 1 Bread, ½ Skim Milk, ½ Slider, 5 Optional Calories

235 Calories, 3 gm Fat, 20 gm Protein, 32 gm Carbohydrate, 394 mg Sodium, 164 mg Calcium, 1 gm Fiber

DIABETIC: 2 Starch, 1 Meat, ½ Skim Milk

Chicken Vegetable Rice Soup

■ ■ ■ ■ ■ ■ ■ ■

This classic soup is always a family-pleaser, with its wonderful abundance of peas, carrots, and string beans. It's also a great way to stretch a half pound of chicken without stinting on nutrition.

Serves 4 (1½ cups)

8 ounces skinned and boned uncooked chicken breast, cut into 12 pieces
½ cup chopped onion
1 cup frozen cut green beans
1 cup frozen sliced carrots

4 cups (two 16-ounce cans) Healthy Request Chicken Broth
2 teaspoons dried parsley flakes
½ cup frozen peas
1 cup (3 ounces) uncooked Minute Rice

In a large saucepan, combine chicken pieces, onion, green beans, carrots, and chicken broth. Bring mixture to a boil. Stir in parsley flakes. Lower heat, cover, and simmer for 10 minutes. Add peas and uncooked rice. Mix well to combine. Cover and continue simmering for 10 minutes, stirring occasionally.

Each serving equals:
HE: 1½ Protein, 1¼ Vegetable, ¾ Bread, 16 Optional Calories

157 Calories, 1 gm Fat, 19 gm Protein, 18 gm Carbohydrate, 538 mg Sodium, 41 mg Calcium, 3 gm Fiber

DIABETIC: 1½ Meat, 1 Vegetable, 1 Starch

Frankly Corn Chowder

■ ■ ■ ■ ■ ■ ■ ■

You'll find, as I have, that healthy frankfurters are a great help in preparing speedy suppers that are as healthy as they are quick. Here's a full-bodied soup whipped up in only minutes—serve it on a crisp fall night when the kids have spent hours jumping in piles of leaves! *Serves 4 (1⅓ cups)*

1½ cups water ☆
1 cup (5 ounces) diced raw
   potatoes
¾ cup shredded carrots
¼ cup chopped onion
1 cup (one 8-ounce can)
   cream-style corn
½ cup frozen whole-kernel
   corn
1 (10¾-ounce) can

Healthy Request Cream of
   Mushroom Soup
8 ounces Healthy Choice
   97% fat-free
   frankfurters, diced
¾ cup (3 ounces) shredded
   Kraft reduced-fat
   Cheddar cheese
1 teaspoon dried parsley
   flakes

In a large saucepan, combine 1 cup water, potatoes, carrots, and onion. Bring mixture to a boil. Lower heat, cover, and simmer for 10 minutes. Stir in cream-style corn, frozen corn, mushroom soup, and remaining ½ cup water. Add frankfurters, Cheddar cheese, and parsley flakes. Mix well to combine. Continue simmering for 5 minutes, or until mixture is heated through and cheese is melted, stirring often.

Each serving equals:

HE: 2⅓ Protein, 1 Bread, ½ Vegetable, ½ Slider, 1 Optional Calorie

271 Calories, 7 gm Fat, 17 gm Protein, 35 gm Carbohydrate, 963 mg Sodium, 217 mg Calcium, 2 gm Fiber

DIABETIC: 2 Meat, 2 Starch, ½ Vegetable

Frankfurter Noodle Soup

■ ■ ■ ■ ■ ■ ■ ■

Here's a truly kid-pleasing tomato soup that brims over with cozy noodles and child-size bites of hot dog! I doubt there's a toddler anywhere who wouldn't gobble it up with a smile!

Serves 4 (1½ cups)

2 cups Healthy Request
tomato juice or any
reduced-sodium tomato
juice
1 cup water
½ cup finely chopped onion
½ cup finely chopped
celery
1 teaspoon dried parsley
flakes

1 teaspoon chili seasoning
1¾ cups (3 ounces)
uncooked noodles
8 ounces Healthy Choice
97% fat-free
frankfurters, diced
1 (10¾-ounce) can
Healthy Request
Tomato Soup

In a large saucepan, combine tomato juice, water, onion, and celery. Bring mixture to a boil. Stir in parsley flakes, chili seasoning, uncooked noodles, and frankfurters. Lower heat and simmer for 10 minutes. Add tomato soup. Mix well to combine. Continue simmering for 5 minutes, or until mixture is heated through, stirring often.

Each serving equals:

HE: 1½ Vegetable, 1⅓ Protein, 1 Bread, ½ Slider, 5 Optional Calories

235 Calories, 3 gm Fat, 13 gm Protein, 39 gm Carbohydrate, 836 mg Sodium, 39 mg Calcium, 3 gm Fiber

DIABETIC: 2 Starch, 1 Vegetable, 1 Meat

Green Bean and Ham Chowder

■ ■ ■ ■ ■ ■ ■ ■ ■

Green beans have been voted the favorite veggie of the kids we feed every day in the local day-care center, so I made a point of gathering lots of green bean recipes for this cookbook. This one is so hearty and full of flavor, the whole family will elect it in a landslide!

Serves 4 (1½ cups)

3 cups frozen cut green
  beans, thawed
1 full cup (6 ounces) diced
  Dubuque 97% fat-free
  ham or any extra-lean
  ham
½ cup chopped onion
1 cup (5 ounces) diced raw
  potatoes

1½ cups water
1 (10¾-ounce) can
  Healthy Request Cream
  of Mushroom Soup
1 cup skim milk
¾ cup (3 ounces) shredded
  Kraft reduced-fat
  Cheddar cheese
¼ teaspoon black pepper

In a large saucepan, combine green beans, ham, onion, potatoes, and water. Bring mixture to a boil. Lower heat, cover, and simmer for 15 minutes. Stir in mushroom soup, skim milk, Cheddar cheese, and black pepper. Continue simmering for 5 minutes or until mixture is heated through and cheese has melted, stirring often.

HINT: Thaw green beans by placing in a colander and rinsing under hot water for one minute.

Each serving equals:
HE: 2 Protein, 1¾ Vegetable, ¼ Bread, ¼ Skim Milk, ½ Slider, 1 Optional Calorie

227 Calories, 7 gm Fat, 18 gm Protein, 23 gm Carbohydrate, 894 mg Sodium, 316 mg Calcium, 4 gm Fiber

DIABETIC: 2 Meat, 1½ Vegetable, 1 Starch/Carbohydrate

Hamburger Milk Gravy
Potato Chowder

■ ■ ■ ■ ■ ■ ■

This one's for Tommy, my son who could live on hamburger milk gravy three meals a day! (Well, almost . . .) I wanted to create a soup with all the taste satisfaction of this heartland classic—and he agreed that I did.   *Serves 4 (1 full cup)*

8 ounces ground 90% lean turkey or beef	1⅓ cups (3 ounces) instant potato flakes
½ cup chopped onion	1 teaspoon dried parsley flakes
½ cup diced celery	¼ teaspoon black pepper
3 cups skim milk	

In a large saucepan sprayed with butter-flavored cooking spray, brown meat, onion, and celery. Stir in skim milk, potato flakes, parsley flakes, and black pepper. Lower heat and simmer for 10 minutes, stirring occasionally.

Each serving equals:
HE: 1½ Protein, 1 Bread, ¾ Skim Milk, ½ Vegetable

209 Calories, 5 gm Fat, 18 gm Protein, 23 gm Carbohydrate, 178 mg Sodium, 242 mg Calcium, 2 gm Fiber

DIABETIC: 1½ Meat, 1 Starch, 1 Skim Milk

Meatball Soup

■ ■ ■ ■ ■ ■ ■ ■

My kids always thought it was fun to find the tiny meatballs in their bowls of soup—sort of like a treasure hunt for extra added goodness. If your family enjoys extra-spicy flavor, why not experiment by increasing (gradually!) the amount of chili seasoning? *Serves 6 (1½ cups)*

16 ounces ground 90% lean turkey or beef
2 teaspoons dried onion flakes
1 teaspoon dried parsley flakes
3 cups Healthy Request tomato juice or any reduced-sodium tomato juice

2 cups (one 16-ounce can) Healthy Request Chicken Broth
2 cups (one 16-ounce can) cream-style corn
1 teaspoon chili seasoning
⅔ cup (2 ounces) uncooked Minute Rice

In a large bowl, combine meat, onion flakes, and parsley flakes. Form into 24 (1-inch) meatballs. Place meatballs in a large skillet sprayed with olive oil–flavored cooking spray. Cook for about 10 minutes or until meatballs are browned. Meanwhile, in a large saucepan, combine tomato juice, chicken broth, cream-style corn, and chili seasoning. Bring mixture to a boil. Stir in uncooked rice. Gently add browned meatballs. Lower heat, cover, and simmer for 15 minutes, stirring occasionally.

Each serving equals:
HE: 2 Protein, 1 Vegetable, 1 Bread, 6 Optional Calories

222 Calories, 6 gm Fat, 17 gm Protein, 25 gm Carbohydrate, 545 mg Sodium, 13 mg Calcium, 2 gm Fiber

DIABETIC: 2 Meat, 1 Vegetable, 1 Starch

Tommy's Chili

■ ■ ■ ■ ■ ■ ■ ■

Tommy was my last child to leave home, so he joined Cliff in lots of taste testing over the years. This unbelievably quick chili dish was one recipe he took off to college with him, so try it on your teenagers, too! (He hates kidney beans, so his chili has celery, corn, and onions instead!)   *Serves 4 (1 cup)*

8 ounces ground 90% lean
   turkey or beef
1 cup finely chopped celery
½ cup chopped onion
1 (10¾-ounce) can
   Healthy Request
   Tomato Soup

1 cup water
1 teaspoon chili seasoning
1½ cups frozen whole-
   kernel corn

In a large saucepan sprayed with butter-flavored cooking spray, brown meat, celery, and onion. Stir in tomato soup, water, and chili seasoning. Add corn. Mix well to combine. Lower heat and simmer for 15 minutes, stirring occasionally.

Each serving equals:

HE: 1½ Protein, ¾ Bread, ¾ Vegetable, ½ Slider, 5 Optional Calories

193 Calories, 5 gm Fat, 13 gm Protein, 24 gm Carbohydrate, 313 mg Sodium, 25 mg Calcium, 3 gm Fiber

DIABETIC: 1½ Meat, 1½ Starch

Sandwiches

■ ■ ■ ■ ■ ■ ■ ■

Carrot–Peanut Butter
   Sandwiches

Cream Cheese and Peanut
   Sandwiches

Pimiento Cheese
   Sandwiches

Veggie Egg Salad Pitas

Tuna Vegetable Pitas

Tuna-Cheese Sandwich
   Burgers

Tuna Sandwich Melts

Hot Swiss-Tuna Buns

Chicken-Fruit Sandwiches

Roman Burger Melts

Italian Beef Sandwiches

Taco Burgers

Hot Dog Bundles

Ham and Egg Salad
   Sandwiches

Carrot—Peanut Butter Sandwiches

■ ■ ■ ■ ■ ■ ■ ■ ■

This combination sounds unusual, but if your kids have ever stuck a carrot stick into a jar of peanut butter and said yum, here's a delicious, nutritious sandwich they're bound to relish!

Serves 4

¼ cup Peter Pan reduced-
  fat chunky peanut butter
¼ cup apricot spreadable
  fruit spread

1 cup shredded carrots
8 slices reduced-calorie
  whole-wheat bread

In a small bowl, combine peanut butter and fruit spread. Stir in carrots. For each sandwich, spread about ¼ cup filling mixture between 2 slices of bread. Serve at once or refrigerate until ready to serve.

Each serving equals:

HE: 1 Bread, 1 Fruit, 1 Fat, 1 Protein, ½ Vegetable

226 Calories, 6 gm Fat, 9 gm Protein, 34 gm Carbohydrate,
315 mg Sodium, 43 mg Calcium, 7 gm Fiber

DIABETIC: 1 Starch, 1 Fruit, ½ Fat, ½ Meat *or* 2 Starch/
Carbohydrate, ½ Fat, ½ Meat, ½ Vegetable

Cream Cheese and Peanut Sandwiches

■ ■ ■ ■ ■ ■ ■ ■

You send a healthy lunch to school, but do you worry that your kids will trade it away for junk food goodies? Here's a sandwich that tastes so much like a treat, they'll be tempted to gobble it down even before the lunch bell rings!   *Serves 4*

½ *cup (4 ounces)*
  Philadelphia fat-free
  cream cheese
2 *tablespoons Cary's*
  Sugar Free Maple Syrup

¼ *cup (1 ounce) chopped*
  dry roasted peanuts
8 *slices reduced-calorie*
  whole-wheat bread

In a medium bowl, stir cream cheese with a spoon until soft. Stir in maple syrup. Add peanuts. Mix well to combine. For each sandwich, spread about 3 tablespoons filling mixture between 2 slices of bread. Serve at once or refrigerate until ready to serve.

Each serving equals:
HE: 1 Bread, ¾ Protein, ½ Fat, 5 Optional Calories

169 Calories, 5 gm Fat, 11 gm Protein, 20 gm Carbohydrate, 417 mg Sodium, 40 mg Calcium, 6 gm Fiber

DIABETIC: 1 Starch, 1 Meat, ½ Fat

Pimiento Cheese Sandwiches

■ ■ ■ ■ ■ ■ ■ ■

This kid-tested saucy cheese sandwich bakes up in minutes, a wonderful choice for hungry children after Saturday morning Little League practice. When food is this much fun, even your fussy eaters will surprise you. *Serves 4*

¾ *cup (3 ounces) shredded*
Kraft reduced-fat
Cheddar cheese
¼ *cup Kraft fat-free*
mayonnaise
1 *teaspoon Worcestershire*
sauce

¼ *cup (one 2-ounce jar)*
chopped pimiento,
drained
4 *reduced-calorie*
hamburger buns

Preheat oven to 400 degrees. In a medium bowl, combine Cheddar cheese, mayonnaise, Worcestershire sauce, and pimiento. Spread about ¼ cup filling mixture between each bun. Wrap buns in foil. Place wrapped buns on baking sheet and bake for 10 minutes. Serve hot.

Each serving equals:
HE: 1 Bread, 1 Protein, 10 Optional Calories

149 Calories, 5 gm Fat, 8 gm Protein, 18 gm Carbohydrate, 500 mg Sodium, 157 mg Calcium, 1 gm Fiber

DIABETIC: 1 Starch, 1 Meat

Veggie Egg Salad Pitas

■ ■ ■ ■ ■ ■ ■ ■

Everyone loves sandwiches in a pita because they're so "handy," so easy to eat. This crunchy egg salad combines fresh and tangy vegetables in a creamy filling that's good—and good for you, too.

Serves 4

¾ cup shredded carrots
½ cup finely chopped
  celery
¼ cup finely chopped green
  onion
4 hard-boiled eggs,
  chopped

½ cup Kraft fat-free
  mayonnaise
1 teaspoon dried parsley
  flakes
½ cup finely shredded
  lettuce
2 pita rounds, halved

In a large bowl, combine carrots, celery, onion, and eggs. Add mayonnaise and parsley flakes. Mix well to combine. For each sandwich, spoon 2 tablespoons lettuce and ½ cup egg mixture into a pita half. Serve at once or cover and refrigerate until ready to serve.

HINT: To make opening pita rounds easier, place pita halves on a paper towel and microwave on HIGH for 10 seconds. Remove and gently press open.

Each serving equals:
HE: 1 Vegetable, 1 Bread, 1 Protein (limited), ¼ Slider

194 Calories, 6 gm Fat, 9 gm Protein, 26 gm Carbohydrate,
505 mg Sodium, 67 mg Calcium, 2 gm Fiber

DIABETIC: 1½ Starch, 1 Vegetable, 1 Meat

Tuna Vegetable Pitas

■ ■ ■ ■ ■ ■ ■ ■

Getting your family to gobble their vegetables is often easier when they're shredded and tucked inside a flavorful, easy-to-eat sandwich like this one. If you're taking these on a picnic, bring the filling and pitas separately, then spoon the filling in just before eating.
Serves 4

> 1 (6-ounce) can white tuna, packed in water, drained and flaked
> ¾ cup shredded carrots
> ¼ cup finely chopped onion
> ¼ cup Kraft fat-free mayonnaise
>
> ½ teaspoon lemon pepper
> 1 teaspoon dried parsley flakes
> 2 pita rounds, halved

In a medium bowl, combine tuna, carrots, and onion. Add mayonnaise, lemon pepper, and parsley flakes. Mix gently to combine. For each sandwich, spoon about ⅓ cup filling mixture into a pita half. Serve at once or cover and refrigerate until ready to serve.

HINT: To make opening pita rounds easier, place pita halves on a paper towel and microwave on HIGH for 10 seconds. Remove and gently press open.

Each serving equals:
HE: 1 Bread, ¾ Protein, ½ Vegetable, 10 Optional Calories

153 Calories, 1 gm Fat, 14 gm Protein, 22 gm Carbohydrate, 443 mg Sodium, 40 mg Calcium, 1 gm Fiber

DIABETIC: 1½ Meat, 1 Starch, ½ Vegetable

Tuna-Cheese Sandwich Burgers

■ ■ ■ ■ ■ ■ ■

Here's another easy family favorite that is great for picnics and school lunches. I don't know why the combo of tuna and cheese is so much fun, but every kid I checked with agreed that it is!

Serves 6

⅓ cup Kraft fat-free
   mayonnaise
1 teaspoon dried onion
   flakes
1 teaspoon dried parsley
   flakes
⅛ teaspoon black pepper
1 (6-ounce) can white
   tuna, packed in water,
   drained and flaked

1 cup finely chopped celery
Full ½ cup (2¼ ounces)
   shredded Kraft reduced-
   fat Cheddar cheese
1 cup finely shredded
   lettuce
6 reduced-calorie
   hamburger buns

In a large bowl, combine mayonnaise, onion flakes, parsley flakes, and black pepper. Add tuna, celery, and Cheddar cheese. Mix well to combine. For each sandwich, place about 3 tablespoons lettuce and ⅓ cup filling mixture between a bun. Serve at once or cover and refrigerate until ready to serve.

Each serving equals:
HE: 1 Bread, 1 Protein, ⅔ Vegetable, 9 Optional Calories

147 Calories, 3 gm Fat, 12 gm Protein, 18 gm Carbohydrate, 476 mg Sodium, 85 mg Calcium, 1 gm Fiber

DIABETIC: 1½ Meat, 1 Starch

Tuna Sandwich Melts

■ ■ ■ ■ ■ ■ ■ ■

Here's another scrumptious tuna-cheese combo with just a touch of crunch that's very tasty. The flavors blend beautifully during the baking time, and the sandwiches emerge from the oven cozy-warm and oh-so-good!   *Serves 4*

1 (6-ounce) can white
   tuna, packed in water,
   drained and flaked
½ cup Kraft fat-free
   mayonnaise
¾ cup (3 ounces) shredded
   Kraft reduced-fat
   Cheddar cheese

¾ cup finely chopped
   celery
¼ cup chopped onion
1 teaspoon dried parsley
   flakes
4 reduced-calorie
   hamburger buns

Preheat oven to 350 degrees. In a large bowl, combine tuna, mayonnaise, and Cheddar cheese. Add celery, onion, and parsley flakes. Mix well to combine. Evenly spoon about ⅓ cup tuna mixture between each bun. Wrap buns in foil. Place wrapped sandwiches on a baking sheet and bake for 20 minutes. Serve hot.

Each serving equals:
HE: 1¾ Protein, 1 Bread, ½ Vegetable, ¼ Slider

209 Calories, 5 gm Fat, 19 gm Protein, 22 gm Carbohydrate, 679 mg Sodium, 173 mg Calcium, 1 gm Fiber

DIABETIC: 2 Meat, 1½ Starch/Carbohydrate

Hot Swiss-Tuna Buns

■ ■ ■ ■ ■ ■ ■ ■

If your children love grilled cheese, and they love tuna fish sandwiches, they're going to adore these yummies! The Swiss cheese flavor is a bit more grown-up than American or Cheddar, but mild enough for kids to enjoy. *Serves 4*

1 (6-ounce) can white tuna, packed in water, drained and flaked
3 (¾-ounce) slices Kraft reduced-fat Swiss cheese, shredded
1 cup finely chopped celery
¼ cup Kraft fat-free mayonnaise
2 tablespoons Heinz Light Harvest Ketchup or any reduced-sodium ketchup
1 teaspoon lemon juice
⅛ teaspoon black pepper
1 teaspoon dried parsley flakes
4 reduced-calorie hamburger buns

Preheat oven to 350 degrees. In a large bowl, combine tuna, Swiss cheese, and celery. Add mayonnaise, ketchup, lemon juice, black pepper, and parsley flakes. Mix well to combine. Evenly spread about ½ cup tuna mixture between each bun. Wrap buns in foil. Place wrapped sandwiches on a baking sheet and bake for 20 minutes. Serve hot.

Each serving equals:
HE: 1½ Protein, 1 Bread, ½ Vegetable, 18 Optional Calories

174 Calories, 2 gm Fat, 18 gm Protein, 21 gm Carbohydrate, 560 mg Sodium, 174 mg Calcium, 1 gm Fiber

DIABETIC: 2 Meat, 1½ Starch/Carbohydrate

Chicken-Fruit Sandwiches

■ ■ ■ ■ ■ ■ ■ ■

My grandson Zach adores pineapple, and when I combined it with some leftover chicken and a few walnuts, he gave me the biggest smile . . . before munching away like crazy! Because the ingredients are so finely chopped, even young children can enjoy this one.   *Serves 6*

*1 cup (5 ounces) finely
  chopped cooked chicken
  breast*
*1 cup (one 8-ounce can)
  crushed pineapple,
  packed in fruit juice,
  drained*

*¼ cup (1 ounce) finely
  chopped walnuts*
*½ cup Kraft fat-free
  mayonnaise*
*12 slices reduced-calorie
  bread*

In a medium bowl, combine chicken, pineapple, and walnuts. Add mayonnaise. Mix gently to combine. For each sandwich, spread about ⅓ cup mixture between 2 slices of bread. Serve at once or cover and refrigerate until ready to serve.

HINT: If you don't have leftovers, purchase a chunk of cooked chicken breast from your local deli.

Each serving equals:
HE: 1 Bread, 1 Protein, ⅓ Fat, ⅓ Fruit, 13 Optional Calories

197 Calories, 5 gm Fat, 12 gm Protein, 26 gm Carbohydrate, 422 mg Sodium, 49 mg Calcium, 5 gm Fiber

DIABETIC: 1½ Starch/Carbohydrate, 1 Meat, ½ Fat

Rooman Burger Melts

■ ■ ■ ■ ■ ■ ■ ■

My healthy version of pizza burgers adds pizazz and home-cooked goodness to that restaurant favorite. It just shows that you can subtract the fat and keep the flavor—and the fun!

Serves 6

6 tablespoons (1½ ounces)
  dried fine bread crumbs
2 teaspoons Italian
  seasoning ☆
¼ cup water
16 ounces ground 90% lean
  turkey or beef
1 (10¾-ounce) can

Healthy Request Tomato
  Soup
6 (¾-ounce) slices Kraft
  reduced-fat mozzarella
  cheese
6 reduced-calorie
  hamburger buns

In a large bowl, combine bread crumbs, 1 teaspoon Italian seasoning, and water. Add meat. Mix well to combine. Using a ⅓ cup measuring cup as a guide, form into 6 patties. Place patties in a large skillet sprayed with olive oil–flavored cooking spray. Brown patties for 3 minutes on each side. In a medium bowl, combine tomato soup and remaining 1 teaspoon Italian seasoning. Pour soup mixture evenly over browned patties. Lower heat, cover, and simmer for 10 minutes. Place 1 slice of mozzarella cheese over each patty. Continue simmering, uncovered, for 2 to 3 minutes or until cheese starts to melt. For each sandwich, place 1 patty between hamburger bun and spoon about 2 tablespoons sauce mixture over top. Serve at once.

Each serving equals:
HE: 3 Protein, 1⅓ Bread, ¼ Slider, 10 Optional Calories

273 Calories, 9 gm Fat, 23 gm Protein, 25 gm Carbohydrate, 570 mg Sodium, 159 mg Calcium, 1 gm Fiber

DIABETIC: 2½ Meat, 1½ Starch/Carbohydrate

Italian Beef Sandwiches

■ ■ ■ ■ ■ ■ ■ ■ ■

This tangy concoction makes everyday roast beef into party food! It takes just minutes to fix, but the cheers you'll hear from adults and kids alike will persuade you to serve it again and again.   *Serves 6*

> 3 full cups (16 ounces)   ⅓ cup Kraft Fat Free
>   thinly sliced cooked lean   Italian Dressing
>   roast beef   1 teaspoon Italian
> 1 (10¾-ounce) can   seasoning
>   Healthy Request   6 reduced-calorie
>   Tomato Soup   hamburger buns

In a large skillet sprayed with olive oil–flavored cooking spray, sauté roast beef for 5 minutes. In a small bowl, combine tomato soup, Italian dressing, and Italian seasoning. Add soup mixture to roast beef. Mix well to combine. Lower heat and simmer for 15 minutes, stirring occasionally. For each serving, spoon about ½ cup meat mixture between a hamburger bun.

HINT: If you don't have leftovers, purchase a chunk of lean cooked roast beef from your local deli or use Healthy Choice Deli slices.

Each serving equals:

HE: 2⅔ Protein, 1 Bread, ¼ Slider, 17 Optional Calories

196 Calories, 4 gm Fat, 17 gm Protein, 23 gm Carbohydrate, 946 mg Sodium, 8 gm Calcium, 1 gm Fiber

DIABETIC: 2½ Meat, 1½ Starch/Carbohydrate

Taco Burgers

Tacos are fun to eat but take a little extra effort to prepare and serve at home. Why not enjoy these spicy Mexican sandwiches that deliver all that South-of-the-Border spirit in one tasty bundle?   *Serves 8*

16 ounces ground 90% lean turkey or beef
1 cup (one 8-ounce can) Hunt's Tomato Sauce
2 teaspoons taco seasoning
1 teaspoon Worcestershire sauce
1 teaspoon prepared mustard

8 reduced-calorie hamburger buns
1 cup finely shredded lettuce
¾ cup (3 ounces) shredded Kraft reduced-fat Cheddar cheese

In a large skillet sprayed with olive oil–flavored cooking spray, brown meat. Stir in tomato sauce, taco seasoning, Worcestershire sauce, and mustard. Lower heat and simmer for 10 minutes, stirring occasionally. For each sandwich, spoon about ⅓ cup meat mixture between a bun and sprinkle 2 tablespoons lettuce and 1½ tablespoons Cheddar cheese over top of meat mixture. Serve at once.

HINT: Good topped with 1 teaspoon fat-free sour cream, but don't forget to count the few additional calories.

Each serving equals:
HE: 2 Protein, 1 Bread, ¾ Vegetable

196 Calories, 8 gm Fat, 15 gm Protein, 16 gm Carbohydrate, 527 mg Sodium, 81 mg Calcium, 1 gm Fiber

DIABETIC: 2 Meat, 1 Starch, ½ Vegetable

Hot Dog Bundles

■ ■ ■ ■ ■ ■ ■ ■

Tired of serving the same old frankfurters on buns to your family but don't have time to fuss? You'll love these frank-and-egg-and-cheese-stuffed buns baked in the oven—and so will your kids!

Serves 4

8 ounces Healthy Choice 97% fat-free frankfurters, cooked, cooled, and chopped
2 hard-boiled eggs, chopped
⅓ cup (1½ ounces) shredded Kraft reduced-fat Cheddar cheese
2 tablespoons Kraft fat-free mayonnaise
2 tablespoons hot dog relish
2 tablespoons Heinz Light Harvest Ketchup or any reduced-sodium ketchup
4 reduced-calorie hamburger buns

Preheat oven to 350 degrees. In a medium bowl, combine frankfurters, eggs, and Cheddar cheese. Add mayonnaise, hot dog relish, and ketchup. Mix well to combine. Evenly spread about ½ cup mixture between each bun. Wrap buns in foil. Place wrapped buns on a baking sheet and bake for 20 minutes. Serve hot.

Each serving equals:
HE: 2⅓ Protein (½ limited), 1 Bread, ¼ Slider

174 Calories, 6 gm Fat, 11 gm Protein, 19 gm Carbohydrate, 642 mg Sodium, 83 mg Calcium, 1 gm Fiber

DIABETIC: 1½ Meat, 1 Starch

Ham and Egg Salad Sandwiches

■ ■ ■ ■ ■ ■ ■ ■

Here's a happy combination of two classic sandwich fillings. They've always been great on their own, but inviting ham salad and egg salad to tango together will make lunchtime extra-special fun! *Serves 4*

2 hard-boiled eggs, diced
1 full cup (6 ounces) finely diced Dubuque 97% fat-free ham or any extra-lean ham
1 teaspoon dried onion flakes
¼ cup Kraft fat-free mayonnaise

2 tablespoons sweet pickle relish
1 teaspoon prepared mustard
8 slices reduced-calorie bread
Lettuce leaves

In a medium bowl, combine eggs, ham, and onion flakes. Add mayonnaise, pickle relish, and mustard. Mix well to combine. For each sandwich, spread about ¼ cup filling mixture on a slice of bread, cover with lettuce leaves, and top with another slice of bread. Serve at once or cover and refrigerate until ready to serve.

Each serving equals:
HE: 1½ Protein (½ limited), 1 Bread, 18 Optional Calories

193 Calories, 5 gm Fat, 15 gm Protein, 22 gm Carbohydrate, 822 mg Sodium, 51 mg Calcium, 5 gm Fiber

DIABETIC: 1½ Meat, 1½ Starch/Carbohydrate

(Yes, You've Got to Eat Your) Veggies and Salads

■ ■ ■ ■ ■ ■ ■ ■

Why is it hard to get your family to eat veggies and salads? Often, it's because Daddy turns his nose up at them, and the kids automatically follow his lead. In our house, my son James always hated peas—in fact, he's had a personal vendetta against them ever since he was a little boy! His father tried to force him to eat them, saying, "You're going to eat those peas or else," which I think is the wrong tactic. Now, of course, he never eats peas.

I suggest you don't force your children to eat what they insist they don't like, but do keep trying different ways to serve a new food, especially vegetables. Sooner or later, they will give them a try, and they may discover that they like them after all. Sometimes, in fact, they'll eat your version of something they won't try elsewhere.

My son Tommy always refused, and still refuses, to eat kidney beans. In fact, when he was six and he went to the hospital because he hurt his foot, they asked if he was allergic to anything and he answered, "Just kidney beans."

Some parents whose kids hate veggies try pureeing them in the blender, and mixing them into sauces and soups. Nine out of ten kids will probably not figure it out; it's worth a try. But just don't

make a thing of it, saying, "See, you ate peas and you liked them."
If you trick them, they won't trust you ever again.

This section is more fun than it sounds, with an abundance of recipes to tickle your family's taste buds! Besides all kinds of tasty vegetable side dishes (like **Fruit-Glazed Carrots** and **Green Beans and Potatoes in Mushroom Sauce**), I've included luscious fruit salads, tangy coleslaws and other veggie salads, plus some wonderfully filling main dish salads to please the fussiest palate. Won't it be fun to help your children discover how truly tasty veggies and salads can be?

Vegetables

Fruit-Glazed Carrots

Carrot Stuffing Casserole

Comforting Beans and
    Carrots

Creamed Beans and
    Carrots

Green Beans au Gratin

Green Bean Pie

Franco Green Beans

Green Beans and Potatoes
    in Mushroom Sauce

Fiesta Peas au Gratin

Creamy Italian Corn

Corn-Vegetable Medley

Corn in Tomato Basil
    Sauce

Simmered Corn and Beans

Cowpoke Beans

Fruit-Glazed Carrots

■ ■ ■ ■ ■ ■ ■ ■

If your children are picky about their veggies but love fruity flavor, here's a great way to sweeten up an already delicious vegetable. This tasty side dish is a landslide winner at our house! *Serves 4 (1 cup)*

> 4 cups sliced carrots
> 1 cup water
> 1 teaspoon dried parsley
>   flakes
>
> ¼ cup apricot spreadable
>   fruit spread

In a medium saucepan, cook carrots in water for 10 to 12 minutes, or just until tender. Drain, reserving 1 tablespoon liquid. Return carrots to saucepan. Add reserved liquid, parsley flakes, and spreadable fruit. Mix gently to combine. Lower heat and simmer for 10 minutes, stirring occasionally. Serve at once.

Each serving equals:
HE: 2 Vegetable, 1 Fruit

---

76 Calories, 0 gm Fat, 1 gm Protein, 18 gm Carbohydrate, 62 mg Sodium, 38 mg Calcium, 2 gm Fiber

---

DIABETIC: 2 Vegetable, 1 Fruit

Carrot Stuffing Casserole

■ ■ ■ ■ ❊ ■ ■ ■

*L*ooking for ways to slip extra healthy goodness by your vegetable-resistant family? This delectable casserole delivers lots of cheese flavor and mouth satisfaction, not to mention loads of vitamin A. *Serves 6*

1 (10¾-ounce) can Healthy Request Cream of Celery Soup
¼ cup skim milk
1 teaspoon dried parsley flakes
1 teaspoon dried onion flakes
4 cups (two 16-ounce cans)
sliced carrots, rinsed and drained
2 cups (3 ounces) unseasoned dry bread cubes
Full ½ cup (2¼ ounces) shredded Kraft reduced-fat Cheddar cheese

Preheat oven to 350 degrees. Spray an 8-by-8-inch baking dish with butter-flavored cooking spray. In a large bowl, combine celery soup and skim milk. Stir in parsley and onion flakes. Add carrots and bread cubes. Mix gently to combine. Pour mixture into prepared baking dish. Evenly sprinkle Cheddar cheese over top. Bake for 25 minutes. Place baking dish on a wire rack and let set for 5 minutes. Divide into 6 servings.

HINT: Pepperidge Farm bread cubes work great.

Each serving equals:
HE: 1⅓ Vegetable, ⅔ Bread, ½ Protein, ¼ Slider, 11 Optional Calories

131 Calories, 3 gm Fiber, 5 gm Protein, 21 gm Carbohydrate, 558 mg Sodium, 152 mg Calcium, 1 gm Fiber

DIABETIC: 1 Vegetable, 1 Starch, ½ Meat

Comforting Beans and Carrots

❋

Don't worry if your kids prefer the easy-eating taste of canned vegetables. What's important is helping them develop healthy eating habits that include lots of good-for-you veggies like these.

Serves 4 (¾ cup)

2 cups (one 16-ounce can) cut green beans, rinsed and drained
2 cups (one 16-ounce can) sliced carrots, rinsed and drained
1 (10¾-ounce) can Healthy Request Cream of Celery Soup
1 teaspoon dried parsley flakes
1 teaspoon dried onion flakes
⅛ teaspoon black pepper

In a large skillet sprayed with butter-flavored cooking spray, combine green beans and carrots. Add celery soup, parsley flakes, onion flakes, and black pepper. Mix well to combine. Simmer for 10 minutes, or until mixture is heated through, stirring often.

Each serving equals:
HE: 2 Vegetable, ½ Slider, 1 Optional Calorie

78 Calories, 2 gm Fat, 2 gm Protein, 13 gm Carbohydrate, 332 mg Sodium, 88 mg Calcium, 2 gm Fiber

DIABETIC: 2 Vegetable

Creamed Beans and Carrots

■ ■ ■ ❄ ■ ■ ■ ■

Evaporated skim milk is simply magic in a can when you're aiming to create a cream sauce without all that fat! This version celebrates green beans and carrots but would also work with other frozen veggies like zucchini and squash.

Serves 4 (¾ cup)

*2 cups frozen cut green
  beans
2 cups frozen cut carrots
1 cup hot water
3 tablespoons all-purpose
  flour*

*1½ cups (one 12-fluid-
  ounce can) Carnation
  Evaporated Skim Milk
¼ teaspoon black pepper
1 teaspoon dried parsley
  flakes*

In a large saucepan, cook green beans and carrots in water for 15 to 20 minutes, or just until tender. Drain. Return vegetables to saucepan. In a covered jar, combine flour and evaporated skim milk. Shake well to blend. Pour milk mixture over vegetables. Add black pepper and parsley flakes. Mix well to combine. Lower heat and simmer for 10 minutes or until sauce thickens, stirring often.

Each serving equals:
HE: 2 Vegetable, ¾ Skim Milk, ¼ Bread

128 Calories, 0 gm Fat, 9 gm Protein, 23 gm Carbohydrate, 143 mg Sodium, 316 mg Calcium, 2 gm Fiber

DIABETIC: 2 Vegetable, 1 Skim Milk

Green Beans au Gratin

■ ■ ■ ■ ❋ ■ ■ ■ ■

Cliff is my number-one in-house green bean fan, so I'm constantly stirring up tasty new ways to fix them for his dining pleasure. This is one of his absolute favorites, as it features a crunchy cornflake topping. *Serves 4*

1½ cups (12-fluid-ounce can) Carnation Evaporated Skim Milk
3 tablespoons all-purpose flour
Full ½ cup (2¼ ounces) shredded Kraft reduced-fat Cheddar cheese

1 tablespoon dried onion flakes
¼ teaspoon black pepper
4 cups (two 16-ounce cans) cut green beans, rinsed and drained
½ cup (¾ ounce) crushed cornflakes

Preheat oven to 350 degrees. Spray an 8-by-8-inch baking dish with butter-flavored cooking spray. In a covered jar, combine evaporated skim milk and flour. Shake well to blend. Pour mixture into a medium saucepan sprayed with butter-flavored cooking spray. Add Cheddar cheese, onion flakes, and black pepper. Mix well to combine. Cook over medium heat until cheese melts and mixture thickens, stirring constantly. Stir in green beans. Pour mixture into prepared baking dish. Evenly sprinkle cornflakes over top. Bake for 30 minutes. Place baking dish on a wire rack and let set for 5 minutes. Divide into 4 servings.

HINT: A self-seal sandwich bag works great for crushing corn-flakes.

Each serving equals:
HE: 2 Vegetable, ¾ Skim Milk, ¾ Protein, ½ Bread

179 Calories, 3 gm Fat, 13 gm Protein, 25 gm Carbohydrate, 284 mg Sodium, 437 mg Calcium, 2 gm Fiber

DIABETIC: 1½ Vegetable, 1 Skim Milk, ½ Meat, ½ Starch

Green Bean Pie

Here's a fun way to serve veggies to your family—in a quick-and-easy "quiche" that bakes up golden and cheesy-good!

Serves 6

¾ cup Bisquick Reduced
  Fat Baking Mix
⅔ cup Carnation Nonfat
  Dry Milk Powder
1 teaspoon dried onion
  flakes
¾ cup water
4 eggs or equivalent in egg
  substitute

2 cups (one 16-ounce can)
  French-style green
  beans, rinsed and
  drained
¾ cup (3 ounces) shredded
  Kraft reduced-fat
  Cheddar cheese

Preheat oven to 350 degrees. Spray a 9-inch pie plate with butter-flavored cooking spray. In a large bowl, combine baking mix, dry milk powder, and onion flakes. Add water and eggs. Mix well to combine. Fold in green beans and Cheddar cheese. Spread mixture into prepared pie plate. Bake for 30 to 35 minutes or until a knife inserted in center comes out clean. Place pie plate on a wire rack and let set for 5 minutes. Cut into 6 wedges.

Each serving equals:
HE: 1⅓ Protein (⅔ limited), ⅔ Vegetable, ½ Bread, ⅓ Skim Milk

179 Calories, 7 gm Fat, 12 gm Protein, 17 gm Carbohydrate, 388 mg Sodium, 235 mg Calcium, 1 gm Fiber

DIABETIC: 1 Meat, 1 Vegetable, 1 Starch/Carbohydrate

Franco Green Beans

■ ■ ■ ■ ❄ ■ ■ ■ ■

This is a fast and flavorful dish just perfect for nights you're late coming home but still want dinner to be cozy and home cooked. That hot French dressing—*ooh la la!*

Serves 6 (½ cup)

½ cup Kraft Fat Free French Dressing

¼ cup (one 2-ounce jar) chopped pimiento, drained

1 teaspoon dried parsley flakes

1 teaspoon dried onion flakes

6 cups (three 16-ounce cans) whole green beans, rinsed and drained

In a large skillet, combine French dressing, pimiento, parsley flakes, and onion flakes. Stir in green beans. Cook over medium heat for 5 minutes, or until mixture is heated through, stirring occasionally.

Each serving equals:
HE: 2 Vegetable, ¼ Slider, 13 Optional Calories

64 Calories, 0 gm Fat, 1 gm Protein, 15 gm Carbohydrate, 204 mg Sodium, 37 mg Calcium, 2 gm Fiber

DIABETIC: 2 Vegetable

Green Beans and Potatoes in Mushroom Sauce

■ ■ ■ ■ ■ ■ ■ ■

This looks and tastes fancy enough for company, but it's simple enough to serve anytime! Besides lots of yummy flavor, it delivers a nice burst of calcium to help those young bones grow strong.

Serves 4 (1 cup)

1 (10¾-ounce) can
  Healthy Request Cream
  of Mushroom Soup
1 cup skim milk
⅛ teaspoon black pepper
2 cups (one 16-ounce can)
  cut green beans, rinsed
  and drained

½ cup (one 2.5-ounce jar)
  sliced mushrooms,
  drained
12 ounces (one 16-ounce
  can) sliced potatoes,
  rinsed and drained

In a large skillet sprayed with butter-flavored cooking spray, combine mushroom soup, skim milk, and black pepper. Add green beans and mushrooms. Mix well to combine. Stir in potatoes. Cook over medium heat for 8 to 10 minutes or until mixture is heated through. Serve at once.

Each serving equals:
HE: 1¼ Vegetable, ¾ Bread, ¼ Skim Milk, ½ Slider, 1 Optional Calorie

138 Calories, 2 gm Fat, 5 gm Protein, 25 gm Carbohydrate,
426 mg Sodium, 169 mg Calcium, 3 gm Fiber

DIABETIC: 1½ Starch/Carbohydrate, 1 Vegetable

Fiesta Peas au Gratin

■ ■ ■ ■ ❋ ■ ■ ■

Peas are just about always a kid-pleaser—maybe it's their tiny size! This saucy skillet dish whips up quickly and wins applause from every chair at the table. *Olé!* *Serves 4 (¾ cup)*

½ cup *finely chopped onion*
1 (10¾-ounce) can
  Healthy Request Cream
  of Mushroom Soup
½ cup (one 2.5-ounce jar)
  sliced mushrooms,
  undrained

¾ cup (3 ounces) shredded
  Kraft reduced-fat
  Cheddar cheese
¼ cup (one 2-ounce jar)
  chopped pimiento,
  drained
2 cups *frozen peas, thawed*

In a large skillet sprayed with butter-flavored cooking spray, sauté onion for 5 minutes. Stir in mushroom soup, undrained mushrooms, and Cheddar cheese. Continue cooking until cheese melts, stirring often. Add pimiento and peas. Mix gently to combine. Lower heat and simmer for 5 minutes, or until mixture is heated through, stirring often.

HINT: Thaw peas by placing in a colander and rinsing under hot water for one minute.

Each serving equals:
HE: 1 Protein, 1 Bread, ½ Vegetable, ½ Slider, 1 Optional Calorie

173 Calories, 5 gm Fat, 11 gm Protein, 21 gm Carbohydrate, 584 mg Sodium, 228 mg Calcium, 5 gm Fiber

DIABETIC: 1½ Starch/Carbohydrate, 1 Meat

Creamy Italian Corn

■ ■ ■ ■ ■ ■ ■ ■

If you've never "cooked" with salad dressing before, I bet you'll be delighted how much tangy goodness it adds to this easy microwave dish! *Serves 4 (½ cup)*

1 (8-ounce) package
   Philadelphia fat-free
   cream cheese
¼ cup Kraft Fat Free
   Italian Dressing

¼ cup (¾ ounce) grated
   Kraft fat-free Parmesan
   cheese
2 cups frozen whole-kernel
   corn, thawed

In an 8-cup glass measuring cup, stir cream cheese with a spoon until soft. Stir in Italian dressing and Parmesan cheese. Microwave on MEDIUM (50% power) for 1 minute. Stir in corn. Microwave on HIGH (100% power) for 3 minutes, stirring after 2 minutes. Serve at once.

HINT: Thaw corn by placing in a colander and rinsing under hot water for one minute.

Each serving equals:
HE: 1¼ Protein, 1 Bread, 8 Optional Calories

144 Calories, 0 gm Fat, 11 gm Protein, 25 gm Carbohydrate, 611 mg Sodium, 2 mg Calcium, 3 gm Fiber

DIABETIC: 1 Meat, 1 Starch

Corn-Vegetable Medley

■ ■ ■ ■ ■ ■ ■ ■

The rich cheesy-creamy sauce makes this colorful veggie mix appealing to young and old alike. It's so good—and good for you—you'll make it often. *Serves 4 (1 full cup)*

2 cups (one 16-ounce can)
   cream-style corn
⅓ cup Carnation Nonfat
   Dry Milk Powder
½ cup water
4 cups frozen carrot,
   broccoli, and

cauliflower blend, thawed
¾ cup (3 ounces) shredded
   Kraft reduced-fat
   Cheddar cheese
1 teaspoon dried parsley
   flakes

In a large saucepan, combine corn, dry milk powder, and water. Add vegetable blend. Bring mixture to a boil. Lower heat, cover, and simmer for 15 minutes. Stir in Cheddar cheese and parsley flakes. Mix well to combine. Continue simmering for 10 minutes or until mixture is heated through and cheese melts, stirring often.

HINTS:
1. 1½ cups frozen broccoli, 1¼ cups frozen carrots, and 1¼ cups frozen cauliflower may be used in place of blended vegetables.
2. Thaw vegetables by placing in a colander and rinsing under hot water for one minute.

Each serving equals:
HE: 2 Vegetable, 1 Bread, 1 Protein, ¼ Skim Milk

228 Calories, 4 gm Fat, 13 gm Protein, 35 gm Carbohydrate, 637 mg Sodium, 275 mg Calcium, 5 gm Fiber

DIABETIC: 2 Vegetable, 1½ Starch/Carbohydrate, 1 Meat

Corn in Tomato Basil Sauce

■ ■ ■ ■ ■ ■ ■ ■

The basil in this tomato-y sauce will convince your family you stirred it for hours! And you really can't have too many healthy corn concoctions.   *Serves 6 (⅔ cup)*

  ½ cup finely chopped onion   ½ teaspoon dried basil
  1¾ cups (one 15-ounce   3 cups frozen whole kernel
  can) Hunt's Chunky   corn, thawed
  Tomato Sauce
  1 tablespoon Sugar Twin
  or Sprinkle Sweet

In a large skillet sprayed with butter-flavored cooking spray, sauté onion for 5 minutes. Add tomato sauce, Sugar Twin, and basil. Mix well to combine. Stir in corn. Lower heat, cover, and simmer for 10 minutes, or until mixture is heated through, stirring occasionally.

HINT: Thaw corn by placing in a colander and rinsing under hot water for one minute.

Each serving equals:
HE: 1⅓ Vegetable, 1 Bread, 1 Optional Calorie

96 Calories, 0 gm Fat, 3 gm Protein, 21 gm Carbohydrate,
471 mg Sodium, 7 mg Calcium, 3 gm Fiber

DIABETIC: 1 Vegetable, 1 Starch

Simmered Corn and Beans

■ ■ ■ ❋ ■ ■ ■

This amazingly quick dish combines two kid-pleasing vegetables with just a touch of spice. It's great for nights when you're all in a hurry to attend the school basketball playoffs.

Serves 4 (¾ cup)

2 cups (one 16-ounce can)
  whole-kernel corn,
  rinsed and drained
2 cups (one 16-ounce can)
  cut green beans, rinsed
  and drained

1 teaspoon dried onion
  flakes
2 tablespoons water
⅛ teaspoon black pepper

In a large skillet sprayed with butter-flavored cooking spray, combine corn and green beans. Add onion flakes, water, and black pepper. Mix well to combine. Lower heat, cover, and simmer for 10 minutes, or until mixture is heated through, stirring occasionally.

Each serving equals:
HE: 1 Bread, 1 Vegetable

92 Calories, 0 gm Fat, 3 gm Protein, 20 gm Carbohydrate, 15 mg Sodium, 20 mg Calcium, 3 gm Fiber

DIABETIC: 1 Starch, 1 Vegetable

Cowpoke Beans

■ ■ ■ ■ ❄ ■ ■ ■ ■

It'll be your home, not the range, where all the kids rush to the table on nights you serve this flavorful dish. If your family prefers mild to wild, you may prefer to start with a little less chili seasoning. Ring that dinner bell and round 'em up!

Serves 4 (full ¾ cup)

¼ *cup chopped onion*
1¾ *cups (one 14½-ounce can) stewed tomatoes, undrained*
1 *cup (one 8-ounce can) Hunt's Tomato Sauce*
1½ *teaspoons chili seasoning*

1 *tablespoon Brown Sugar Twin*
¼ *teaspoon black pepper*
10 *ounces (one 16-ounce can) pinto beans, rinsed and drained*

In a large skillet sprayed with butter-flavored cooking spray, sauté onion for 5 minutes. Stir in undrained stewed tomatoes, tomato sauce, chili seasoning, Brown Sugar Twin, and black pepper. Add pinto beans. Mix well to combine. Lower heat and simmer for 10 minutes, stirring occasionally.

Each serving equals:
HE: 2 Vegetable, 1¼ Protein

268 Calories, 1 gm Fat, 15 gm Protein, 50 gm Carbohydrate, 719 mg Sodium, 138 mg Calcium, 16 gm Fiber

DIABETIC: 2½ Starch, 2 Vegetable, 1 Meat

Fruit Salads

Cherry Hill Apple Salad

Blueberry-Bonanza
  Gelatin Salad

Ginger Peachy Salad

Lemon Fruit Salad

Heavenly Pistachio Fruit
  Salad

Hawaiian Fruit Salad

Cherry Hill Apple Salad

■ ■ ■ ■ ■ ■ ■ ■

Gelatin salads are a terrific way to persuade picky eaters that healthy fruit is yummy food. This combines luscious colors and textures in a very flavorful fiesta!   *Serves 6*

1 (4-serving) package JELL-O sugar-free cherry gelatin
¾ cup boiling water
1 cup unsweetened apple juice

1 cup (2 small) cored, unpeeled, and chopped Red Delicious apples
1 cup (1 medium) diced banana

In a large bowl, combine dry gelatin and boiling water. Mix well to dissolve gelatin. Stir in apple juice. Add apples and banana. Mix well to combine. Pour mixture into an 8-by-8-inch dish. Refrigerate until firm, about 3 hours. Cut into 6 servings.

HINT: To prevent banana from turning brown, mix with 1 teaspoon lemon juice or sprinkle with Fruit Fresh.

Each serving equals:
HE: 1 Fruit, 7 Optional Calories

60 Calories, 0 gm Fat, 1 gm Protein, 14 gm Carbohydrate, 38 mg Sodium, 6 mg Calcium, 1 gm Fiber

DIABETIC: 1 Fruit

Blueberry-Bonanza Gelatin Salad

■ ■ ■ ■ ■ ■ ■ ■ ■

-ö- It's fun to mix flavors to create your own magical mélange! This party-on-a-plate is so full of fruit, it just might explode! Because it's kind of red, white, and blue, keep it in mind for a summer picnic or potluck. *Serves 6*

1 (4-serving) package
  JELL-O sugar-free
  raspberry gelatin
1 (4-serving) package
  JELL-O sugar-free berry
  blue gelatin
2½ cups boiling water
1 cup (one 8-ounce can)
  crushed pineapple,

packed in fruit juice,
  undrained
¾ cup frozen unsweetened
  blueberries
¾ cup frozen unsweetened
  red raspberries
1 cup (1 medium) diced
  banana

In a large bowl, combine dry gelatins and water. Mix well to dissolve gelatin. Stir in undrained pineapple. Add frozen blueberries and raspberries. Mix well to combine. Fold in banana. Pour mixture into an 8-by-8-inch dish. Refrigerate until firm, about 3 hours. Cut into 6 servings.

HINT: To prevent banana from turning brown, mix with 1 teaspoon lemon juice or sprinkle with Fruit Fresh.

Each serving equals:
HE: 1 Fruit, 13 Optional Calories

80 Calories, 0 gm Fat, 2 gm Protein, 18 gm Carbohydrate,
74 mg Sodium, 12 mg Calcium, 2 gm Fiber

DIABETIC: 1 Fruit

Ginger Peachy Salad

■ ■ ■ ■ ■ ■ ■ ■

Sometimes a surprising blend of ingredients produces a dark horse winner like this sparkling salad. It's got such a fresh and fizzy flavor, you could celebrate a special anniversary or a perfect report card with this instead of champagne! *Serves 6*

1 (4-serving) package
    JELL-O sugar-free
    orange gelatin
1 cup boiling water

1 cup diet ginger ale
2 cups (one 16-ounce can)
    sliced peaches, packed in
    fruit juice, drained

In a large bowl, combine dry gelatin and boiling water. Mix well to dissolve gelatin. Stir in diet ginger ale. Add peaches. Mix well to combine. Pour mixture into an 8-by-8-inch dish. Refrigerate until firm, about 3 hours. Cut into 6 servings.

Each serving equals:
HE: ⅔ Fruit, 7 Optional Calories

32 Calories, 0 gm Fat, 1 gm Protein, 7 gm Carbohydrate,
43 mg Sodium, 3 mg Calcium, 1 gm Fiber

DIABETIC: ½ Fruit

Lemon Fruit Salad

■ ■ ■ ■ ■ ■ ■ ■

Here's a pretty way to blend your kids' favorite fruits—mandarin oranges, bananas, and more—into one delectable salad! The Diet Dew gives it just that extra touch of sparkle.

Serves 8 (⅔ cup)

1 (4-serving) package
JELL-O sugar-free
instant vanilla pudding
1 (4-serving) package
JELL-O sugar-free
lemon gelatin
⅔ cup Carnation Nonfat
Dry Milk Powder
1 cup (one 8-ounce can)
crushed pineapple,
packed in fruit juice,
undrained

¾ cup Diet Mountain Dew
½ cup Cool Whip Free
1 cup (one 8-ounce can)
fruit cocktail, packed in
fruit juice, drained
1 cup (one 11-ounce can)
mandarin oranges,
rinsed and drained
1 cup (1 medium) diced
banana

In a large bowl, combine dry pudding mix, dry gelatin, and dry milk powder. Add undrained pineapple and Diet Mountain Dew. Mix well using a wire whisk. Blend in Cool Whip Free. Add fruit cocktail, mandarin oranges, and banana. Mix gently to combine. Cover and refrigerate for at least 15 minutes. Gently stir again just before serving.

HINT: To prevent banana from turning brown, mix with 1 teaspoon lemon juice or sprinkle with Fruit Fresh.

Each serving equals:
HE: 1 Fruit, ¼ Skim Milk, ¼ Slider, 6 Optional Calories

108 Calories, 0 gm Fat, 3 gm Protein, 24 gm Carbohydrate, 231 mg Sodium, 80 mg Calcium, 1 gm Fiber

DIABETIC: 1 Fruit, ½ Starch/Carbohydrate

Heavenly Pistachio Fruit Salad

■ ■ ■ ■ ■ ■ ■ ■

*J*ust full of sweet surprises, this colorful salad dazzles the appetite with tasty textures too! I've never met a kid (or husband) who didn't love finding those mini-marshmallows!

Serves 6 (¾ cup)

1 (4-serving) package
  JELL-O sugar-free
  instant pistachio
  pudding mix
⅔ cup Carnation Nonfat
  Dry Milk Powder
2 cups (one 16-ounce can)
  fruit cocktail, packed in
  fruit juice, drained, and
  ¼ cup liquid reserved
1 cup (one 8-ounce can)

crushed pineapple, packed
  in fruit juice, drained,
  and ¼ cup liquid
  reserved
½ cup water
¾ cup Yoplait plain fat-
  free yogurt
¾ cup Cool Whip Free
½ cup (1 ounce) miniature
  marshmallows

In a large bowl, combine dry pudding mix, dry milk powder, fruit cocktail and pineapple liquids, and water. Mix well using a wire whisk. Blend in yogurt and Cool Whip Free. Gently stir in fruit cocktail, pineapple, and marshmallows. Cover and refrigerate for at least 30 minutes. Gently stir again just before serving.

Each serving equals:
HE: 1 Fruit, ½ Skim Milk, ½ Slider, 5 Optional Calories

152 Calories, 0 gm Fat, 5 gm Protein, 33 gm Carbohydrate, 286 mg Sodium, 161 mg Calcium, 1 gm Fiber

DIABETIC: 1 Fruit, 1 Starch/Carbohydrate

Hawaiian Fruit Salad

■ ■ ■ ■ ■ ■ ■ ■

Here's a terrific way to brighten up a snowy winter meal—with a lively salad as gorgeous as a Hawaiian sunset! This one is pretty and tasty enough to serve for dessert. *Serves 6*

2 cups (2 medium) sliced
  bananas
2 cups (two 16-ounce cans)
  pineapple chunks,
  packed in fruit juice,
  drained
1 cup (one 11-ounce can)

mandarin oranges, rinsed
  and drained
4 maraschino cherries,
  diced
2 tablespoons flaked
  coconut

In a medium bowl, combine bananas, pineapple, mandarin oranges, and maraschino cherries. Gently stir to combine. Evenly spoon mixture into 6 dessert dishes. Sprinkle 1 teaspoon coconut over top of each. Refrigerate for at least 30 minutes.

HINT: To prevent bananas from turning brown, mix with 1 teaspoon lemon juice or sprinkle with Fruit Fresh.

Each serving equals:
HE: 1⅔ Fruit, 17 Optional Calories

128 Calories, 0 gm Fat, 1 gm Protein, 31 gm Carbohydrate,
7 mg Sodium, 19 mg Calcium, 2 gm Fiber

DIABETIC: 2 Fruit

Veggie Salads

Traditional Coleslaw

Cabbage Apple Salad

Sunshine Carrot Salad

Carrot Raisin
Marshmallow Salad

Sweet Pea Salad

Dilled Carrot and Pea
Salad

Grandma Jo's Lettuce-
Tomato Salad

Riviera Bean Salad

Traditional Coleslaw

■ ■ ■ ■ ■ ■ ■

There's nothing like classic coleslaw—every family's favorite side dish and buffet mainstay during the summer months. Isn't it wonderful to enjoy it as often as you like without worrying whether it's too high in fat or calories? This one is just right!

Serves 6 (⅔ cup)

1 cup Kraft fat-free mayonnaise	*5 cups shredded cabbage*
¾ teaspoon celery seed	*1 cup shredded carrots*
Sugar substitute to equal 2 teaspoons sugar	

In a large bowl, combine mayonnaise, celery seed, and sugar substitute. Add cabbage and carrots. Mix well to combine. Cover and refrigerate for at least 30 minutes. Gently stir again just before serving.

Each serving equals:
HE: 2 Vegetable, ¼ Slider, 1 Optional Calorie

---

103 Calories, 3 gm Fat, 3 gm Protein, 16 gm Carbohydrate, 383 mg Sodium, 244 mg Calcium, 3 gm Fiber

---

DIABETIC: 1 Vegetable, ½ Starch/Carbohydrate

Cabbage Apple Salad

■ ■ ■ ■ ■ ■ ■ ■

I like to slip in a surprise or two when I'm creating a new recipe, and this time my mix of crunchy cabbage and apples sparkles more brightly with a little nutty flavor and the smooth, sweet taste of maple syrup. *Serves 4 (¾ cup)*

2 cups shredded cabbage
1 cup (2 small) cored, unpeeled, and diced Red Delicious apples
¼ cup (1 ounce) chopped dry-roasted peanuts
⅓ cup Kraft fat-free mayonnaise

2 tablespoons Peter Pan reduced-fat peanut butter
2 tablespoons Cary's Sugar Free Maple Syrup

In a medium bowl, combine cabbage, apples, and peanuts. In a small bowl, combine mayonnaise, peanut butter, and maple syrup. Add mayonnaise mixture to cabbage mixture. Toss gently to combine. Cover and refrigerate for at least 30 minutes. Gently stir again just before serving.

Each serving equals:
HE: 1 Vegetable, 1 Fat, ¾ Protein, ½ Fruit, 16 Optional Calories

140 Calories, 7 gm Fat, 5 gm Protein, 16 gm Carbohydrate,
233 mg Sodium, 23 mg Calcium, 2 gm Fiber

DIABETIC: 1 Starch/Carbohydrate, 1 Fat, ½ Meat

Sunshine Carrot Salad

■ ■ ■ ■ ■ ■ ■ ■

This dish looks as good as it tastes, and the aroma of the orange juice blended with apple pie spice is a fragrant promise no one can resist! The smiles on your family's faces will say thank you with every single bite.

Serves 6 (½ cup)

3 cups shredded carrots
1 cup (2 small) cored, unpeeled, and diced Red Delicious apples
1 cup (one 11-ounce can) mandarin oranges, rinsed and drained

½ cup Kraft fat-free mayonnaise
2 tablespoons unsweetened orange juice
Sugar substitute to equal 2 teaspoons sugar
½ teaspoon apple pie spice

In a medium bowl, combine carrots, apples, and mandarin oranges. In a small bowl, combine mayonnaise, orange juice, sugar substitute, and apple pie spice. Add mayonnaise mixture to carrot mixture. Mix gently to combine. Cover and refrigerate for at least 30 minutes. Gently stir again just before serving.

Each serving equals:
HE: 1 Vegetable, ⅔ Fruit, 17 Optional Calories

68 Calories, 0 gm Fat, 1 gm Protein, 16 gm Carbohydrate, 195 mg Sodium, 21 mg Calcium, 2 gm Fiber

DIABETIC: 1 Vegetable, ½ Fruit

Carrot Raisin Marshmallow Salad

■ ■ ■ ■ ■ ■ ■ ■

*S*weet and crunchy, tangy and luscious, this festive blend is a real crowd-pleaser. Kids just seem to love discovering raisins and nuts among their veggies.   *Serves 6 (½ cup)*

3 cups shredded carrots
¾ cup chopped celery
¾ cup raisins
¼ cup (1 ounce) chopped
* walnuts*

½ cup (1 ounce) miniature
* marshmallows*
⅔ cup Kraft fat-free
* mayonnaise*

In a large bowl, combine carrots, celery, and raisins. Stir in walnuts and marshmallows. Add mayonnaise. Mix well to combine. Cover and refrigerate for at least 30 minutes. Gently stir again just before serving.

HINT: To plump up raisins without "cooking," place in a glass measuring cup and microwave on HIGH for 20 seconds.

Each serving equals:
HE: 1¼ Vegetable, 1 Fruit, ⅓ Fat, ¼ Slider, 11 Optional Calories

151 Calories, 3 gm Fat, 2 gm Protein, 29 gm Carbohydrate, 266 mg Sodium, 35 mg Calcium, 2 gm Fiber

DIABETIC: 1 Vegetable, 1 Fruit, ½ Starch/Carbohydrate, ½ Fat *or* 2 Starch/Carbohydrate, ½ Fat

Sweet Pea Salad

∎∎∎∎∎∎∎∎∎

Here's a treat for toddlers to teens, and all you adults too! Aren't those tiny peas irresistibly delicious? My daughter, Becky, could never get enough of them.   *Serves 4 (½ cup)*

2 cups (one 16-ounce can)
  tiny peas, rinsed and
  drained
½ cup finely chopped
  celery

¼ cup sweet pickle relish
⅓ cup Kraft fat-free
  mayonnaise
1 teaspoon dried onion
  flakes

In a medium bowl, combine peas and celery. Add sweet pickle relish, mayonnaise, and onion flakes. Mix gently to combine. Cover and refrigerate for at least 30 minutes. Gently stir again just before serving.

Each serving equals:
HE: 1 Bread, ¼ Vegetable, ¼ Slider, 8 Optional Calories

96 Calories, 0 gm Fat, 4 gm Protein, 20 gm Carbohydrate, 297 mg Sodium, 28 mg Calcium, 4 gm Fiber

DIABETIC: 1 Starch/Carbohydrate

Dilled Carrot and Pea Salad

■ ■ ■ ■ ■ ■ ■ ■

I've always loved the flavor of dill, especially when I snipped it fresh from my garden. Well, most of us now buy it dried, but when it's blended with this pea-carrot combo, your family will insist it's just perfect! *Serves 4 (¾ cup)*

⅓ cup Kraft Fat Free
   French Dressing
2 tablespoons Kraft fat-
   free mayonnaise
1 teaspoon dried dill weed

2 cups frozen peas, thawed
2 cups (one 16-ounce can)
   sliced carrots, rinsed
   and drained

In a medium bowl, combine French dressing, mayonnaise, and dill weed. Add peas and carrots. Mix gently to combine. Cover and refrigerate for at least 30 minutes. Gently stir again just before serving.

HINT: Thaw peas by placing in a colander and rinsing under hot water for one minute.

Each serving equals:
HE: 1 Vegetable, 1 Bread, ¼ Slider, 18 Optional Calories

112 Calories, 0 gm Fat, 4 gm Protein, 24 gm Carbohydrate, 298 mg Sodium, 41 mg Calcium, 5 gm Fiber

DIABETIC: 1 Vegetable, 1 Starch/Carbohydrate

Grandma Jo's Lettuce-Tomato Salad

Don't let your family get bored with good old lettuce and tomato salad—try something fresh and new! This healthy homemade dressing is very easy to stir up, and it'll tickle everyone's taste buds.

Serves 4 (¾ cup)

3 cups shredded lettuce
1¼ cups chopped fresh tomatoes
¼ cup sliced green onion
2 tablespoons Kraft fat-free mayonnaise

2 teaspoons skim milk
Sugar substitute to equal 2 tablespoons sugar
1 tablespoon Heinz Light Harvest Ketchup or any reduced-sodium ketchup

In a large bowl, combine lettuce, tomatoes, and onion. In a small bowl, combine mayonnaise, skim milk, sugar substitute, and ketchup. Add mayonnaise mixture to lettuce mixture. Toss gently to combine. Serve at once.

Each serving equals:
HE: 2¼ Vegetable, 12 Optional Calories

28 Calories, 0 gm Fat, 1 gm Protein, 6 gm Carbohydrate, 104 mg Sodium, 16 mg Calcium, 1 gm Fiber

DIABETIC: 1 Vegetable

Riviera Bean Salad

■ ■ ■ ■ ■ ■ ■ ■

Here's a fun new way to give green beans something to crow about—the sunshiny sizzle of the beaches of the south of France. It's pretty, it's tasty, and because it's so good for you, you may even look forward to bathing suit season!

Serves 4 (¾ cup)

¼ cup Kraft Fat Free
   French Dressing
4 cups (two 16-ounce cans)
   cut green beans, rinsed
   and drained

½ cup sliced red radishes
1 tablespoon Hormel
   Bacon Bits
1 hard-boiled egg, diced

In a medium bowl, combine French dressing and green beans. Add radishes, bacon bits, and egg. Mix gently to combine. Cover and refrigerate for at least 30 minutes. Gently stir again just before serving.

Each serving equals:
HE: 2¼ Vegetable, ¼ Protein (limited), ¼ Slider, 11 Optional Calories

86 Calories, 2 gm Fat, 4 gm Protein, 13 gm Carbohydrate,
234 mg Sodium, 44 mg Calcium, 2 gm Fiber

DIABETIC: 2½ Vegetable

Main Dish Salads

■ ■ ■ ■ ■ ■ ■ ■

Mom's Tuna Salad

Tuna Spaghetti Salad

Chicken Ranch Taco Salad

Grandma's Chicken Salad

Pasta, Ham, and Egg Salad

Ham and Peas Supper Salad

BLT Salad

Olé Taco Layered Salad

Mom's Tuna Salad

▪ ▪ ▪ ▪ ▪ ▪ ▪ ▪ ▪

Don't you agree that the tastes we grow to love in childhood stay with us for a lifetime? My mother's tuna salad made lunchtime special whenever she served it, so I created this healthy version with my loving memories of her in mind.

Serves 4 (½ cup)

2 (6-ounce) cans white
   tuna, packed in water,
   drained and flaked
1 hard-boiled egg, chopped
1 tablespoon sweet pickle
   relish

½ cup finely chopped
   celery
⅔ cup Kraft fat-free
   mayonnaise
1 teaspoon dried onion
   flakes

In a medium bowl, combine tuna, egg, pickle relish, and celery. Add mayonnaise and onion flakes. Mix gently to combine. Cover and refrigerate for at least 30 minutes. Gently stir again just before serving. Good served on lettuce or as a sandwich filling.

Each serving equals:
HE: 1½ Protein (¼ limited), ¼ Vegetable, ¼ Slider, 15 Optional Calories

142 Calories, 2 gm Fat, 23 gm Protein, 9 gm Carbohydrate, 687 mg Sodium, 23 mg Calcium, 0 gm Fiber

DIABETIC: 3 Meat, ½ Starch

Tuna Spaghetti Salad

■ ■ ■ ■ ■ ■ ■ ■

$\mathcal{S}$paghetti makes kids smile, and this easy combo will widen that smile into a grin! The peas and carrots give it a little extra color, and if you remember to break up the spaghetti before cooking, it'll be easy even for little ones to eat.

Serves 4 (1 cup)

1 (6-ounce) can white
    tuna, packed in water,
    drained and flaked
1½ cups cooked spaghetti,
    rinsed and drained
¼ cup dill pickle relish
½ cup Kraft fat-free
    mayonnaise

¼ teaspoon black pepper
1 teaspoon prepared
    mustard
½ cup shredded carrots
½ cup frozen peas, thawed
1 hard-boiled egg, chopped

In a large bowl, combine tuna and spaghetti. Add pickle relish, mayonnaise, black pepper, and mustard. Mix gently to combine. Fold in carrots, peas, and egg. Cover and refrigerate for at least 30 minutes. Gently stir again just before serving.

HINTS:
1. A full 1 cup broken uncooked spaghetti usually cooks to about 1½ cups.
2. Thaw peas by placing in a colander and rinsing under hot water for one minute.

Each serving equals:
HE: 1 Protein, 1 Bread, ¼ Vegetable, ¼ Slider

198 Calories, 2 gm Fat, 16 gm Protein, 29 gm Carbohydrate, 551 mg Sodium, 28 mg Calcium, 2 gm Fiber

DIABETIC: 2 Meat, 2 Starch

Chicken Ranch Taco Salad

■ ■ ■ ■ ■ ■ ■

Ready-made dressings are a busy cook's secret weapon, especially when they come in so many delicious and fat-free flavors. After stirring up just a few ingredients and spicing them with your favorite salsa, you'll feel great about serving this yummy dish to your family!   *Serves 6 (1 cup)*

1½ cups (8 ounces) diced   *¾ cup chunky salsa (mild,*
    cooked chicken breast   *medium, or hot)*
3 cups shredded lettuce   *½ cup (1½ ounces)*
¾ cup (3 ounces) shredded   *crushed Doritos*
    Kraft reduced-fat   *Reduced Fat Tortilla*
    Cheddar cheese   *Chips*
1 cup Kraft Fat Free
    Ranch Dressing

In a large bowl, combine chicken, lettuce, and Cheddar cheese. In a medium bowl, combine Ranch dressing and salsa. Add dressing mixture to chicken mixture. Mix well to combine. Stir in tortilla chips. Serve at once.

HINT: If you don't have leftovers, purchase a chunk of cooked chicken breast from your local deli.

Each serving equals:
HE: 2 Protein, 1¼ Vegetable, ½ Bread, ¾ Slider, 7 Optional Calories

197 Calories, 5 gm Fat, 16 gm Protein, 22 gm Carbohydrate, 739 mg Sodium, 146 mg Calcium, 1 gm Fiber

DIABETIC: 2 Meat, 1 Vegetable, 1 Starch/Carbohydrate

Grandma's Chicken Salad

■ ■ ■ ■ ■ ■ ■ ■

The guests at Grandma's boardinghouse weren't exactly family, but she fed them as if they were! This classic dish is as crisp and tangy as I remember hers was.   *Serves 4 (½ cup)*

1½ cups (8 ounces) diced cooked chicken breast
¾ cup finely chopped celery
¼ cup finely chopped onion
⅔ cup Kraft fat-free mayonnaise

¼ cup (one 2-ounce jar) chopped pimiento, drained
1 teaspoon Worcestershire sauce
¼ teaspoon black pepper

In a medium bowl, combine chicken, celery, and onion. Add mayonnaise, pimiento, Worcestershire sauce, and black pepper. Mix well to combine. Cover and refrigerate for at least 30 minutes. Gently stir again just before serving.

HINTS:
1. If you don't have leftovers, purchase a chunk of cooked chicken breast from your local deli.
2. Good served over lettuce or as a sandwich filling.

Each serving equals:
HE: 2 Protein, ½ Vegetable, ¼ Slider, 7 Optional Calories

126 Calories, 2 gm Fat, 18 gm Protein, 9 gm Carbohydrate, 420 mg Sodium, 22 mg Calcium, 0 gm Fiber

DIABETIC: 2 Meat, ½ Starch/Carbohydrate

Pasta, Ham, and Egg Salad

■ ■ ■ ■ ■ ■ ■ ■

Pasta salads are wonderfully filling and provide lots of healthy carbohydrates for an energetic day's work or play. This one is tasty and a bit tangy, and couldn't be easier for any family member to stir up in a hurry. *Serves 4 (1¼ cups)*

2 cups cold cooked rotini pasta, rinsed and drained
1 full cup (6 ounces) diced Dubuque 97% fat-free ham or any extra-lean ham
2 hard-boiled eggs, chopped

½ cup Kraft fat-free mayonnaise
2 teaspoons prepared mustard
2 tablespoons sweet pickle relish
¼ teaspoon black pepper
Dash paprika

In a large bowl, combine rotini pasta, ham, and eggs. In a small bowl, combine mayonnaise, mustard, pickle relish, and black pepper. Add mayonnaise mixture to pasta mixture. Mix well to combine. Cover and refrigerate for at least 15 minutes. Just before serving, lightly sprinkle paprika over top.

HINT: 1½ cups uncooked rotini pasta usually cooks to about 2 cups.

Each serving equals:
HE: 1½ Protein (½ limited), 1 Bread, ¼ Slider, 8 Optional Calories

213 Calories, 5 gm Fat, 13 gm Protein, 29 gm Carbohydrate, 739 mg Sodium, 22 mg Calcium, 1 gm Fiber

DIABETIC: 2 Starch, 1½ Meat

Ham and Peas Supper Salad

■ ■ ■ ■ ■ ■ ■ ■

My kids are big fans of this salad's creamy dressing. Instead of the same old ham-and-cheese sandwich your family is expecting, why not stir up this ham-and-cheese combo that adds some colorful peas for fun and flavor? *Serves 4 (1 full cup)*

½ cup Kraft fat-free
  mayonnaise
1 tablespoon skim milk
1 teaspoon dried onion
  flakes
1 teaspoon dried parsley
  flakes
¼ teaspoon black pepper
1½ cups cold cooked elbow

macaroni, rinsed and
  drained
½ cup frozen peas, thawed
¾ cup (3 ounces) diced
  Velveeta Light Cheese
1 full cup (6 ounces) diced
  Dubuque 97% fat-free
  ham or any extra-lean
  ham

In a large bowl, combine mayonnaise, skim milk, onion flakes, parsley flakes, and black pepper. Add macaroni, peas, Velveeta cheese, and ham. Mix well to combine. Cover and refrigerate for at least 30 minutes. Gently stir again just before serving.

HINTS:
1. 1 cup of uncooked macaroni usually cooks to about 1½ cups.
2. Thaw peas by placing in a colander and rinsing under hot water for one minute.

Each serving equals:
HE: 2 Protein (¼ limited), 1 Bread, ¼ Slider, 2 Optional Calories

191 Calories, 3 gm Fat, 16 gm Protein, 25 gm Carbohydrate, 625 mg Sodium, 162 mg Calcium, 2 gm Fiber

DIABETIC: 2 Meat, 1½ Starch/Carbohydrate

BLT Salad

■ ■ ■ ■ ■ ■ ■ ■

How can you be eating healthy, you may wonder, when I stir real bacon into this tasty sandwich-in-a-salad? Remember my Healthy Exchanges motto—Moderation!—and enjoy its rich, smoky flavor along with cheese and veggies for a wonderfully satisfying meal! *Serves 6 (1 cup)*

4¼ cups finely shredded
　lettuce
1½ cups cherry tomatoes,
　halved
¼ cup sliced green onion
¾ cup (3 ounces) shredded
　Kraft reduced-fat
　Cheddar cheese
6 tablespoons Hormel
　Bacon Bits

½ cup Kraft Fat Free
　Thousand Island
　Dressing
2 tablespoons Kraft fat-
　free mayonnaise
2 tablespoons sweet pickle
　relish

In a large bowl, combine lettuce, tomatoes, onion, Cheddar cheese, and bacon bits. In a small bowl, combine Thousand Island dressing, mayonnaise, and pickle relish. Add dressing mixture to lettuce mixture. Toss gently to combine. Serve at once.

Each serving equals:
HE: 2 Vegetable, ¾ Protein, ¾ Slider, 7 Optional Calories

124 Calories, 4 gm Fat, 8 gm Protein, 14 gm Carbohydrate,
655 mg Sodium, 114 mg Calcium, 2 gm Fiber

DIABETIC: 1 Vegetable, ½ Starch, ½ Meat, 1 Free Vegetable

Olé Taco Layered Salad

■ ■ ■ ■ ■ ■ ■ ■

It doesn't take much extra time to prepare a salad that's layered instead of tossed together in a bowl. But, oh, the compliments you'll receive from family members when you please their eyes and treat their taste buds with this scrumptious dish. Take a bow!   *Serves 6*

8 ounces ground 90% lean turkey or beef
2 tablespoons taco seasoning
¾ cup water
4 cups finely shredded lettuce
2 cups finely chopped fresh tomatoes
¾ cup (3 ounces) shredded
Kraft reduced-fat Cheddar cheese
1½ cups chunky salsa (mild, medium, or hot)
¾ cup Land O Lakes no-fat sour cream
1 cup (3 ounces) crushed Doritos Reduced Fat Tortilla Chips

In a large skillet sprayed with olive oil–flavored cooking spray, brown meat. Stir in taco seasoning and water. Lower heat and simmer for 10 minutes, stirring occasionally. Remove from heat and allow to cool for 5 minutes. In a 9-by-12-inch dish, layer lettuce, cooled meat mixture, tomatoes, and Cheddar cheese. In a medium bowl, combine salsa and sour cream. Evenly spread salsa mixture over top. Refrigerate for at least 30 minutes. Sprinkle tortilla chips evenly over salsa mixture. Cover and refrigerate for at least 1 hour. Divide into 6 servings.

Each serving equals:
HE: 2½ Vegetable, 1⅔ Protein, ⅔ Bread, ¼ Slider, 10 Optional Calories

224 Calories, 8 gm Fat, 14 gm Protein, 24 gm Carbohydrate, 953 mg Sodium, 227 mg Calcium, 2 gm Fiber

DIABETIC: 2 Vegetable, 1½ Meat, 1 Starch, 1 Free Vegetable

Fill-'Em-Up Main Dishes

■ ■ ■ ■ ■ ■ ■

Of all of my children, James is the one who enjoys cooking most. He's like his mom in that he doesn't care to do dishes, but he's very creative in the kitchen! Even as a child, he cooked. He makes the very best pot roast in America bar none. Even Cliff raves about it! In fact, although James is married now with kids of his own, at least once a year he makes his famous pot roast and the whole family comes to dinner.

In sixth grade he made his own chili—and it was so hot and spicy I thought I was going to die! When he gave some to our next-door neighbor to take home, I must admit I was concerned, but he came back a half hour later to tell us he wanted more, that it was the best chili he'd ever had! Another time, he fixed a spaghetti meal for Father Kuntz, one of his teachers when he was in sixth or seventh grade. James did all the cooking, and the meal was a big success. But while he gets his creativity from me, I think he got his love of cooking from my mom and grandmother. I always loved to help Grandma cook in her boardinghouse when I was a young girl, just six or seven years old. In fact, she made me an apron to match hers. I was so proud, I wore it every time I visited her house and we cooked together on her wood-burning stove.

What pleases me most about this section is the variety. You'll find dozens of family favorites made healthy and easy to prepare. Whether your children beg for cheeseburgers (**Cheeseburger Milk Gravy Skillet**), tuna casserole (**Tuna Krispie Bake**), or hot dogs (**Creamy Franks and Rice**), you'll find new ways of serving the foods they love.

Fill-'Em-Up Main Dishes

French Potato Casserole

Rio Grande Rice

Vegetable Tetrazzini

Creamy Macaroni and Cheese with Green Beans

Pronto Pizza

Fish Italiano

Savory Fish Fillets

Tuna Krispie Bake

Creamy Tuna-Potato Scallop

Salmon Noodle Bake

Italian Glazed Chicken

Cheesy Chicken Pot Biscuit Cups

Chicken Parmesan Noodle Bake

Country Chicken and Biscuits

Oven-Baked Turkey Hash

Deep-Dish Turkey Pot Pie

Quick Turkey and Dressing

Tom's Easy Cheesy Skillet

Cheeseburger Milk Gravy Skillet

Grande Meatloaf with Potato Stuffing

Lazy-Day Lasagna

Pizza Popover Pie

Cheeseburger Pie

Aloha "Steaks" with
  Island Sauce

Baked Gringo Steaks

Italian Braised Steak

Mulligan Stew

Machaca Beef Tortillas

Baked BBQ Pork Tenders

Quick Pork Parmigiana

Baked Pork Cutlets with
  Rice-Tomato Stuffing

Scalloped Peas and
  Potatoes with Ham

Ham-Corn Custard Bake

Macaroni and Cheese with
  Frankfurters

Idaho Hot Dog Bake

Frankly Good Hot Dish

Taco Dogs

Creamy Franks and Rice

French Potato Casserole

■ ■ ■ ■ ■ ■ ■ ■ ■

Tired of serving the same old foods the same old way? Here's a quick and tasty way to enjoy mashed potatoes and still get the healthy nutrition of cottage cheese. Your oven works like magic to transform a bowl of ingredients into a little bit of heaven on a plate! *Serves 4*

1⅔ cups boiling water
1⅓ cups (3 ounces) instant potato flakes
2 teaspoons dried onion flakes
2 cups fat-free cottage cheese

1 egg or equivalent in egg substitute
⅛ teaspoon black pepper
¼ cup (¾ ounce) grated Kraft fat-free Parmesan cheese

Preheat oven to 350 degrees. Spray an 8-by-8-inch baking dish with butter-flavored cooking spray. In a large bowl, combine boiling water, potato flakes, and onion flakes. Stir in cottage cheese, egg, and black pepper. Add Parmesan cheese. Mix well to combine. Spread mixture into prepared baking dish. Bake for 45 to 50 minutes. Place baking dish on a wire rack and let set for 5 minutes. Divide into 4 servings.

Each serving equals:
HE: 1½ Protein (¼ limited), 1 Bread

165 Calories, 1 gm Fat, 19 gm Protein, 20 gm Carbohydrate, 566 mg Sodium, 60 mg Calcium, 2 gm Fiber

DIABETIC: 2 Meat, 1½ Starch

Rio Grande Rice

■ ■ ■ ✳ ■ ■ ■

The kids who visit JO's Kitchen Cafe just love rice, so I'm always thinking up new ways to incorporate one of their favorite tastes. This tangy concoction is rich in flavor and texture, and full of things kids like!   *Serves 4*

¼ cup chopped onion
¾ cup finely chopped
  celery
1 (10¾-ounce) can
  Healthy Request Cream
  of Mushroom Soup
1¾ cups (one 15-ounce
  can) Hunt's Chunky
  Tomato Sauce

1½ cups (6 ounces)
  shredded Kraft reduced-
  fat Cheddar cheese
1 teaspoon chili seasoning
½ cup (one 2.5-ounce jar)
  sliced mushrooms,
  drained
2 cups hot cooked rice
⅛ teaspoon black pepper

Preheat oven to 350 degrees. Spray an 8-by-8-inch baking dish with butter-flavored cooking spray. In a large skillet sprayed with butter-flavored cooking spray, sauté onion and celery for 8 to 10 minutes. Stir in mushroom soup, tomato sauce, Cheddar cheese, and chili seasoning. Continue cooking until cheese melts, stirring often. Add mushrooms, rice, and black pepper. Mix well to combine. Spread mixture into prepared baking dish. Bake for 30 minutes. Place baking dish on a wire rack and let set for 5 minutes. Divide into 4 servings.

HINT: 1⅓ cups uncooked rice usually cooks to about 2 cups.

Each serving equals:
HE: 2½ Vegetable, 2 Protein, 1 Bread, ½ Slider, 1 Optional Calorie

277 Calories, 9 gm Fat, 16 gm Protein, 33 gm Carbohydrate, 995 mg Sodium, 376 mg Calcium, 3 gm Fiber

DIABETIC: 2½ Vegetable, 2 Meat, 1½ Starch

Vegetable Tetrazzini

■ ■ ■ ■ ❋ ■ ■ ■ ■

A creamy spaghetti dish featuring your family's favorite veggies is a true tummy pleaser on a chilly fall night. And the aroma of cheese melting always brings my kids to the table in a hurry—how about yours?   *Serves 4 (1½ cups)*

½ cup chopped onion
1 (10¾-ounce) can
   Healthy Request Cream
   of Mushroom Soup
½ cup skim milk
1½ cups (6 ounces)
   shredded Kraft reduced-
   fat Cheddar cheese
¼ cup (one 2-ounce jar)
   chopped pimiento,
   drained
¼ cup chopped fresh

parsley or 1 tablespoon
   dried parsley flakes
2 cups hot cooked
   spaghetti, rinsed and
   drained
2 cups (one 16-ounce can)
   sliced carrots, rinsed
   and drained
2 cups (one 16-ounce can)
   cut green beans, rinsed
   and drained

In a large skillet sprayed with butter-flavored cooking spray, sauté onion for 5 minutes. Stir in mushroom soup, skim milk, Cheddar cheese, pimiento, and parsley. Continue cooking until cheese melts, stirring often. Add spaghetti, carrots, and green beans. Mix well to combine. Lower heat and simmer for 5 minutes, or until mixture is heated through, stirring occasionally.

HINT: 1½ cups broken uncooked spaghetti usually cooks to about 2 cups.

Each serving equals:

HE: 2 Protein, 1¼ Vegetable, 1 Bread, ½ Slider, 13 Optional Calories

313 Calories, 9 gm Fat, 19 gm Protein, 39 gm Carbohydrate, 746 mg Sodium, 458 mg Calcium, 4 gm Fiber

DIABETIC: 2 Meat, 1½ Starch, 1 Vegetable

Creamy Macaroni and Cheese with Green Beans

■ ■ ■ ✻ ■ ■ ■

You can never have too many ways to prepare this Midwestern family favorite, which Cliff could eat at least three times a week! It's so fast, you'll have time to relax with your kids before dinner. *Serves 4*

1½ cups hot cooked elbow macaroni, rinsed and drained
2 cups (one 16-ounce can) cut green beans, rinsed and drained
1½ cups (6 ounces) shredded Kraft reduced-fat Cheddar cheese
1 (10¾-ounce) can Healthy Request Cream of Mushroom Soup
½ teaspoon black pepper
6 small fat-free saltine crackers, crushed
1 teaspoon dried parsley flakes

Preheat oven to 350 degrees. Spray an 8-by-8-inch baking dish with butter-flavored cooking spray. In a large bowl, combine macaroni, green beans, and Cheddar cheese. Add mushroom soup and black pepper. Mix well to combine. Pour mixture into prepared baking dish. In a small bowl, combine cracker crumbs and parsley flakes. Sprinkle mixture evenly over top. Lightly spray crumbs with butter-flavored cooking spray. Bake for 25 to 30 minutes. Place baking dish on a wire rack and let set for 5 minutes. Divide into 4 servings.

HINTS:
1. 1 full cup uncooked elbow macaroni usually cooks to about 1½ cups.
2. A self-seal sandwich bag works great for crushing crackers.

Each serving equals:

HE: 2 Protein, 1 Bread, 1 Vegetable, ½ Slider, 1 Optional Calorie

265 Calories, 9 gm Fat, 16 gm Protein, 30 gm Carbohydrate, 676 mg Sodium, 301 mg Calcium, 2 gm Fiber

DIABETIC: 2 Meat, 1½ Starch, 1 Vegetable

Pronto Pizza

■ ■ ■ ■ ❊ ■ ■ ■ ■

Tasty, healthy pizza you can prepare at home in minutes? *Delicioso* is the only word for it! And feel free to add some mushrooms or pepper slices on top for a little extra color and flavor.

Serves 6

1 (7.5-ounce) can Pillsbury
   refrigerated buttermilk
   biscuits
1 teaspoon dried onion
   flakes
1 teaspoon Italian
   seasoning
¼ cup (¾ ounce) grated

Kraft fat-free Parmesan
   cheese
1 cup (one 8-ounce can)
   Hunt's Tomato Sauce
1 scant cup (3¾ ounces)
   shredded Kraft reduced-
   fat mozzarella cheese

Preheat oven to 450 degrees. Spray a 12-inch pizza pan with olive oil–flavored cooking spray. Flatten biscuits and pat into prepared pan being sure to press together to cover pizza pan and forming a ridge around the outside. In a medium bowl, combine onion flakes, Italian seasoning, Parmesan cheese, and tomato sauce. Spread sauce mixture evenly over biscuit crust. Evenly sprinkle mozzarella cheese over top. Bake for 10 to 12 minutes. Place pan on a wire rack and let set for 2 to 3 minutes. Cut into 6 servings.

Each serving equals:
HE: 1¼ Bread, 1 Protein, ⅔ Vegetable

160 Calories, 4 gm Fat, 9 gm Protein, 22 gm Carbohydrate,
785 mg Sodium, 139 mg Calcium, 3 gm Fiber

DIABETIC: 1½ Starch, 1 Meat, ½ Vegetable

Fish Italiano

■ ■ ■ ■ ■ ■ ■

If you want your family to eat more healthy fish for supper, why not tempt them with this simple but sensational recipe? The shouts of "Bravo" will echo through the house! *Serves 4*

⅓ cup Kraft fat-free
   mayonnaise
¼ cup (¾ ounce) grated
   Kraft fat-free Parmesan
   cheese
2 tablespoons skim milk
1 teaspoon Italian
   seasoning

16 ounces white fish, cut
   into 4 pieces
⅓ cup (1½ ounces)
   shredded Kraft reduced-
   fat mozzarella cheese

Preheat oven to 375 degrees. Spray an 8-by-8-inch baking dish with butter-flavored cooking spray. In a medium bowl, combine mayonnaise, Parmesan cheese, skim milk, and Italian seasoning. Rinse fish pieces and pat dry. Evenly arrange fish in prepared baking dish. Spread mayonnaise mixture evenly over fish pieces. Evenly sprinkle mozzarella cheese over top. Bake for 15 to 20 minutes or until fish flakes easily. Divide into 4 servings.

Each serving equals:
HE: 2¼ Protein, 16 Optional Calories

---

159 Calories, 3 gm Fat, 25 gm Protein, 8 gm Carbohydrate, 449 mg Sodium, 121 mg Calcium, 0 gm Fiber

---

DIABETIC: 3½ Meat, ½ Starch

Savory Fish Fillets

■ ■ ■ ■ ■ ■ ■ ■

The French dressing gives these fillets a great tangy taste and pretty color, too. Remember that fish is "brain food," so serving this will help your kids be the best they can be! **Serves 4**

*16 ounces white fish, cut
into 4 pieces*
*½ cup Kraft Fat Free
French Dressing*

*1 teaspoon dried parsley
flakes*
*1 teaspoon dried onion
flakes*

Preheat oven to 350 degrees. Spray an 8-by-8-inch baking dish with butter-flavored cooking spray. Rinse fish pieces and pat dry. Evenly arrange fish in prepared baking dish. In a small bowl, combine French dressing, parsley flakes, and onion flakes. Drizzle dressing mixture evenly over top. Bake for 20 to 25 minutes or until fish flakes easily.

Each serving equals:
HE: 1½ Protein, ½ Slider, 10 Optional Calories

149 Calories, 1 gm Fiber, 23 gm Protein, 12 gm Carbohydrate, 392 mg Sodium, 45 mg Calcium, 1 gm Fiber

DIABETIC: 3 Meat, ½ Starch

Tuna Krispie Bake

■ ■ ■ ■ ❄ ■ ■ ■ ■

𝕯on't you just love the kind of cooking that tells you to put a few ingredients in a bowl, stir 'em up, bake 'em, and enjoy? This tuna casserole is comfort food with a capital *C* and reheats beautifully in the microwave.   *Serves 4*

1 (6-ounce) can white
   tuna, packed in water,
   drained and flaked
3 cups (3 ounces) Rice
   Krispies
½ cup chopped onion
1 teaspoon dried parsley
   flakes

1 (10¾-ounce) can
   Healthy Request Cream
   of Mushroom Soup
¾ cup (3 ounces) shredded
   Kraft reduced-fat
   Cheddar cheese

Preheat oven to 350 degrees. Spray an 8-by-8-inch baking dish with butter-flavored cooking spray. In a large bowl, combine tuna, Rice Krispies, onion, and parsley flakes. Add mushroom soup and Cheddar cheese. Mix well to combine. Spread mixture evenly into prepared baking dish. Bake for 30 to 35 minutes. Place baking dish on a wire rack and let set for 5 minutes. Divide into 4 servings.

Each serving equals:
HE: 1¾ Protein, 1 Bread, ¼ Vegetable, ½ Slider, 1 Optional Calorie

---

242 Calories, 6 gm Fat, 19 gm Protein, 28 gm Carbohydrate, 796 mg Sodium, 217 mg Calcium, 1 gm Fiber

---

DIABETIC: 2 Meat, 1½ Starch

Creamy Tuna-Potato Scallop

Here's another speedy solution to the nightly question, "What's for dinner, Mom?" This one just bubbles with cozy goodness and gets your taste buds primed! You could also try this with slices of reduced-fat Swiss cheese for a change.

Serves 4

1 (10¾-ounce) can
   Healthy Request Cream
   of Celery Soup
¼ cup skim milk
¼ cup Land O Lakes no-
   fat sour cream
1 teaspoon dried parsley
   flakes
1 teaspoon dried onion
   flakes
½ teaspoon prepared
   mustard
3 full cups (16 ounces)
   diced cooked potatoes
2 (6-ounce) cans white
   tuna, packed in water,
   drained and flaked
Dash paprika

Preheat oven to 350 degrees. Spray an 8-by-8-inch baking dish with butter-flavored cooking spray. In a large bowl, combine celery soup and skim milk. Add sour cream, parsley flakes, onion flakes, and mustard. Mix well to combine. Stir in potatoes and tuna. Spread mixture into prepared baking dish. Bake for 30 minutes. Lightly sprinkle paprika over top. Place baking dish on a wire rack and let set for 5 minutes. Divide into 4 servings.

Each serving equals:

HE: 1½ Protein, 1 Bread, ¾ Slider, 1 Optional Calorie

254 Calories, 2 gm Fat, 26 gm Protein, 33 gm Carbohydrate, 629 mg Sodium, 105 mg Calcium, 1 gm Fiber

DIABETIC: 3 Meat, 2 Starch

Salmon Noodle Bake

■ ■ ■ ❄ ■ ■ ■

Here's a great way to serve another one of those good-for-you fish dishes in quick-and-easy fashion! Combined with peas and noodles, this is a hearty entree that will warm everybody's hearts—and tummies, too!   *Serves 6*

1½ cups (one 12-fluid-
　　ounce can) Carnation
　　Evaporated Skim Milk
3 tablespoons all-purpose
　　flour
1 tablespoon dried onion
　　flakes
¼ cup Kraft fat-free
　　mayonnaise

½ teaspoon lemon pepper
1 (14¾-ounce) can pink
　　salmon, drained, boned,
　　and flaked
1 cup frozen peas, thawed
2 cups hot cooked noodles,
　　rinsed and drained
3 tablespoons (¾ ounce)
　　dried fine bread crumbs

Preheat oven to 350 degrees. Spray an 8-by-8-inch baking dish with butter-flavored cooking spray. In a covered jar, combine evaporated skim milk and flour. Shake well to blend. Pour mixture into a medium saucepan sprayed with butter-flavored cooking spray. Cook over medium heat until mixture thickens, stirring constantly. Remove from heat. Stir in onion flakes, mayonnaise, and lemon pepper. Add salmon, peas, and noodles. Mix gently to combine. Pour mixture into prepared baking dish. Evenly sprinkle bread crumbs over top. Lightly spray crumbs with butter-flavored cooking spray. Bake for 30 minutes. Place baking dish on a wire rack and let set for 5 minutes. Divide into 6 servings.

HINTS:
1. Thaw peas by placing in a colander and rinsing under hot water for one minute.
2. 1¾ cups uncooked noodles usually cooks to about 2 cups.

Each serving equals:

HE: 1⅔ Protein, 1⅓ Bread, ½ Skim Milk, 6 Optional Calories

248 Calories, 4 gm Fat, 22 gm Protein, 31 gm Carbohydrate, 536 mg Sodium, 305 mg Calcium, 2 gm Fiber

DIABETIC: 2½ Meat, 1½ Starch, ½ Skim Milk *or* 2½ Meat, 2 Starch/ Carbohydrate

Italian Glazed Chicken

■ ■ ■ ■ ■ ❊ ■ ■ ■ ■ ■

Here's a culinary composition that'll convince your family they're on a Roman holiday! I think fat-free dressings are a heaven-sent aid to healthy cooking, even on nights when salad's nowhere on the menu!   *Serves 4*

> *16 ounces skinned and*   *¼ cup Kraft Fat Free*
>   *boned uncooked chicken*   *Italian Dressing*
>   *breast, cut into 4 pieces*   *⅛ teaspoon black pepper*
> *¼ cup Heinz Light*
>   *Harvest Ketchup or any*
>   *reduced-sodium ketchup*

Preheat oven to 350 degrees. Spray an 8-by-8-inch baking dish with butter-flavored cooking spray. Arrange chicken pieces in prepared baking dish. In a small bowl, combine ketchup, Italian dressing, and black pepper. Drizzle sauce mixture evenly over chicken pieces. Bake for 35 to 40 minutes or until chicken is tender.

Each serving equals:
HE: 3 Protein, ¼ Slider, 3 Optional Calories

138 Calories, 2 gm Fat, 26 gm Protein, 4 gm Carbohydrate, 344 mg Sodium, 13 mg Calcium, 0 gm Fiber

DIABETIC: 3 Meat

Cheesy Chicken Pot Biscuit Cups

■ ■ ■ ■ ❄ ■ ■ ■ ■

$\mathcal{S}$omething about this recipe's perfectly kid-size portions makes them irresistible to children of every age! The flaky crust, the cheesy sauce, and the tasty chunks of chicken make any meal a real treat! *Serves 5 (2 each)*

1 (7.5-ounce) can Pillsbury
    refrigerated buttermilk
    biscuits
1 cup (5 ounces) diced
    cooked chicken breast
1 (10¾-ounce) can
    Healthy Request Cream
    of Chicken Soup

Scant ⅔ cup (2½ ounces)
    shredded Kraft reduced-
    fat Cheddar cheese
1 teaspoon dried parsley
    flakes
¼ teaspoon black pepper

Preheat oven to 400 degrees. Separate biscuits and place each biscuit in a cup of an ungreased 12-hole muffin pan, pressing dough up sides to edge of cup. In a medium bowl, combine chicken, chicken soup, Cheddar cheese, parsley flakes, and black pepper. Mix well to combine. Evenly spoon chicken mixture into prepared biscuit cups. Bake for 12 to 15 minutes or until golden brown. Remove from oven. Place muffin pan on a wire rack and let set for 2 to 3 minutes. Serve at once.

HINTS:
1. If you don't have leftovers, purchase a chunk of cooked chicken breast from your local deli.
2. Fill unused muffin wells with water. It protects the muffin pan and ensures even baking.

Each serving equals:
HE: 1⅔ Protein, 1½ Bread, ¼ Slider, 16 Optional Calories

230 Calories, 6 gm Fat, 17 gm Protein, 27 gm Carbohydrate, 763 mg Sodium, 114 mg Calcium, 2 gm Fiber

DIABETIC: 1½ Meat, 1½ Starch/Carbohydrate

Chicken Parmesan Noodle Bake

■ ■ ■ ■ ❋ ■ ■ ■ ■

Umm-ummm! This dish is so fragrant as it bakes, the world will beat a path to your dinner table! It's incredibly flavorful, yet as healthy as can be. *Serves 4*

¼ cup chopped onion
1¾ cups (one 14½-ounce can) stewed tomatoes, coarsely chopped and undrained
1½ teaspoons Italian seasoning
2 teaspoons Sugar Twin or Sprinkle Sweet

½ cup (one 2.5-ounce jar) sliced mushrooms, drained
¼ cup (¾ ounce) grated Kraft fat-free Parmesan cheese
1½ cups (8 ounces) diced cooked chicken breast
2 cups hot cooked noodles, rinsed and drained

Preheat oven to 375 degrees. Spray an 8-by-8-inch baking dish with olive oil–flavored cooking spray. In a large skillet sprayed with olive oil–flavored cooking spray, sauté onion for 5 minutes. Stir in undrained stewed tomatoes, Italian seasoning, Sugar Twin, and mushrooms. Add Parmesan cheese, chicken, and noodles. Mix well to combine. Spread mixture into prepared baking dish. Bake for 30 minutes. Place baking dish on a wire rack and let set for 5 minutes. Divide into 4 servings.

HINTS:
1. If you don't have leftovers, purchase a chunk of cooked chicken breast from your local deli.
2. 1¾ cups uncooked noodles usually cooks to about 2 cups.

Each serving equals:
HE: 2¼ Protein, 1¼ Vegetable, 1 Bread, 1 Optional Calorie

251 Calories, 3 gm Fat, 24 gm Protein, 32 gm Carbohydrate, 558 mg Sodium, 77 mg Calcium, 3 gm Fiber

DIABETIC: 2½ Meat, 1½ Starch, 1 Vegetable

Country Chicken and Biscuits

■ ■ ■ ❋ ■ ■ ■

*C*liff just loves old-fashioned chicken and biscuits—in fact, most Midwestern families do. I created this better-for-you version so this beloved dish isn't just for Sunday supper anymore.

Serves 6

1 (10¾-ounce) can
Healthy Request Cream
of Celery or Mushroom
Soup
¼ cup skim milk
1 teaspoon dried onion
flakes
1 teaspoon dried parsley
flakes

1½ cups (8 ounces) diced
cooked chicken breast
2 cups (one 16-ounce can)
cut green beans, rinsed
and drained
1 (7.5-ounce) can Pillsbury
refrigerated buttermilk
biscuits

Preheat oven to 375 degrees. Spray an 8-by-8-inch baking dish with butter-flavored cooking spray. In a large skillet sprayed with butter-flavored cooking spray, combine celery soup, skim milk, onion flakes, and parsley flakes. Add chicken and green beans. Mix well to combine. Cook for 5 minutes or until heated through, stirring often. Spread mixture into prepared baking dish. Separate biscuits and cut each biscuit into 4 pieces. Evenly sprinkle biscuit pieces over top. Lightly spray tops with butter-flavored cooking spray. Bake for 12 to 15 minutes or until golden brown. Place baking dish on a wire rack and let set for 5 minutes. Divide into 6 servings.

HINT: If you don't have leftovers, purchase a chunk of cooked chicken breast from your local deli.

Each serving equals:
HE: 1⅓ Protein, 1¼ Bread, ⅔ Vegetable, ¼ Slider, 11 Optional Calories

192 Calories, 4 gm Fat, 15 gm Protein, 24 gm Carbohydrate,
538 mg Sodium, 65 mg Calcium, 2 gm Fiber

DIABETIC: 1½ Meat, 1½ Starch, 1 Vegetable

Oven-Baked Turkey Hash

■ ■ ■ ■ ❄ ■ ■ ■ ■

ॱ᷍ऀ᷍
I was raised by a mother whose magic with leftover bits and pieces was a legend in our family. I know she'd be pleased that her daughter inherited her gift for making meals that are as tasty as they are thrifty!   *Serves 4*

*1½ cups (8 ounces) diced
    cooked turkey breast*
*1½ cups (8 ounces) diced
    cooked potatoes*
*⅔ cup Carnation Nonfat
    Dry Milk Powder*
⅔ cup water
*1 teaspoon dried parsley
    flakes*
*1 teaspoon dried onion
    flakes*

*¼ cup (one 2-ounce jar)
    chopped pimiento,
    drained*
*1 teaspoon Worcestershire
    sauce*
*5 (¾-ounce) Ritz Reduced
    Fat Crackers, made into
    crumbs*

Preheat oven to 350 degrees. Spray an 8-by-8-inch baking dish with butter-flavored cooking spray. In a large bowl, combine turkey and potatoes. In a small bowl, combine dry milk powder and water. Stir in parsley flakes, onion flakes, pimiento, and Worcestershire sauce. Add milk mixture to turkey mixture. Mix well to combine. Spread mixture into prepared baking dish. Evenly sprinkle cracker crumbs over top. Bake for 30 minutes. Place baking dish on a wire rack and let set for 5 minutes. Divide into 4 servings.

HINT: If you don't have leftovers, purchase a chunk of cooked turkey breast from your local deli.

Each serving equals:
HE: 2 Protein, ¾ Bread, ½ Skim Milk

211 Calories, 3 gm Fat, 23 gm Protein, 23 gm Carbohydrate, 185 mg Sodium, 161 mg Calcium, 1 gm Fiber

DIABETIC: 2 Meat, 1 Starch, ½ Skim Milk

Deep-Dish Turkey Pot Pie

■ ■ ■ ■ ❄ ■ ■ ■ ■

You'll think you've gone time traveling when you bite into this wonderfully old-fashioned, meaty pot pie that just over-flows with cozy goodness! I can close my eyes and almost be back at the big table in Grandma's boardinghouse.   *Serves 4*

1½ cups (one 12-fluid-ounce can) Carnation Evaporated Skim Milk
3 tablespoons all-purpose flour
1 full cup (6 ounces) diced cooked turkey breast
Scant 1 cup (4 ounces) diced cooked potatoes
½ cup frozen peas, thawed
1 cup frozen sliced carrots, thawed

½ cup (one 2.5-ounce jar) sliced mushrooms, drained
¼ teaspoon black pepper
9 tablespoons Bisquick Reduced Fat Baking Mix
⅓ cup Carnation Nonfat Dry Milk Powder
1 teaspoon dried parsley flakes
½ cup water

Preheat oven to 375 degrees. In a covered jar, combine evaporated skim milk and flour. Shake well to blend. Pour mixture into a medium saucepan sprayed with butter-flavored cooking spray. Cook over medium heat until mixture thickens, stirring constantly. Stir in turkey, potatoes, peas, carrots, mushrooms, and black pepper. Mix well to combine. Evenly spoon mixture into 4 individual casseroles. In a medium bowl, combine baking mix, dry milk powder, and parsley flakes. Add water. Mix well to combine. Spoon about ¼ cup batter over top of each casserole. Bake for 20 minutes. Place casseroles on a wire rack and let set for 5 minutes.

HINTS:
1. If you don't have leftovers, purchase a chunk of cooked turkey breast from your local deli.
2. Thaw peas and carrots by placing in a colander and rinsing under hot water for one minute.

Each serving equals:
HE: 1½ Protein, 1½ Bread, 1 Skim Milk, ¾ Vegetable

295 Calories, 3 gm Fat, 26 gm Protein, 41 gm Carbohydrate, 464 mg Sodium, 386 mg Calcium, 3 gm Fiber

DIABETIC: 1½ Meat, 1½ Starch, 1 Skim Milk, 1 Vegetable

Quick Turkey and Dressing

■ ■ ■ ■ ❄ ■ ■ ■ ■

*B*ut it's not Thanksgiving or Christmas," your kids will say, delight in their eyes, when you serve this holiday treat in June or October! Don't reserve this scrumptious dish for only a few special days each year—enjoy it often. *Serves 4*

½ cup chopped onion
1 cup finely chopped celery
1 (10¾-ounce) can
  Healthy Request Cream
  of Chicken Soup
⅓ cup Carnation Nonfat
  Dry Milk Powder
½ cup water
1½ teaspoons poultry
  seasoning

1 teaspoon dried parsley
  flakes
2 cups (3 ounces)
  unseasoned dry bread
  cubes
1½ cups (8 ounces) diced
  cooked turkey breast

Preheat oven to 350 degrees. Spray an 8-by-8-inch baking dish with butter-flavored cooking spray. In a large skillet sprayed with butter-flavored cooking spray, sauté onion and celery for 5 minutes. In a small bowl, combine chicken soup, dry milk powder, water, poultry seasoning, and parsley flakes. Stir soup mixture into vegetable mixture. Add bread cubes and turkey. Mix well to combine. Pour mixture into prepared baking dish. Bake for 30 minutes. Place baking dish on a wire rack and let set for 2 to 3 minutes. Divide into 4 servings.

HINTS:
  1. Pepperidge Farm bread cubes work great.
  2. If you don't have leftovers, purchase a chunk of cooked turkey breast from your local deli.

Each serving equals:

HE: 2 Protein, 1 Bread, ¾ Vegetable, ¼ Skim Milk, ½ Slider, 5 Optional Calories

260 Calories, 4 gm Fat, 25 gm Protein, 31 gm Carbohydrate, 653 mg Sodium, 100 mg Calcium, 2 gm Fiber

DIABETIC: 2 Meat, 2 Starch

Tom's Easy Cheesy Skillet

■ ■ ■ ■ ❋ ■ ■ ■ ■

If you haven't yet cooked with fat-free gravy, you'll be delighted how rich it tastes, even with the fat whisked out! This satisfying concoction, made even heartier with corn and pasta, is just perfect for growing boys and girls.　*Serves 4 (1 cup)*

8 ounces ground 90% lean
　turkey or beef
½ cup chopped onion
1 (12-ounce) jar Heinz Fat
　Free Beef Gravy
¾ cup (3 ounces) shredded
　Kraft reduced-fat
　Cheddar cheese

½ cup (one 2.5-ounce jar)
　sliced mushrooms,
　drained
1½ cups hot cooked rotini
　pasta, rinsed and
　drained
½ cup frozen whole-kernel
　corn, thawed

In a large skillet sprayed with olive oil–flavored cooking spray, brown meat and onion. Stir in gravy and Cheddar cheese. Continue cooking until cheese melts, stirring often. Add mushrooms, rotini pasta, and corn. Mix well to combine. Lower heat and simmer for 5 minutes, or until mixture is heated through, stirring often.

HINTS:

1. A full 1 cup uncooked rotini pasta usually cooks to about 1½ cups.
2. Thaw corn by placing in a colander and rinsing under hot water for one minute.

Each serving equals:
HE: 2½ Protein, 1 Bread, ½ Vegetable, ¼ Slider, 3 Optional Calories

269 Calories, 9 gm Fat, 21 gm Protein, 26 gm Carbohydrate, 830 mg Sodium, 163 mg Calcium, 2 gm Fiber

DIABETIC: 2 Meat, 1½ Starch/Carbohydrate

Cheeseburger Milk Gravy Skillet

Another entry for my son Tommy's cheeseburger milk gravy recipe collection! Whenever he comes home to visit, I always stir up something new to please his palate, and he voted this creamy skillet supper one of his favorites.

Serves 4 (1 full cup)

8 ounces ground 90% lean
    turkey or beef
1 cup finely chopped celery
½ cup chopped onion
1 (10¾-ounce) can
    Healthy Request Cream
    of Mushroom Soup
1⅓ cups skim milk

1⅓ cups (4 ounces)
    uncooked Minute Rice
¾ cup (3 ounces) shredded
    Kraft reduced-fat
    Cheddar cheese
1 teaspoon dried parsley
    flakes
¼ teaspoon black pepper

In a large skillet sprayed with butter-flavored cooking spray, brown meat, celery, and onion. Stir in mushroom soup and skim milk. Add uncooked rice, Cheddar cheese, parsley flakes, and black pepper. Mix well to combine. Lower heat, cover, and simmer for 6 to 8 minutes, or until rice is tender, stirring occasionally.

Each serving equals:
HE: 2½ Protein, 1 Bread, ¾ Vegetable, ⅓ Skim Milk, ½ Slider, 1 Optional Calorie

223 Calories, 7 gm Fat, 15 gm Protein, 25 gm Carbohydrate, 424 mg Sodium, 172 mg Calcium, 1 gm Fiber

DIABETIC: 2 Meat, 1½ Starch/Carbohydrate

Grande Meatloaf with Potato Stuffing

■ ■ ■ ❄ ■ ■ ■

If you looked up the definition of comfort food in a kitchen dictionary, you'd probably find a picture of a meatloaf in all its homey glory! There are so many delectable ways to prepare this classic, but few are more full of flavor than this one, which has a potato surprise at its heart. *Serves 6*

1 cup (2¼ ounces) instant potato flakes
⅔ cup hot water
⅓ cup Land O Lakes no-fat sour cream
1 teaspoon dried parsley flakes
½ cup finely chopped onion
½ cup finely chopped green bell pepper
½ cup + 1 tablespoon dried fine bread crumbs

1 teaspoon chili seasoning
1 cup (one 8-ounce can) Hunt's Tomato Sauce ☆
16 ounces ground 90% lean turkey or beef
⅓ cup (1½ ounces) shredded Kraft reduced-fat Cheddar cheese
1 tablespoon Brown Sugar Twin

Preheat oven to 350 degrees. Spray a 9-by-5-inch loaf pan with olive oil–flavored cooking spray. In a medium bowl, combine potato flakes, water, sour cream, and parsley flakes. Mix well and set aside. In a large bowl, combine onion, green pepper, bread crumbs, chili seasoning, and ⅓ cup tomato sauce. Add meat. Mix well to combine. Pat half of mixture into prepared loaf pan. Spread potato mixture evenly over top. Pat remaining meat mixture over potato mixture. Stir Cheddar cheese and Brown Sugar Twin into remaining tomato sauce. Spoon sauce mixture evenly over top. Bake for 55 to 60 minutes. Place loaf pan on a wire rack and let set for 5 minutes. Cut into 6 servings.

Each serving equals:

HE: 2⅓ Protein, 1 Bread, 1 Vegetable, 15 Optional Calories

220 Calories, 8 gm Fat, 18 gm Protein, 19 gm Carbohydrate,
502 mg Sodium, 87 mg Calcium, 2 gm Fiber

DIABETIC: 2 Meat, 1 Starch/Carbohydrate, 1 Vegetable

Lazy-Day Lasagna

▪▪▪▪ ❋ ▪▪▪▪

℘oes your family love this hearty pasta dish, but you think it takes too much time to prepare except for special occasions? I came up with a way to enjoy it often and without a lot of fuss— and of course, it had to be healthy and delicious. While it bakes, why not spend a few minutes enjoying your garden!

Serves 4

8 ounces ground 90% lean turkey or beef
1¾ cups (one 15-ounce can) Hunt's Chunky Tomato Sauce
1 teaspoon Italian seasoning
2 teaspoons Sugar Twin or Sprinkle Sweet

2 cups hot cooked mini lasagna noodles, rinsed and drained ☆
1 cup fat-free cottage cheese
4 (¾-ounce) slices Kraft reduced-fat mozzarella cheese

Preheat oven to 375 degrees. Spray an 8-by-8-inch baking dish with olive oil–flavored cooking spray. In a large skillet sprayed with olive oil–flavored cooking spray, brown meat. Stir in tomato sauce, Italian seasoning, and Sugar Twin. Arrange 1 cup noodles in prepared baking dish. Spoon 1¼ cups meat sauce and cottage cheese over top. Arrange remaining 1 cup noodles over cottage cheese. Evenly place mozzarella cheese slices over noodles and spoon remaining meat sauce over top. Bake for 30 to 35 minutes. Place baking dish on a wire rack and let set for 5 minutes. Cut into 4 servings.

HINTS:
1. 1¾ cups uncooked lasagna noodles usually cooks to about 2 cups.
2. Regular noodles may be used in place of lasagna noodles.

Each serving equals:

HE: 3 Protein, 1¾ Vegetable, 1 Bread, 1 Optional Calorie

292 Calories, 8 gm Fat, 28 gm Protein, 27 gm Carbohydrate,
984 mg Sodium, 167 mg Calcium, 3 gm Fiber

DIABETIC: 3 Meat, 2 Vegetable, 1 Starch

Pizza Popover Pie

■ ■ ❄ ■ ■

This blue-ribbon dinner-in-a-dish is a winner with kids and adults alike! When it emerges from the oven golden-brown and fragrant with cheese, meat, and spices, it'll perk up the fussiest appetite.   *Serves 6*

8 ounces ground 90% lean turkey or beef
¾ cup chopped green bell pepper
¾ cup chopped onion
1¾ cups (one 15-ounce can) Hunt's Chunky Tomato Sauce
1½ teaspoons pizza seasoning
¾ cup (3 ounces) shredded Kraft reduced-fat mozzarella cheese
⅓ cup (1½ ounces) shredded Kraft reduced-fat Cheddar cheese

1 cup + 2 tablespoons all-purpose flour
⅔ cup Carnation Nonfat Dry Milk Powder
1 cup water
2 eggs, slightly beaten, or equivalent in egg substitute
2 tablespoons Kraft Fat Free Italian Dressing
¼ cup (¾ ounce) grated Kraft fat-free Parmesan cheese

Preheat oven to 375 degrees. Spray a deep-dish 10-inch pie plate with olive oil–flavored cooking spray. In a large skillet sprayed with olive oil–flavored cooking spray, brown meat, green pepper, and onion. Stir in tomato sauce and pizza seasoning. Bring mixture to a boil. Spoon mixture into prepared pie plate. Sprinkle mozzarella cheese and Cheddar cheese evenly over top. In a medium bowl, combine flour, dry milk powder, water, eggs, and Italian dressing. Mix well to combine. Spoon batter evenly over meat mixture. Evenly sprinkle Parmesan cheese over top. Bake for 30 minutes or until lightly browned and top is set. Place pie plate on a wire rack and let set for 5 minutes. Cut into 6 servings.

Each serving equals:

HE: 2½ Protein (⅓ limited), 1⅔ Vegetable, 1 Bread, ⅓ Skim Milk, 3 Optional Calories

293 Calories, 9 gm Fat, 21 gm Protein, 32 gm Carbohydrate, 854 mg Sodium, 257 mg Calcium, 3 gm Fiber

DIABETIC: 2½ Meat, 1½ Starch/Carbohydrate, 1½ Vegetable

Cheeseburger Pie

■ ■ ■ ■ ❋ ■ ■ ■

Even if your children are passionate about cheeseburgers, you'll be delighted by their smiles when you serve this instead! It's fun to find your cheeseburger flavor in a flaky, crusty pie, and it looks just beautiful when you carry it to the table. The only fast food in your house tonight will be Mom-made!　　*Serves 8*

> 1 Pillsbury unbaked
>   refrigerated 9-inch
>   piecrust
> 8 ounces ground 90% lean
>   turkey or beef
> ½ cup chopped onion
> ½ cup dill pickle relish
> 3 tablespoons all-purpose
>   flour
>
> ⅔ cup **Carnation Nonfat**
>   **Dry Milk Powder**
> ½ cup water
> ¾ cup (3 ounces) shredded
>   **Kraft reduced-fat**
>   **Cheddar cheese** ☆

Preheat oven to 415 degrees. Place piecrust in a 9-inch pie plate. Flute edges and prick bottom and sides with tines of a fork. Bake for 9 to 12 minutes, or until lightly browned. Meanwhile, in a large skillet sprayed with butter-flavored cooking spray, brown meat and onion. Stir in dill pickle relish. In a covered jar, combine flour, dry milk powder, and water. Shake well to blend. Add milk mixture to meat mixture. Mix gently to combine. Stir in ¼ cup Cheddar cheese. Pour mixture into piecrust. Continue baking for 15 minutes. Sprinkle remaining ½ cup Cheddar cheese over top and continue baking for 4 to 5 minutes or until cheese melts. Place pie plate on a wire rack and let set for 5 minutes. Cut into 8 servings.

Each serving equals:
HE: 1¼ Protein, ½ Bread, ¼ Skim Milk, ¼ Vegetable, ¾ Slider, 2 Optional Calories

---

234 Calories, 10 gm Fat, 11 gm Protein, 25 gm Carbohydrate, 364 mg Sodium, 151 mg Calcium, 1 gm Fiber

---

DIABETIC: 1½ Starch/Carbohydrate, 1 Meat, 1 Fat

Aloha "Steaks" with Island Sauce

■ ■ ■ ■ ■ ■ ■ ■ ■

These sweet-and-tangy burgers may not actually convince you that you're in Hawaii, but their scrumptious flavor is irresistible! My grandbabies, the pineapple lovers in the family, always request these.   *Serves 6*

*1 cup (one 8-ounce can)
    crushed pineapple,
    packed in fruit juice,
    drained, and ¼ cup
    liquid reserved*
*6 tablespoons (1½ ounces)
    dried fine bread crumbs*
*1 teaspoon dried onion
    flakes*
*1 cup (one 8-ounce can)
    Hunt's Tomato Sauce ☆*

*16 ounces ground 90% lean
    turkey or beef*
*2 tablespoons Brown
    Sugar Twin*
*2 teaspoons Worcestershire
    sauce*
*1 teaspoon dried onion
    flakes*
*1 teaspoon dried parsley
    flakes*

In a large bowl, combine drained pineapple, bread crumbs, onion flakes, and ¼ cup tomato sauce. Add meat. Mix well to combine. Using a ⅓-cup measuring cup as a guide, form into 6 patties. Place patties in a large skillet sprayed with butter-flavored cooking spray. Brown patties about 5 minutes on each side. In a medium bowl, combine remaining ¾ cup tomato sauce, reserved pineapple juice, Brown Sugar Twin, Worcestershire sauce, onion flakes, and parsley flakes. Spoon mixture evenly over browned patties. Lower heat, cover, and simmer for 10 minutes. When serving, evenly spoon any remaining sauce over top of "steaks."

Each serving equals:
HE: 2 Protein, ⅔ Vegetable, ⅓ Fruit, ⅓ Bread, 1 Optional Calorie

166 Calories, 6 gm Fat, 14 gm Protein, 14 gm Carbohydrate,
411 mg Sodium, 24 mg Calcium, 1 gm Fiber

DIABETIC: 2 Meat, 1 Starch/Carbohydrate

Baked Gringo Steaks

■ ■ ■ ■ ■ ■ ■ ■

My boys always loved minute steaks, so I like to find new ways to use these handy meat portions. The cheese, salsa, and sour cream topping is as pretty as a South-of-the-Border sunset!

Serves 4

4 (4 ounce) lean beef
  minute or cube steaks
1 (10¾-ounce) can
  Healthy Request
  Tomato Soup
½ cup chunky salsa (mild,
  medium, or hot)
1 tablespoon Brown Sugar
  Twin

1 teaspoon dried parsley
  flakes
3 tablespoons (¾ ounce)
  shredded Kraft reduced-
  fat Cheddar cheese
¼ cup Land O Lakes
  no-fat sour cream

Spray an 8-by-8-inch baking dish with olive oil–flavored cooking spray. In a large skillet sprayed with olive oil–flavored cooking spray, brown meat for 3 to 4 minutes on each side. Place browned meat in prepared baking dish. In a small bowl, combine tomato soup, salsa, Brown Sugar Twin, and parsley flakes. Spoon soup mixture evenly over meat. Cover and bake for 30 minutes. Uncover. Evenly sprinkle Cheddar cheese over top. Continue baking for 3 to 4 minutes. For each serving, place 1 piece of meat on plate, spoon sauce evenly over meat, and top with 1 tablespoon sour cream.

Each serving equals:
HE: 3¼ Protein, ¼ Vegetable, ¾ Slider

232 Calories, 8 gm Fat, 27 gm Protein, 13 gm Carbohydrate, 464 mg Sodium, 108 mg Calcium, 0 gm Fiber

DIABETIC: 3 Meat, 1 Starch

Italian Braised Steak

■ ■ ■ ■ ❄ ■ ■ ■ ■

Here's another "soup-er" solution to the nightly task of what to make for dinner! It's a great recipe for preteens and teenagers to make on evenings they're on their own, and it's easy to double or triple this when cooking for a crowd.   *Serves 4*

4 (4-ounce) lean   Healthy Request Tomato
   tenderized minute or   Soup
   cube steaks   ¼ cup Kraft Fat Free
1 (10¾-ounce) can   Italian Dressing

In a large skillet sprayed with olive oil–flavored cooking spray, brown meat 3 to 4 minutes on each side. In a medium bowl, combine tomato soup and Italian dressing. Spoon soup mixture evenly over meat. Lower heat, cover, and simmer for 20 to 25 minutes, or until meat is tender. When serving, evenly spoon sauce over meat.

Each serving equals:
HE: 3 Protein, ½ Slider, 13 Optional Calories

203 Calories, 7 gm Fat, 25 gm Protein, 10 gm Carbohydrate, 440 mg Sodium, 12 mg Calcium, 0 gm Fiber

DIABETIC: 3 Meat, ½ Starch

Mulligan Stew

■ ■ ■ ❄ ■ ■ ■

In some kitchens, this flavorful dish cooks for hours, but if you haven't got the time, don't worry about it! This speedy stew simmers in less than an hour and tastes sooo good everyone will ask for seconds! *Serves 4 (1 cup)*

8 ounces lean beef stew
 meat, cut into small
 pieces
1 (10¾-ounce) can
 Healthy Request
 Tomato Soup
1 cup water

1 teaspoon dried parsley
 flakes
1½ cups sliced carrots
2 cups (10 ounces) diced
 raw potatoes
½ cup chopped onion
1 cup sliced celery

In a large skillet sprayed with butter-flavored cooking spray, brown meat for 10 minutes. Stir in tomato soup, water, and parsley flakes. Add carrots, potatoes, onion, and celery. Mix well to combine. Lower heat, cover, and simmer for 35 to 45 minutes or until meat and vegetables are tender, stirring occasionally.

HINT: Lean round steak may be substituted for stew meat.

Each serving equals:
HE: 1½ Protein, 1½ Vegetable, ½ Bread, ½ Slider, 5 Optional Calories

239 Calories, 7 gm Fat, 20 gm Protein, 24 gm Carbohydrate,
452 mg Sodium, 50 mg Calcium, 3 gm Fiber

DIABETIC: 1½ Meat, 1 Vegetable, 1 Starch

Machaca Beef Tortillas

■ ■ ■ ■ ■ ■ ■ ■

For a meal in just minutes, these tasty roll-ups provide a quick and healthy alternative to microwaved frozen dinners. If there's nothing in the house for dinner, isn't it nice to know that you can pick up everything you need for this dish at the deli?

Serves 4

1½ cups (8 ounces) diced cooked lean roast beef
½ cup chunky salsa (mild, medium, or hot)
¼ cup Heinz Light Harvest Ketchup or any reduced-sodium ketchup

1 teaspoon dried parsley flakes
4 (6-inch) warm flour tortillas

In a large skillet sprayed with olive oil–flavored cooking spray, combine roast beef, salsa, ketchup, and parsley flakes. Cook over medium heat until mixture is heated through, stirring often. For each serving, spoon about ½ cup meat mixture on a tortilla and roll up.

HINTS:
1. If you don't have leftovers, purchase a chunk of cooked roast beef from your local deli.
2. Warm tortillas in microwave for about 30 seconds.

Each serving equals:
HE: 2 Protein, 1 Bread, ¼ Vegetable, 15 Optional Calories

202 Calories, 6 gm Fat, 19 gm Protein, 18 gm Carbohydrate, 417 mg Sodium, 54 mg Calcium, 0 gm Fiber

DIABETIC: 2 Meat, 1 Starch

Baked BBQ Pork Tenders

∎ ∎ ∎ ∎ ✳ ∎ ∎ ∎ ∎

Feel like the taste of barbecue but don't want to fire up the grill? You don't have to; just stir up my homemade-healthy tangy sauce, smother your meat, and bake up a storm!

Serves 4

4 (4-ounce) lean pork
   tenderloins or cutlets
1 cup (one 8-ounce can)
   Hunt's Tomato Sauce
2 tablespoons Sugar Twin
   or Sprinkle Sweet

2 tablespoons Brown
   Sugar Twin
1 teaspoon lemon juice
½ cup finely chopped onion

Preheat oven to 350 degrees. Spray an 8-by-8-inch baking dish with butter-flavored cooking spray. Evenly arrange meat in prepared baking dish. In a small bowl, combine tomato sauce, Sugar Twin, Brown Sugar Twin, and lemon juice. Add onion. Mix well to combine. Pour sauce mixture evenly over meat. Cover and bake for 45 minutes. Uncover and continue baking for 15 minutes, or until meat is tender. Place baking dish on a wire rack and let set for 5 minutes. When serving, evenly spoon sauce over meat.

Each serving equals:
HE: 3 Protein, 1¼ Vegetable, 5 Optional Calories

178 Calories, 6 gm Fat, 26 gm Protein, 5 gm Carbohydrate, 475 mg Sodium, 28 mg Calcium, 1 gm Fiber

DIABETIC: 3 Meat, 1 Vegetable

Quick Pork Parmigiana

■ ■ ■ ■ ❋ ■ ■ ■

Can you believe it—a crusty, cheesy, tomatoey version of this restaurant favorite that is healthy but doesn't taste it? Instead of avoiding the foods you love, why not reinvent them as I like to do—you'll be delighted instead of deprived! *Serves 4*

4 (3 ounce) lean pork
   tenderloins
6 tablespoons Kraft Fat
   Free Italian Dressing ☆
6 tablespoons (1½ ounces)
   dried fine bread crumbs
¼ cup (¾ ounce) grated
   Kraft fat-free Parmesan
   cheese
1¾ cups (one 15-ounce

can) Hunt's Chunky
   Tomato Sauce
1 teaspoon Italian
   seasoning
1 teaspoon Sugar Twin or
   Sprinkle Sweet
⅓ cup (1½ ounces)
   shredded Kraft reduced-
   fat mozzarella cheese

Place tenderloins between waxed paper and pound with a meat mallet until each is about ⅛ inch thick. Pour ¼ cup Italian dressing into a saucer. In a pie plate, combine bread crumbs and Parmesan cheese. Dip tenderloins first into Italian dressing, then into crumb mixture. Pour remaining 2 tablespoons Italian dressing into a large skillet and cook over medium heat until hot. Place tenderloins in hot skillet and brown tenderloins about 5 minutes on each side. Remove tenderloins and keep warm. Pour tomato sauce into same skillet. Add Italian seasoning and Sugar Twin. Mix well to combine. Continue cooking until mixture is heated through. For each serving, place a tenderloin on a plate, spoon about ⅓ cup sauce mixture over top, and sprinkle a scant 2 tablespoons mozzarella cheese over sauce. Serve at once.

HINT: Do not overcook meat as it will become tough.

Each serving equals:

HE: 3 Protein, 1¾ Vegetable, ½ Bread, 13 Optional Calories

235 Calories, 7 gm Fat, 24 gm Protein, 19 gm Carbohydrate, 1251 mg Sodium, 107 mg Calcium, 3 gm Fiber

DIABETIC: 3 Meat, 2 Vegetable, ½ Starch

Baked Pork Cutlets with Rice-Tomato Stuffing

■ ■ ■ ■ ❄ ■ ■ ■ ■

Here's a perfect example of how spicing up an old standby with a savory blend can produce culinary fireworks! The rice-tomato stuffing is especially moist and good.   *Serves 4*

  4 (4-ounce) lean   *½ cup finely diced onion*
    tenderized pork cutlets   *⅛ teaspoon black pepper*
    or tenderloins   *1 teaspoon dried parsley*
  1 cup hot cooked rice   *flakes*
  1 (10¾-ounce) can
    Healthy Request
    Tomato Soup

Preheat oven to 350 degrees. Spray an 8-by-8-inch baking dish with butter-flavored cooking spray. In a large skillet sprayed with butter-flavored cooking spray, lightly brown meat on both sides. Meanwhile, in a medium bowl, combine rice, tomato soup, onion, black pepper, and parsley flakes. Spoon mixture evenly into prepared baking dish. Evenly arrange browned meat over rice mixture. Cover and bake for 30 minutes. Uncover and continue baking for 10 minutes. Place baking dish on a wire rack and let set for 5 minutes. Divide into 4 servings.

HINTS:
1. Do not overbrown meat, as it will become tough.
2. ⅔ cup uncooked rice usually cooks to about 1 cup.

Each serving equals:
HE: 3 Protein, ½ Bread, ¼ Vegetable, ½ Slider, 5 Optional Calories

255 Calories, 7 gm Fat, 27 gm Protein, 21 gm Carbohydrate, 378 mg Sodium, 97 mg Calcium, 1 gm Fiber

DIABETIC: 3 Meat, 1 Starch

Scalloped Peas and Potatoes with Ham

■ ■ ■ ■ ❋ ■ ■ ■ ■

Here's a luscious main-dish custard that cooks up golden-brown and irresistible! For a wintertime lunch or weekend supper, this is a great way to show your family how much you care.   *Serves 6*

1½ cups (one 12-fluid-
   ounce can) Carnation
   Evaporated Skim Milk
3 tablespoons all-purpose
   flour
2 teaspoons dried onion
   flakes
⅛ teaspoon black pepper
2 cups frozen peas, thawed

3 full cups (16 ounces)
   diced cooked potatoes
¼ cup (one 2-ounce jar)
   chopped pimiento,
   drained
1½ cups (9 ounces) diced
   Dubuque 97% fat-free
   ham or any extra-lean
   ham

Preheat oven to 350 degrees. Spray an 8-by-8-inch baking dish with butter-flavored cooking spray. In a covered jar, combine evaporated skim milk and flour. Shake well to blend. Pour mixture into a large saucepan sprayed with butter-flavored cooking spray. Add onion flakes and black pepper. Mix well to combine. Cook over medium heat until mixture thickens, stirring often. Add peas, potatoes, pimiento, and ham. Mix well to combine. Spread mixture into prepared baking dish. Bake for 30 minutes. Place baking dish on a wire rack and let set for 5 minutes. Divide into 6 servings.

HINT: Thaw peas by placing in a colander and rinsing under hot water for one minute.

Each serving equals:
HE: 1½ Bread, 1 Protein, ½ Skim Milk

186 Calories, 2 gm Fat, 15 gm Protein, 28 gm Carbohydrate, 400 mg Sodium, 204 mg Calcium, 4 gm Fiber

DIABETIC: 1½ Starch, 1 Meat, ½ Skim Milk

Ham-Corn Custard Bake

■ ■ ■ ■ ■ ■ ■

*C*orn "puddings" are a wonderful Midwestern tradition, and
this one is especially creamy good! Rich in calcium and oh-so-
tasty, this Iowa classic is bound to be a family favorite at your
house as it is at ours.   *Serves 6*

*1½ cups (one 12-fluid-
    ounce can) Carnation
    Evaporated Skim Milk
2 eggs or equivalent in egg
    substitute
½ teaspoon prepared
    mustard
1 tablespoon Sugar Twin
    or Sprinkle Sweet*

*1 teaspoon dried parsley
    flakes
3 cups frozen whole-kernel
    corn, thawed
1 full cup (6 ounces) diced
    Dubuque 97% fat-free
    ham or any extra-lean
    ham*

Preheat oven to 350 degrees. Spray an 8-by-8-inch baking dish
with butter-flavored cooking spray. In a large bowl, combine
evaporated skim milk, eggs, mustard, Sugar Twin, and parsley
flakes. Add corn and ham. Mix well to combine. Pour mixture
into prepared baking dish. Bake for 45 minutes or until mixture
is set in center. Place baking dish on a wire rack and let set for 5
minutes. Divide into 6 servings.

HINT: Thaw corn by placing in a colander and rinsing under
hot water for one minute.

Each serving equals:
HE: 1 Bread, 1 Protein (⅓ limited), ½ Skim Milk, 1 Optional Calorie

170 Calories, 2 gm Fat, 14 gm Protein, 24 gm Carbohydrate,
344 mg Sodium, 196 mg Calcium, 2 gm Fiber

DIABETIC: 1 Starch, 1 Meat, ½ Skim Milk

Macaroni and Cheese with Frankfurters

■ ■ ■ ❋ ■ ■ ■

Sometimes eating healthy is about making what's good better—and it has to be true when it comes to this yummy dish! Homemade macaroni and cheese combined with the tanginess of hot dogs is better than better—it's irresistible!

Serves 4

1 (10¾-ounce) can
Healthy Request Cream
of Mushroom Soup
⅓ cup skim milk
1 teaspoon prepared
mustard
1 teaspoon dried parsley
flakes
1 scant cup (3¾ ounces)

shredded Kraft reduced-fat
Cheddar cheese
2 cups hot cooked elbow
macaroni, rinsed and
drained
8 ounces Healthy Choice
97% fat-free
frankfurters, diced

Preheat oven to 350 degrees. Spray an 8-by-8-inch baking dish with butter-flavored cooking spray. In a large skillet, combine mushroom soup, skim milk, mustard, and parsley flakes. Stir in Cheddar cheese. Cook over medium heat until cheese melts, stirring often. Add macaroni and frankfurters. Mix well to combine. Pour mixture into prepared baking dish. Bake for 30 minutes. Place baking dish on a wire rack and let set for 5 minutes. Divide into 4 servings.

HINT: 1⅓ cups uncooked macaroni usually cooks to about 2 cups.

Each serving equals:
HE: 2½ Protein, 1 Bread, ½ Slider, 14 Optional Calories

284 Calories, 8 gm Fat, 20 gm Protein, 33 gm Carbohydrate, 963 mg Sodium, 286 mg Calcium, 1 gm Fiber

DIABETIC: 2½ Meat, 2 Starch

Idaho Hot Dog Bake

❉

No, you don't have to head for Boise in order to enjoy this savory casserole, but the flavor of these cheesy mashed potatoes is as big as the Rockies! As with all frankfurter recipes served to children, make certain the hot dog is diced small, so every bite goes down easily.

Serves 4

1⅓ cups (3 ounces) instant
  potato flakes
¾ cup (3 ounces) shredded
  Kraft reduced-fat
  Cheddar cheese
½ cup Land O Lakes no-
  fat sour cream
2 teaspoons dried onion
  flakes

1 teaspoon dried parsley
  flakes
1½ cups boiling water
8 ounces Healthy Choice
  97% fat-free
  frankfurters, diced
1 cup (one 8-ounce can)
  cut green beans, rinsed
  and drained

Preheat oven to 350 degrees. Spray an 8-by-8-inch baking dish with butter-flavored cooking spray. In a large bowl, combine potato flakes, Cheddar cheese, sour cream, onion flakes, and parsley flakes. Add boiling water. Mix well to combine. Stir in frankfurters and green beans. Spread mixture evenly into pre-pared baking dish. Bake for 25 to 30 minutes. Place baking dish on a wire rack and let set for 5 minutes. Divide into 4 servings.

Each serving equals:
HE: 2⅓ Protein, 1 Bread, ¼ Vegetable, ¼ Slider, 10 Optional Calories

---

209 Calories, 5 gm Fat, 16 gm Protein, 25 gm Carbohydrate,
827 mg Sodium, 201 mg Calcium, 2 gm Fiber

DIABETIC: 2 Meat, 1 Starch, ½ Vegetable

Frankly Good Hot Dish

■ ■ ■ ❋ ■ ■ ■

Here's something a little new and different to do with plain old spaghetti. It's filling, and it's fun to discover the bits of hot dog and green beans amid the noodles. *Serves 4 (1 cup)*

2 cups hot cooked
 spaghetti, rinsed and
 drained
1 (10¾-ounce) can
 Healthy Request
 Tomato Soup
1 teaspoon dried onion
 flakes
¼ cup (¾ ounce) grated

Kraft fat-free Parmesan
 cheese
8 ounces Healthy Choice
 97% fat-free
 frankfurters, diced
2 cups (one 16-ounce can)
 sliced green beans,
 rinsed and drained

In an 8-cup glass measuring bowl, combine spaghetti, tomato soup, onion flakes, and Parmesan cheese. Stir in frankfurters and green beans. Cover and microwave on HIGH (100% power) for 6 to 7 minutes or until mixture is hot, stirring after 4 minutes. Let set, covered, for 2 to 3 minutes. Stir again just before serving.

HINT: 1½ cups broken uncooked spaghetti usually cooks to about 2 cups.

Each serving equals:
HE: 1½ Protein, 1 Bread, 1 Vegetable, ½ Slider, 10 Optional Calories

247 Calories, 3 gm Fat, 13 gm Protein, 42 gm Carbohydrate, 919 mg Sodium, 31 mg Calcium, 3 gm Fiber

DIABETIC: 2 Starch, 1½ Meat, 1 Vegetable

Taco Dogs

■ ■ ■ ■ ■ ■ ■ ■

Surprise your family with this unique combination that mingles spicy Mexican flavors with good old American frankfurters! Two traditions, double the cheese, and lots of chewing satisfaction. *Serves 4*

4 Healthy Choice 97% fat-
free frankfurters
4 (¾-ounce) slices Kraft
reduced-fat Cheddar
cheese
4 (6-inch) flour tortillas
1 cup (one 8-ounce can)
Hunt's Tomato Sauce

½ cup chunky salsa (mild,
medium, or hot)
⅓ cup (1½ ounces)
shredded Kraft reduced-
fat Cheddar cheese
¼ cup Land O Lakes
no-fat sour cream

Preheat oven to 350 degrees. Spray an 8-by-8-inch baking dish with butter-flavored cooking spray. Wrap each frankfurter in a slice of cheese, then place each on one end of a tortilla and roll up. Place each seam-side down in prepared baking dish. In a small bowl, combine tomato sauce and salsa. Evenly spoon sauce mixture over tortillas and sprinkle shredded Cheddar cheese over top. Bake for 30 minutes. When serving, top each with 1 tablespoon sour cream.

Each serving equals:
HE: 3 Protein, 1¼ Vegetable, 1 Bread, 19 Optional Calories

234 Calories, 8 gm Fat, 18 gm Protein, 27 gm Carbohydrate, 1409 mg Sodium, 273 mg Calcium, 1 gm Fiber

DIABETIC: 2 Meat, 1½ Starch, 1 Vegetable

Creamy Franks and Rice

■ ■ ■ ■ ❄ ■ ■ ■ ■

"M*mm-hmm*" was the only response I got when I asked the people sampling this recipe if they liked it! They were too busy munching away to stop and say more. If your kids have been particularly noisy, maybe serving this will make mealtime more peaceful!   *Serves 4 (1 cup)*

1 cup finely chopped celery	*½ cup (one 2.5-ounce jar)*
8 ounces Healthy Choice	*sliced mushrooms,*
97% fat-free	*drained*
frankfurters, diced	*1 teaspoon dried parsley*
1 (10¾-ounce) can	*flakes*
Healthy Request Cream	*¼ teaspoon black pepper*
of Mushroom Soup	*1⅓ cups (4 ounces)*
¼ cup skim milk	*uncooked Minute Rice*

In a large skillet sprayed with butter-flavored cooking spray, sauté celery and frankfurters for 10 minutes. Add mushroom soup, skim milk, mushrooms, parsley flakes, and black pepper. Mix well to combine. Bring mixture to a boil. Stir in uncooked rice. Cover, remove from heat, and let set for 5 minutes. Gently stir again just before serving.

Each serving equals:
HE: 1⅓ Protein, 1 Bread, ¾ Vegetable, ½ Slider, 4 Optional Calories

171 Calories, 3 gm Fat, 10 gm Protein, 26 gm Carbohydrate, 994 mg Sodium, 90 mg Calcium, 1 gm Fiber

DIABETIC: 1½ Meat, 1½ Starch, ½ Vegetable

Delicious Desserts for Good Girls and Boys

▪ ▪ ▪ ▪ ▪ ▪ ▪ ▪

I remember when my grandson Zach was about two years old, maybe even one and a half, and just learning to walk really well. We'd been having a birthday party for our employees, and there was still a piece of Blueberry Mountain Cheesecake on the table. When James, Pam, and Zach arrived, Zachie saw that piece of dessert, and he just went straight over to that table, took a spoon, and started into it! Now, every time he comes to visit, as soon as the door opens, he says, "Pie, Gamma, pie!" (It doesn't matter what the dessert is, he always calls it pie.) He loves to help me stir up all of his favorite desserts, and he uses a whisk really well.

Will your kids eat my healthy desserts? A recent letter I received answered that question with a definite "Yes!" Before leaving to go to work, this woman had whipped up a recipe called Crunchy Munchy Banana Party Pie (from one of my earlier books). Later that day, she got a phone call from her eighteen-year-old son at home. He said, "Mom, that pie in the fridge was fabulous. Could you please stop and pick up another one on your way home, because my friends and I just finished the whole thing!"

But this really made me smile: a woman at an autographing shared with me that her four-year-old granddaughter comes over every week to watch my public television cooking show. And just before the show starts, she says to her grandma, "Here comes the Yum-Yum Lady!"

Some health professionals may suggest that a healthy dessert means a piece of fruit or tell you that treats like pie and cake should be saved for special occasions. Certainly, I hope you'll encourage your children to eat some healthy fruit every day. But Healthy Exchanges desserts like my **Cherry Skillet Pudding with "Dumplings"** or my **Sweetheart Strawberry Silk Pie** don't have to be saved for once in a while. They're made from the healthiest ingredients I can find, and they provide real nutrition, not empty calories. So invite your family to savor a healthy sweet treat just as often as you please!

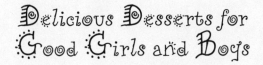

Delicious Desserts for Good Girls and Boys

Banana Split Parfait

Baked Apple with Caramel Cream Sauce

Root Beer Float Pudding

Mud Pudding

Chocolate Peanut Butter Truffles

Ambrosia Pudding

Black Forest Mousse

Festive Glorified Rice

Orange Rice Pudding

Coconut Peach Melba Custard

Pear and Blueberry Bread Pudding

Pumpkin-Mallow Dessert

Mexican Peach Dessert Cups

Baby Ruthy Delites

Cherry Almond Tarts

Cherry Skillet Pudding
with "Dumplings"

Hawaiian Delight Cobbler

Easy Strawberry
Shortcakes

Maple Banana Upside-
Down Cake

Lemon Strawberry Pie

Sweetheart Strawberry Silk
Pie

Chocolate Pear Pie

Peanut Butter, Jelly, and
Banana Pie

Layered Chocolate-
Pineapple Crumb Pie

Chocolate Express Pie

Scrumptious White
Chocolate Cheesecake

Rocky Road Quick Cake

Triple Treat Chocolate
Poke Cake

Pineapple Carrot Cake

Banana Split Parfait

■ ■ ■ ■ ❄ ■ ■ ■ ■

My husband, Cliff, is always coming up with great new ideas to make the "House That Recipes Built" even better—and I always reward him with a new "Banana Split" recipe. Here's a wonderfully fruity ice cream concoction that will make any man, young or just young at heart, smile! *Serves 6*

*2 cups sliced fresh
  strawberries
1 cup (1 medium) diced
  banana
1 cup (one 8-ounce can)
  crushed pineapple,
  packed in fruit juice,
  undrained
2 tablespoons Sugar Twin
  or Sprinkle Sweet*

*3 cups Wells' Blue Bunny
  sugar- and fat-free
  strawberry ice cream or
  any sugar- and fat-free
  ice cream
6 tablespoons Cool Whip
  Lite
3 maraschino cherries,
  halved*

Place strawberries in a medium bowl. Slightly crush with a potato masher or fork. Stir in banana. In a medium saucepan, combine undrained pineapple and Sugar Twin. Cook over medium heat until mixture starts to boil, stirring often. Pour hot pineapple mixture over strawberry mixture. Refrigerate for 10 minutes. Spoon 2 tablespoons strawberry mixture into 6 parfait glasses. Top each with ½ cup strawberry ice cream. Spoon scant 2 tablespoons strawberry mixture over each. Top each with 1 tablespoon Cool Whip Lite and garnish with half a maraschino cherry. Serve at once or freeze. If freezing, remove from freezer 10 minutes before serving.

HINT: To prevent banana from turning brown, mix with 1 teaspoon lemon juice or sprinkle with Fruit Fresh.

Each serving equals:

HE: 1 Fruit, ¾ Slider, 17 Optional Calories

160 Calories, 0 gm Fat, 4 gm Protein, 36 gm Carbohydrate, 51 mg Sodium, 134 mg Calcium, 1 gm Fiber

DIABETIC: 1 Fruit, 1 Starch/Carbohydrate

Baked Apple with Caramel Cream Sauce

■ ■ ■ ■ ■ ■ ■

There's just something so cozy and satisfying about baked apples fresh from the oven. But these are even more special, stuffed with raisins and marshmallows and topped with scrumptious caramel! *Mmmmm . . . these are almost too good to eat!*

Serves 4

1⅓ cups + 2 tablespoons water ☆
4 small cored and unpeeled cooking apples
2 tablespoons raisins
½ cup (1 ounce) miniature marshmallows
1 (4-serving) package

JELL-O sugar-free vanilla cook-and-serve pudding mix
⅔ cup Carnation Nonfat Dry Milk Powder
¼ cup fat-free caramel sauce

Preheat oven to 400 degrees. Spray an 8-by-8-inch baking dish with butter-flavored cooking spray and pour 2 tablespoons water into bottom. Evenly fill center of apples with raisins and marshmallows. Place filled apples in prepared baking dish. Cover and bake for 30 minutes. Prepare sauce 10 minutes before apples are finished baking. In a medium saucepan, combine dry pudding mix, dry milk powder, and remaining 1⅓ cups water. Cook over medium heat until mixture thickens and starts to boil, stirring constantly. Stir in caramel sauce. Lower heat and simmer until apples are baked, stirring often. For each serving, place 1 apple on a plate and spoon about ⅓ cup warm sauce over top.

Each serving equals:
HE: 1¼ Fruit, ½ Skim Milk, ½ Slider, 13 Optional Calories

124 Calories, 0 gm Fat, 4 gm Protein, 27 gm Carbohydrate, 180 mg Sodium, 144 mg Calcium, 1 gm Fiber

DIABETIC: 1 Fruit, ½ Skim Milk, ½ Starch/Carbohydrate

Root Beer Float Pudding

■ ■ ■ ■ ■ ■ ■ ■

Some grown-ups may think this sounds "gross," but most children are sure to cheer! If your family adores the flavor of this old-fashioned soft drink, why not surprise them with a dessert that makes it the star of the show?   *Serves 4*

1 (4-serving) package   ⅔ cup Carnation Nonfat
   JELL-O sugar-free   Dry Milk Powder
   instant vanilla pudding   1½ cups diet root beer
   mix   ½ cup Cool Whip Lite ☆

In a medium bowl, combine dry pudding mix and dry milk powder. Add diet root beer. Mix well using a wire whisk. Blend in ¼ cup Cool Whip Lite. Evenly spoon mixture into 4 dessert dishes. Top each with 1 tablespoon Cool Whip Lite. Refrigerate for at least 15 minutes.

Each serving equals:
HE: ½ Skim Milk, ¼ Slider, 13 Optional Calories

89 Calories, 1 gm Fat, 4 gm Protein, 16 gm Carbohydrate,
411 mg Sodium, 138 mg Calcium, 0 gm Fiber

DIABETIC: ½ Skim Milk, ½ Starch/Carbohydrate, *or* 1 Starch/
Carbohydrate

Mud Pudding

■ ■ ■ ■ ■ ■ ■ ■

𝔇id your kids ever try to taste a real mud pie when they were little? I bet you still smile at the memory of those disappointed faces. Well, this creamy treat looks more than a little like the real thing, but it tastes oh so much better!!   *Serves 6*

1 (4-serving) package
    JELL-O sugar-free
    instant vanilla pudding
    mix
⅔ cup Carnation Nonfat
    Dry Milk Powder
1 cup water

¾ cup Yoplait plain fat-
    free yogurt
¾ cup Cool Whip Free
18 (2½-inch) Nabisco
    chocolate graham
    cracker squares, made
    into crumbs ☆

In a large bowl, combine dry pudding mix, dry milk powder, and water. Mix well using a wire whisk. Blend in yogurt and Cool Whip Free. Reserve 6 tablespoons chocolate graham cracker crumbs. Stir remaining crumbs into pudding mixture. Evenly spoon mixture into 6 dessert dishes and top each with 1 tablespoon cracker crumbs. Refrigerate for at least 15 minutes.

HINT: A self-seal sandwich bag works great for crushing graham crackers.

Each serving equals:
HE: 1 Bread, ½ Skim Milk, ¼ Slider, 12 Optional Calories

117 Calories, 1 gm Fat, 5 gm Protein, 22 gm Carbohydrate, 355 mg Sodium, 148 mg Calcium, 0 gm Fiber

DIABETIC: 1 Starch/Carbohydrate, ½ Skim Milk

Chocolate Peanut Butter Truffles

∎ ∎ ∎ ∎ ∎ ∎ ∎ ∎

If you've ever tasted a richer-than-rich truffle candy, one bite will tell you I'm not kidding when I named this dessert after it! It takes a little magic to make a little peanut butter deliver so much goodness, but I'm willing to share my secret. *Serves 4*

¾ cup purchased graham cracker crumbs or 12 (2½-inch) graham cracker squares, made into crumbs
¼ cup Peter Pan reduced-fat peanut butter (chunky or creamy)
¼ cup Sugar Twin or Sprinkle Sweet ☆

1 (4-serving) package JELL-O sugar-free instant chocolate pudding mix
1 cup Carnation Nonfat Dry Milk Powder ☆
1¾ cups water
¾ cup Yoplait plain fat-free yogurt
1 teaspoon vanilla extract
½ cup Cool Whip Free

In a medium bowl, combine graham cracker crumbs, peanut butter, and 2 tablespoons Sugar Twin. In another medium bowl, combine dry pudding mix, ⅔ cup dry milk powder, and water. Mix well using a wire whisk. In a small bowl, combine yogurt and remaining ⅓ cup dry milk powder. Blend in vanilla extract, Cool Whip Free, and remaining 2 tablespoons Sugar Twin. Reserve ¼ cup cracker crumb mixture. To assemble, sprinkle 2 tablespoons cracker crumb mixture into 4 dessert dishes, top each with ¼ cup pudding mixture, and spoon about 3 tablespoons yogurt mixture on top. Repeat layers, then top each with 1 tablespoon reserved cracker crumbs. Refrigerate for at least 15 minutes.

HINT: A self-seal sandwich bag works great for crushing graham crackers.

Each serving equals:

HE: 1 Bread, 1 Protein, 1 Fat, 1 Skim Milk, ½ Slider, 11 Optional Calories

315 Calories, 7 gm Fat, 15 gm Protein, 48 gm Carbohydrate, 671 mg Sodium, 299 mg Calcium, 2 gm Fiber

DIABETIC: 2 Starch/Carbohydrate, 1 Skim Milk, ½ Meat, ½ Fat

Ambrosia Pudding

■ ■ ■ ■ ■ ■ ■ ■

Each spoonful of this sweet treat seems to deliver another great flavor, and together they're enough to earn five stars! There's so much heavenly taste, you'll wonder if angels had something to do with it!

Serves 4

1 (4-serving) package
   JELL-O sugar-free
   instant vanilla pudding
   mix
⅔ cup Carnation Nonfat
   Dry Milk Powder
1 cup (one 8-ounce can)
   crushed pineapple,
   packed in fruit juice,
   undrained
½ cup unsweetened orange
   juice

½ cup Cool Whip Free
1 teaspoon coconut extract
2 tablespoons purchased
   graham cracker crumbs
   or 2 (2½-inch) graham
   cracker squares, made
   into fine crumbs
2 tablespoons flaked
   coconut

In a large bowl, combine dry pudding mix, dry milk powder, undrained pineapple, and orange juice. Mix well using a wire whisk. Blend in Cool Whip Free and coconut extract. Evenly spoon mixture into 4 dessert dishes. In a small bowl, combine graham cracker crumbs and coconut. Sprinkle about 1 tablespoon crumb mixture over top of each. Refrigerate for at least 15 minutes.

HINT: A self-seal sandwich bag works great for crushing graham crackers.

Each serving equals:
HE: ¾ Fruit, ½ Skim Milk, ½ Slider, 16 Optional Calories

---

157 Calories, 1 gm Fat, 5 gm Protein, 32 gm Carbohydrate,
426 mg Sodium, 150 mg Calcium, 1 gm Fiber

DIABETIC: 1 Fruit, ½ Skim Milk, ½ Starch/Carbohydrate

Black Forest Mousse

■ ■ ■ ■ ❄ ■ ■ ■ ■

*W*hen a pudding dessert is so thick and rich you want to close your eyes and just savor every spoonful, you might be enjoying this magnificent mousse! It looks lovely when you bring it to the table, but the pleasure is in the tasting! *Serves 6*

1 (4-serving) package JELL-O sugar-free vanilla cook-and-serve pudding mix

1 (4-serving) package JELL-O sugar-free cherry gelatin

2 cups (one 16-ounce can) tart red cherries, packed in water, drained, and ½ cup liquid reserved

1¾ cups water ☆

1 (4-serving) package JELL-O sugar-free instant chocolate fudge pudding mix

⅔ cup Carnation Nonfat Dry Milk Powder

¾ cup Yoplait plain fat-free yogurt

1 teaspoon vanilla extract

¾ cup Cool Whip Free

In a medium saucepan, combine dry cook-and-serve pudding mix, dry gelatin, reserved cherry liquid, and ¾ cup water. Stir in cherries. Cook over medium heat until mixture thickens and starts to boil, stirring often and being careful not to crush the cherries. Remove from heat. Place saucepan on a wire rack and let cool for 30 minutes. In a large bowl, combine dry instant pudding, dry milk powder, and remaining 1 cup water. Mix well using a wire whisk. Blend in yogurt, vanilla extract, and Cool Whip Free. Add cooled cherry mixture. Mix gently to combine. Evenly spoon mixture into 6 dessert dishes. Refrigerate for at least 15 minutes.

Each serving equals:

HE: ⅔ Fruit, ½ Skim Milk, ¾ Slider, 2 Optional Calories

128 Calories, 0 gm Fat, 6 gm Protein, 26 gm Carbohydrate, 406 mg Sodium, 157 mg Calcium, 1 gm Fiber

DIABETIC: 1 Fruit, ½ Skim Milk, ½ Starch/Carbohydrate

Festive Glorified Rice

■ ■ ■ ■ ■ ■ ■

Kids like foods that look like a party—in fact, so do many adults! What could be more colorful and fun than this fruity rice dessert? *Serves 6*

¾ cup Cool Whip Free
5 to 6 drops red food coloring
1 cup (one 8-ounce can) crushed pineapple, packed in fruit juice, drained

2 cups cold cooked rice
½ cup (1 ounce) miniature marshmallows
1 cup (1 medium) diced banana
6 maraschino cherries, quartered

In a large bowl, gently combine Cool Whip Free and red food coloring. Stir in pineapple. Add rice, marshmallows, banana, and maraschino cherries. Mix gently to combine. Evenly spoon mixture into 6 dessert dishes. Refrigerate for at least 15 minutes.

HINTS:
1. 1⅓ cups uncooked rice usually cooks to about 2 cups.
2. To prevent banana from turning brown, mix with 1 teaspoon lemon juice or sprinkle with Fruit Fresh.

Each serving equals:
HE: ⅔ Bread, ⅔ Fruit, ¼ Slider, 13 Optional Calories

136 Calories, 0 gm Fat, 1 gm Protein, 33 gm Carbohydrate, 9 mg Sodium, 12 mg Calcium, 1 gm Fiber

DIABETIC: 1 Starch/Carbohydrate, 1 Fruit

☼Orange Rice Pudding

■ ■ ■ ■ ■ ■ ■

Rice pudding is a family favorite in so many homes, I've discovered, but it's fun to serve it in a fresh, new way! The orange juice adds a truly intense flavor to this beloved comfort food.

Serves 4

1 (4-serving) package
   JELL-O sugar-free
   vanilla cook-and-serve
   pudding mix
⅔ cup Carnation Nonfat
   Dry Milk Powder
1½ cups water

½ cup unsweetened orange
   juice
1 cup (one 11-ounce can)
   mandarin oranges,
   rinsed and drained
1 cup cold cooked rice
¼ cup Cool Whip Lite

In a medium saucepan, combine dry pudding mix, dry milk powder, water, and orange juice. Cook over medium heat until mixture thickens and starts to boil, stirring constantly. Remove from heat. Stir in oranges and rice. Evenly spoon mixture into 4 dessert dishes. Refrigerate for at least 1 hour. Just before serving, top each with 1 tablespoon Cool Whip Lite.

HINT: ⅔ cup uncooked rice usually cooks to about 1 cup.

Each serving equals:
HE: ¾ Fruit, ½ Skim Milk, ½ Bread, ¼ Slider, 10 Optional Calories

140 Calories, 0 gm Fat, 5 gm Protein, 30 gm Carbohydrate,
182 mg Sodium, 151 mg Calcium, 0 gm Fiber

DIABETIC: 1 Fruit, ½ Skim Milk, ½ Starch/Carbohydrate *or* 1 Fruit,
1 Starch/Carbohydrate

Coconut Peach Melba Custard

■ ■ ■ ■ ■ ■ ■ ■

*N*ot just any treat is special enough to name after the famous singer Nellie Melba, who couldn't get enough of peaches and raspberries! But this cool and creamy combo will inspire everyone to "sing" your praises—just serve it and see!　　*Serves 4*

2 cups (one 16-ounce can) sliced peaches, packed in fruit juice, drained, and ½ cup liquid reserved
1½ cups frozen unsweetened raspberries, thawed and drained
1 (4-serving) package JELL-O sugar-free
vanilla cook-and-serve pudding mix
⅔ cup Carnation Nonfat Dry Milk Powder
1½ cups water
1 teaspoon coconut extract
¼ cup Cool Whip Lite
1 tablespoon + 1 teaspoon flaked coconut

Coarsely chop peaches, then evenly divide peaches and raspberries into 4 parfait or dessert dishes. In a large saucepan, combine dry pudding mix, dry milk powder, reserved peach juice, and water. Cook over medium heat until mixture thickens and starts to boil, stirring often. Remove from heat. Stir in coconut extract. Evenly spoon hot mixture into parfait dishes. Refrigerate for at least 30 minutes. Just before serving, top each with 1 tablespoon Cool Whip Lite and 1 teaspoon coconut.

Each serving equals:
HE: 1½ Fruit, ½ Skim Milk, ¼ Slider, 15 Optional Calories

161 Calories, 1 gm Fat, 5 gm Protein, 33 gm Carbohydrate, 188 mg Sodium, 156 mg Calcium, 4 gm Fiber

DIABETIC: 1 Fruit, ½ Skim Milk, ½ Starch/Carbohydrate

Pear and Blueberry Bread Pudding

■ ■ ■ ■ ❄ ■ ■ ■ ■

I decided to invent a new way to serve my favorite dessert, and this bread pudding was the result! What a great way to use up leftover bread, especially when you couldn't resist bringing home a couple of pints of really ripe berries!   *Serves 6*

2 cups (one 16-ounce can) pears, packed in fruit juice, drained, and ½ cup liquid reserved
2 cups water
1 (4-serving) package JELL-O sugar-free vanilla cook-and-serve pudding mix

⅔ cup Carnation Nonfat Dry Milk Powder
¼ teaspoon ground nutmeg
1 teaspoon vanilla extract
12 slices stale reduced-calorie white bread, torn into medium-size pieces
1½ cups fresh blueberries

Preheat oven to 350 degrees. Spray an 8-by-8-inch baking dish with butter-flavored cooking spray. In a large bowl, combine reserved pear liquid, water, dry pudding mix, and dry milk powder. Stir in nutmeg and vanilla extract. Add bread pieces. Mix well to combine. Coarsely chop pears. Stir pears and blueberries into bread mixture. Pour mixture into prepared baking dish. Bake for 45 to 50 minutes. Place baking dish on a wire rack and let set for at least 5 minutes. Divide into 6 servings. Good served warm or cold.

Each serving equals:
HE: 1 Fruit, 1 Bread, ⅓ Skim Milk, 13 Optional Calories

193 Calories, 1 gm Fat, 8 gm Protein, 38 gm Carbohydrate, 354 mg Sodium, 134 mg Calcium, 8 gm Fiber

DIABETIC: 1½ Starch/Carbohydrate, 1 Fruit

Pumpkin-Mallow Dessert

■ ■ ■ ■ ■ ■ ■ ■

Remember serving sweet potatoes with marshmallows on Thanksgiving? My family loves them, so I thought, why not try it with pumpkin to create a holiday taste you can enjoy all year long? My kids said thank you with their smiles and happy faces!

Serves 8

12 (2½-inch) graham
   cracker squares ☆
2 cups (one 16-ounce can)
   pumpkin
1 teaspoon pumpkin pie
   spice
1 (4-serving) package
   JELL-O sugar-free

vanilla cook-and-serve
   pudding mix
⅔ cup Carnation Nonfat
   Dry Milk Powder
½ cup water
1 cup (2 ounces) miniature
   marshmallows
1 cup Cool Whip Free

Place 9 graham crackers in a 9-by-9-inch cake pan. In a medium saucepan, combine pumpkin, pumpkin pie spice, dry pudding mix, dry milk powder, water, and marshmallows. Cook over medium heat until mixture starts to boil and marshmallows are melted, stirring constantly. Remove from heat. Place saucepan on a wire rack and allow to cool completely. Gently fold Cool Whip Free into cooled pumpkin mixture. Carefully spread mixture evenly over graham crackers. Crush remaining 3 graham crackers. Evenly sprinkle cracker crumbs over top. Refrigerate for at least 2 hours. Cut into 8 servings.

HINT: A self-seal sandwich bag works great for crushing graham crackers.

Each serving equals:
HE: ½ Bread, ½ Vegetable, ¼ Skim Milk, ¼ Slider, 18 Optional Calories

104 Calories, 0 gm Fat, 3 gm Protein, 23 gm Carbohydrate, 133 mg Sodium, 85 mg Calcium, 2 gm Fiber

DIABETIC: 1½ Starch/Carbohydrate

Mexican Peach Dessert Cups

■ ■ ■ ■ ■ ■ ■

If you want to pretend you're on a family vacation on the Mexican Riviera, this peachy treat will help you enjoy the fantasy even more! If you can't get away for real, let your taste buds run a little wild—and enjoy the trip. *Serves 4*

2 cups (4 medium) peeled and sliced fresh peaches
2 tablespoons Sugar Twin or Sprinkle Sweet
2 cups Wells' Blue Bunny sugar- and fat-free vanilla ice cream or any

sugar- and fat-free ice cream, softened
1 teaspoon ground cinnamon
1 (4-serving) package sponge cake dessert cups

In a medium bowl, combine peaches and Sugar Twin. Set aside. In a medium bowl, stir ice cream just until softened. Add cinnamon. Mix well to combine. For each serving, place 1 sponge cake on a serving plate, spoon about ½ cup ice cream mixture over sponge cake, and top with ½ cup peach mixture. Serve at once.

Each serving equals:
HE: 1 Fruit, 1 Starch, ¾ Slider, 3 Optional Calories

237 Calories, 1 gm Fat, 7 gm Protein, 50 gm Carbohydrate, 169 mg Sodium, 158 mg Calcium, 2 gm Fiber

DIABETIC: 2 Starch, 1 Fruit

Baby Ruthy Delites

■ ■ ■ ■ ■ ■ ■ ■

Isn't it amazing that such a delicious list of ingredients—peanut butter, chocolate syrup, chocolate *and* butterscotch puddings—bakes up into a sweet and still healthy dessert the whole family will cheer? If you always loved the candy bar, this tasty treat will hit a home run with you!   *Serves 8*

2 tablespoons + 2
   teaspoons reduced-
   calorie margarine
¼ cup Brown Sugar Twin
¼ cup Peter Pan reduced-
   fat chunky peanut butter
1 teaspoon vanilla extract
1 cup (3 ounces) quick
   oats
1 (4-serving) package
   JELL-O sugar-free
   instant chocolate
   pudding mix

1 (4-serving) package
   JELL-O sugar-free
   instant butterscotch
   pudding mix
⅔ cup Carnation Nonfat
   Dry Milk Powder
2 cups water
¾ cup Cool Whip Lite
2 teaspoons Hershey's Lite
   Chocolate Syrup

Preheat oven to 375 degrees. In a small saucepan, combine margarine and Brown Sugar Twin. Cook over medium heat until margarine melts. Stir in peanut butter and vanilla extract. Continue cooking until peanut butter melts, stirring constantly. Add oats. Mix well to combine. Pat mixture into an 8-by-8-inch baking dish. Bake for 10 minutes. Place baking dish on a wire rack and allow to cool. In a medium bowl, combine dry pudding mixes. Add dry milk powder and water. Mix well using a wire whisk. Spread pudding mixture evenly over cooled crust. Refrigerate until set, about 30 minutes. Spread Cool Whip Lite evenly over set pudding layer. Drizzle chocolate syrup evenly over top. Refrigerate for at least 15 minutes. Cut into 8 servings.

Cherry Almond Tarts

■ ■ ■ ■ ❄ ■ ■ ■ ■

This is my version of a healthy cherry cheesecake-in-a-cup, one I just know your family will love. If you haven't got a biscuit cutter, you can use a small glass to cut out the circles of dough.

Serves 8 (2 each)

1 Pillsbury refrigerated
    unbaked 9-inch piecrust
1 (4-serving) package
    JELL-O sugar-free
    vanilla cook-and-serve
    pudding mix
1 (4-serving) package
    JELL-O sugar-free
    cherry gelatin

2 cups (one 16-ounce can)
    tart red cherries, packed
    in water, drained, and
    ½ cup liquid reserved
¼ cup water
1 teaspoon almond extract
2 tablespoons (½ ounce)
    slivered almonds

Preheat oven to 400 degrees. Unfold piecrust. Using a (2½-inch) biscuit cutter, cut 12 circles. Press dough scraps together and cut 4 more circles, for a total of 16 circles. Place pastry circles into 16 miniature muffin cups. Press into cups to form shells. In a medium saucepan, combine dry pudding mix, dry gelatin, reserved cherry liquid, and water. Cook over medium heat until mixture thickens and starts to boil, stirring often. Remove from heat. Stir in cherries and almond extract. Evenly spoon mixture into prepared pastry shells. Sprinkle about ¼ teaspoon almonds over top of each. Bake for 18 to 22 minutes. Place pans on a wire rack and allow to cool for 10 minutes. Carefully remove tarts from pans and allow to cool completely.

Each serving equals:
HE: ½ Bread, ½ Fruit, ¾ Slider, 12 Optional Calories

168 Calories, 8 gm Fat, 2 gm Protein, 22 gm Carbohydrate, 189 mg Sodium, 12 mg Calcium, 1 gm Fiber

DIABETIC: 1 Starch/Carbohydrate, 1 Fat, ½ Fruit

Cherry Skillet Pudding with "Dumplings"

■■■■■■■■

My taste testers loved the name of this recipe so much, they lined up to wait with plates in hand! It's wonderfully sweet and a luscious color, but it's the combination of the dumplings topped with hot cherry sauce that makes it so special.

Serves 6

1 (4-serving) package
    JELL-O sugar-free
    vanilla cook-and-serve
    pudding mix
1 (4-serving) package
    JELL-O sugar-free
    cherry gelatin
1 cup unsweetened orange
    juice ☆
½ cup water

2 cups (one 16-ounce can)
    tart red cherries, packed
    in water, undrained
1 cup + 2 tablespoons
    Bisquick Reduced Fat
    Baking Mix
2 tablespoons Brown
    Sugar Twin
⅓ cup skim milk

In a large skillet, combine dry pudding mix, dry gelatin, ¾ cup orange juice, water, and undrained cherries. Cook over medium heat until mixture starts to boil, stirring often and being careful not to crush cherries. In a medium bowl, combine baking mix, Brown Sugar Twin, skim milk, and remaining ¼ cup orange juice. Drop batter by tablespoonful into hot cherry mixture to form 6 dumplings. Lower heat, cover, and simmer for 10 minutes. Uncover and continue simmering for 6 to 8 minutes or until dumplings are cooked.

Each serving equals:
HE: 1 Fruit, 1 Bread, ¼ Slider, 7 Optional Calories

153 Calories, 1 gm Fat, 4 gm Protein, 32 gm Carbohydrate, 388 mg Sodium, 47 mg Calcium, 1 gm Fiber

DIABETIC: 1 Fruit, 1 Starch/Carbohydrate

Hawaiian Delight Cobbler

■ ■ ■ ❄ ■ ■ ■

This tropical concoction is so full of great fruit flavor, it's as good as hopping on a plane and taking the kids to Maui! The coconut and pecans give it a special-occasion crunch, don't you think?   *Serves 6*

*1 (4-serving) package
    JELL-O sugar-free
    vanilla cook-and-serve
    pudding mix
2 cups (two 8-ounce cans)
    pineapple tidbits,
    packed in fruit juice,
    drained, and ¼ cup
    liquid reserved
¾ cup water
1 cup (one 11-ounce can)
    mandarin oranges,
    rinsed and drained*

*1 teaspoon coconut extract
1 cup + 2 tablespoons
    Bisquick Reduced Fat
    Baking Mix
2 tablespoons Sugar Twin
    or Sprinkle Sweet
2 tablespoons (½ ounce)
    chopped pecans
¼ teaspoon ground
    cinnamon
½ cup skim milk
2 tablespoons flaked
    coconut*

Preheat oven to 375 degrees. Spray an 8-by-8-inch baking dish with butter-flavored cooking spray. In a large saucepan, combine dry pudding mix, reserved pineapple liquid, and water. Stir in pineapple and mandarin oranges. Cook over medium heat until mixture thickens and starts to boil, stirring often and being careful not to crush fruit. Remove from heat. Stir in coconut extract. Spoon hot mixture into prepared baking dish. In a medium bowl, combine baking mix, Sugar Twin, pecans, and cinnamon. Add skim milk. Mix gently just to combine. Drop by spoonfuls onto hot fruit mixture to form 6 mounds. Sprinkle coconut evenly over mounds. Bake for 20 minutes or until biscuits are done. Place baking dish on a wire rack and let set for at least 5 minutes. Divide into 6 servings.

◯ **HINT:** If you can't find tidbits, use chunk pineapple and coarsely chop.

Each serving equals:
HE: 1 Fruit, 1 Bread, ⅓ Fat, ¼ Slider, 1 Optional Calorie

200 Calories, 4 gm Fat, 3 gm Protein, 38 gm Carbohydrate,
355 mg Sodium, 62 mg Calcium, 1 gm Fiber

DIABETIC: 1½ Starch/Carbohydrate, 1 Fruit

Easy Strawberry Shortcakes

■ ■ ■ ■ ■ ■ ■ ■

Love the taste of this all-American dessert but figure it takes too much time to fix? Not anymore, when you whip up my speedy but sensational dish that piles those fresh berries oh-so-high!   *Serves 5*

5 cups sliced fresh
  strawberries ☆
¾ cup Sugar Twin or
  Sprinkle Sweet ☆
¼ teaspoon ground
  cinnamon

1 (7.5-ounce) can Pillsbury
  refrigerated buttermilk
  biscuits
10 tablespoons Cool Whip
  Lite

Preheat oven to 400 degrees. In a large bowl, mash 2 cups strawberries with a fork or potato masher. Stir in ½ cup Sugar Twin. Add remaining 3 cups strawberries. Mix well to combine. Refrigerate while preparing shortcakes. In a small saucer, combine cinnamon and ¼ cup Sugar Twin. Separate dough into 10 biscuits. Place one biscuit on top of another and firmly press together to form 5 shortcakes. Lightly spray each shortcake with butter-flavored cooking spray, then dip shortcakes in cinnamon mixture. Place shortcakes on an ungreased baking sheet. Bake for 10 to 12 minutes or until golden brown. For each serving, split 1 shortcake, spoon ⅓ cup strawberry sauce over bottom, replace top, spoon about ⅓ cup strawberries over top, and garnish with 2 tablespoons Cool Whip Lite.

Each serving equals:
HE: 1½ Bread, 1 Fruit, ¼ Slider, 14 Optional Calories

171 Calories, 3 gm Fat, 4 gm Protein, 32 gm Carbohydrate,
366 mg Sodium, 20 mg Calcium, 4 gm Fiber

DIABETIC: 1 Starch/Carbohydrate, 1 Fruit

Maple Banana Upside-Down Cake

■ ■ ■ ■ ■ ■ ■ ■

Ever since childhood, haven't you loved the idea of a cake that turns magical when you turn it out of the pan? Here's a new way to share that fun with your family, a cake that's rich with maple flavor and crunchy-sweet! *Serves 4*

¼ cup Cary's Sugar Free
   Maple Syrup
¼ cup (1 ounce) chopped
   walnuts
2 cups (2 medium) sliced
   bananas
¾ cup all-purpose flour
1 teaspoon baking powder
1 teaspoon apple pie spice

⅓ cup Sugar Twin or
   Sprinkle Sweet
1 egg, slightly beaten, or
   equivalent in egg
   substitute
1 teaspoon vanilla extract
2 tablespoons unsweetened
   applesauce

Preheat oven to 350 degrees. Spoon 1 tablespoon maple syrup into four (1-cup) custard dishes. Place 1 tablespoon walnuts and ½ cup bananas in each. In a large bowl, combine flour, baking powder, apple pie spice, and Sugar Twin. Add egg, vanilla extract, and applesauce. Mix well to combine. Spoon about ¼ cup batter into each custard dish. Place custard dishes on a baking sheet. Bake for 25 minutes or until a toothpick inserted in center comes out clean. Place baking sheet on a wire rack and let set for at least 3 minutes. Good warm or cold.

Each serving equals:
HE: 1 Fruit, 1 Bread, ½ Fat, ½ Protein (¼ limited), ¼ Slider, 2 Optional Calories

238 Calories, 6 gm Fat, 6 gm Protein, 40 gm Carbohydrate, 174 mg Sodium, 89 mg Calcium, 3 gm Fiber

DIABETIC: 1½ Starch/Carbohydrate, 1 Fruit, ½ Fat, ½ Meat

Lemon Strawberry Pie

■ ■ ■ ■ ■ ■ ■ ■

*W*hen the strawberries are at their sweetest, there's just no more delightful way to serve them than in this light and pretty pie. (Take the kids strawberry picking for a special treat!) Blending the ripe berry taste with the tangy, tart lemon is almost as sensational as a sunset! *Serves 8*

2 cups halved fresh
   strawberries ☆
1 (6-ounce) Keebler
   shortbread piecrust
1 (4-serving) package
   JELL-O sugar-free
   instant vanilla pudding
   mix

1 (4-serving) package
   JELL-O sugar-free
   lemon gelatin
⅔ cup Carnation Nonfat
   Dry Milk Powder
1¼ cups Diet Mountain
   Dew
¾ cup Cool Whip Lite ☆

Reserve 8 strawberry halves. Place remaining strawberries in bottom of piecrust. In a medium bowl, combine dry pudding mix, dry gelatin, dry milk powder, and Diet Mountain Dew. Mix well using a wire whisk. Blend in ¼ cup Cool Whip Lite. Spread mixture evenly over strawberries. Refrigerate for at least 10 minutes. Evenly drop remaining Cool Whip Lite by tablespoon over top of pie to form 8 mounds. Garnish each mound with a reserved strawberry half. Refrigerate for at least 1 hour. Cut into 8 servings.

Each serving equals:
HE: ½ Bread, ¼ Fruit, ¼ Skim Milk, ¾ Slider, 19 Optional Calories

166 Calories, 6 gm Fat, 4 gm Protein, 24 gm Carbohydrate,
362 mg Sodium, 74 mg Calcium, 1 gm Fiber

DIABETIC: 1½ Starch/Carbohydrate, 1 Fat

Sweetheart Strawberry Silk Pie

■ ■ ■ ■ ■ ■ ■ ■

*J*ust as that wonderful old song says, "Let me call you sweetheart" and show you how much I care with this luscious strawberry pie! There's no better way to show your love than with this creamy delight! *Serves 8*

¼ cup Diet Mountain Dew
2 cups sliced fresh
   strawberries
1 (4-serving) package
   JELL-O sugar-free
   instant vanilla pudding
   mix

⅔ cup Carnation Nonfat
   Dry Milk Powder
1 cup Cool Whip Free ☆
1 (6-ounce) Keebler
   shortbread piecrust

In a blender container, combine Diet Mountain Dew and strawberries. Cover and process on BLEND for 20 seconds or until mixture is smooth. In a large bowl, combine dry pudding mix and dry milk powder. Add blended strawberry mixture. Mix well using a wire whisk. Blend in ½ cup Cool Whip Free. Spread mixture into piecrust. Refrigerate for at least 2 hours. Cut into 8 servings. Just before serving, garnish each with 1 tablespoon Cool Whip Free and additional strawberry pieces, if desired.

Each serving equals:
HE: ½ Bread, ¼ Fruit, ¼ Skim Milk, ¾ Slider, 18 Optional Calories

161 Calories, 5 gm Fat, 3 gm Protein, 26 gm Carbohydrate, 337 mg Sodium, 74 mg Calcium, 1 gm Fiber

DIABETIC: 1½ Starch/Carbohydrate, ½ Fat

Chocolate Pear Pie

■ ■ ■ ■ ■ ■ ■ ■

Isn't it wonderful that you can whip up a great dessert in just minutes when you've got a piecrust and some delectable canned pears? This scrumptious dessert takes no time to fix, but you'll keep hearing compliments all night long! *Serves 8*

2 cups (one 16-ounce can) pear halves, packed in fruit juice, drained, and ½ cup liquid reserved
1 (6-ounce) Keebler chocolate piecrust
1 (4-serving) package JELL-O sugar-free chocolate fudge pudding mix

⅔ cup Carnation Nonfat Dry Milk Powder
½ cup water
1 teaspoon almond extract
¾ cup Cool Whip Free
2 tablespoons (½ ounce) slivered almonds

Coarsely chop pears and arrange in bottom of piecrust. In a large bowl, combine dry pudding mix, dry milk powder, water, and reserved pear liquid. Mix well using a wire whisk. Blend in almond extract and Cool Whip Free. Spread mixture evenly over pears. Evenly sprinkle almonds over top. Refrigerate for at least 1 hour. Cut into 8 servings.

Each serving equals:
HE: ½ Bread, ½ Fruit, ¼ Skim Milk, 1 Slider, 5 Optional Calories

206 Calories, 6 gm Fat, 4 gm Protein, 34 gm Carbohydrate, 303 mg Sodium, 78 mg Calcium, 2 gm Fiber

DIABETIC: 1½ Starch/Carbohydrate, 1 Fat, ½ Fruit *or* 2 Starch/Carbohydrate, 1 Fat

Peanut Butter, Jelly, and Banana Pie

Creating pies to please children of all ages is even easier when I recall their favorite sandwiches! This dessert version combining peanut butter and bananas will bring back cozy childhood memories when Mom made your favorite lunch.   *Serves 8*

1 cup (1 medium) diced banana
1 (6-ounce) Keebler graham cracker piecrust
1 (4-serving) package JELL-O sugar-free instant vanilla pudding mix
⅔ cup Carnation Nonfat Dry Milk Powder
1¼ cups water

6 tablespoons Peter Pan reduced-fat peanut butter (chunky or creamy)
¼ cup grape spreadable fruit spread
¾ cup Cool Whip Lite
1 tablespoon (¼ ounce) chopped dry-roasted peanuts

Layer banana in bottom of piecrust. In a medium bowl, combine dry pudding mix, dry milk powder, and water. Mix well using a wire whisk. Blend in peanut butter. Pour mixture over banana. Refrigerate for 5 minutes. Evenly spread spreadable fruit over pudding mixture. Spread Cool Whip Lite evenly over top. Garnish with peanuts. Refrigerate for at least 1 hour. Cut into 8 servings.

HINTS:
1. To prevent banana from turning brown, mix with 1 teaspoon lemon juice or sprinkle with Fruit Fresh.
2. Peanut butter blends best at room temperature.
3. Any flavor spreadable fruit may be used. Spreadable fruit spreads best at room temperature.

Layered Chocolate-Pineapple Crumb Pie

■ ■ ■ ■ ■ ■ ■ ■

This festive concoction looks extra-delicious somehow because of the layers—and it tastes even better than that! Does your family adore pineapple as much as mine does? *Serves 8*

1 (4-serving) package JELL-O sugar-free instant chocolate pudding mix

1⅓ cups Carnation Nonfat Dry Milk Powder ☆

1¾ cups water ☆

1 (6-ounce) Keebler chocolate piecrust

1 (4-serving) package JELL-O sugar-free instant vanilla pudding mix

1 cup (one 8-ounce can) crushed pineapple, packed in fruit juice, undrained

½ cup Cool Whip Free

2 (2½-inch) Nabisco chocolate graham crackers, made into crumbs

In a medium bowl, combine dry chocolate pudding mix, ⅔ cup dry milk powder, and 1¼ cups water. Mix well using a wire whisk. Pour mixture into piecrust. Refrigerate while preparing topping. In a large bowl, combine dry vanilla pudding mix, remaining ⅔ cup dry milk powder, remaining ½ cup water, and undrained pineapple. Mix well using a wire whisk. Blend in Cool Whip Free. Spread topping mixture evenly over chocolate layer. Evenly sprinkle chocolate graham cracker crumbs over the top. Refrigerate for at least 1 hour. Cut into 8 servings.

◯HINT: A self-seal sandwich bag is great for crushing graham crackers.

Each serving equals:
HE: ½ Bread, ½ Skim Milk, ¼ Fruit, 1 Slider, 12 Optional Calories

205 Calories, 5 gm Fat, 6 gm Protein, 34 gm Carbohydrate, 500 mg Sodium, 143 mg Calcium, 1 gm Fiber

DIABETIC: 2 Starch/Carbohydrate, 1 Fat

Chocolate Express Pie

■ ■ ■ ■ ■ ■ ■ ■

It's simple, and it's super-good. Just chocolate, chocolate, and more chocolate flavor—for anyone who knows that too much chocolate is just enough! (Would that describe your kids to a T?)

Serves 8

1 (4-serving) package
    JELL-O sugar-free
    instant chocolate
    pudding mix
⅔ cup Carnation Nonfat
    Dry Milk Powder
1¼ cups water
¾ cup Cool Whip Free

12 (2½-inch) Nabisco
    chocolate graham
    cracker squares, made
    into crumbs ☆
1 (6-ounce) Keebler
    chocolate piecrust
1 tablespoon (¼ ounce)
    mini chocolate chips

In a large bowl, combine dry pudding mix, dry milk powder, and water. Mix well using a wire whisk. Blend in Cool Whip Free. Reserve 2 tablespoons graham cracker crumbs. Add remaining crumbs to pudding mixture. Mix gently to combine. Spread mixture into piecrust. Evenly sprinkle reserved graham cracker crumbs and chocolate chips over top. Refrigerate for at least 1 hour. Cut into 8 servings.

HINT: A self-seal sandwich bag works great for crushing graham crackers.

Each serving equals:
HE: 1 Bread, ¼ Skim Milk, 1 Slider, 1 Optional Calorie

186 Calories, 6 gm Fat, 4 gm Protein, 29 gm Carbohydrate,
333 mg Sodium, 69 mg Calcium, 1 gm Fiber

DIABETIC: 2 Starch/Carbohydrate, 1 Fat

Scrumptious White Chocolate Cheesecake

■ ■ ■ ■ ■ ■ ■ ■ ■

*W*hen everyone yells "We want chocolate for dessert!" be ready with this irresistible surprise. If one of your kids has been very, very good, invite him or her to help you by drizzling the chocolate syrup over the top!   *Serves 8*

2 (8-ounce) packages
    Philadelphia fat-free
    cream cheese
1 (4-serving) package
    JELL-O sugar-free
    white chocolate pudding
    mix
⅔ cup Carnation Nonfat
    Dry Milk Powder

1 cup water
¼ cup Cool Whip Free
2 tablespoons (½ ounce)
    mini chocolate chips
1 (6-ounce) Keebler
    chocolate piecrust
2 teaspoons Hershey's Lite
    Chocolate Syrup

In a large bowl, stir cream cheese with a spoon until soft. Add dry pudding mix, dry milk powder, and water. Mix well using a wire whisk. Blend in Cool Whip Free. Gently fold in chocolate chips. Spread mixture into piecrust. Drizzle chocolate syrup evenly over top. Refrigerate for at least 1 hour. Cut into 8 servings.

Each serving equals:
HE: 1 Protein, ½ Bread, ¼ Skim Milk, 1 Slider, 2 Optional Calories

202 Calories, 6 gm Fat, 11 gm Protein, 26 gm Carbohydrate, 639 mg Sodium, 70 mg Calcium, 1 gm Fiber

DIABETIC: 1½ Starch/Carbohydrate, 1 Fat, 1 Meat

Rocky Road Quick Cake

■ ■ ■ ■ ■ ■ ■ ■

If you thought a healthy lifestyle meant no more desserts with those "rocky road" flavors, you'll be pleasantly surprised to try this one! It's a great example of how using small amounts of favorite treats will convince your taste buds you're enjoying the real thing!   *Serves 4*

¾ cup Bisquick Reduced
  Fat Baking Mix
¼ cup Nestlé Quik sugar-
  free chocolate mix
¼ cup Sugar Twin or
  Sprinkle Sweet
¼ cup (1 ounce) chopped
  walnuts ☆

½ cup water
2 tablespoons Kraft fat-
  free mayonnaise
1 teaspoon vanilla extract
¼ cup (½ ounce)
  miniature marshmallows
1 tablespoon (¼ ounce)
  mini chocolate chips

Preheat oven to 375 degrees. Spray four (1-cup) glass custard dishes with butter-flavored cooking spray. In a large bowl, combine baking mix, dry Nestlé Quik, Sugar Twin, and 3 tablespoons walnuts. Add water, mayonnaise, and vanilla extract. Mix well to combine. Evenly spoon mixture into prepared custard dishes. Sprinkle 1 tablespoon marshmallows over top of each. In a small bowl, combine chocolate chips and remaining 1 tablespoon walnuts. Evenly sprinkle about 1½ teaspoons of mixture over each. Place custard dishes on a baking sheet and bake for 16 to 18 minutes. Place baking sheet on a wire rack and allow cakes to cool for at least 5 minutes. Good warm or cold.

Each serving equals:
HE: 1 Bread, ½ Fat, ¼ Protein, ½ Slider, 7 Optional Calories

179 Calories, 7 gm Fat, 3 gm Protein, 26 gm Carbohydrate,
351 mg Sodium, 26 mg Calcium, 2 gm Fiber

DIABETIC: 1½ Starch/Carbohydrate, 1 Fat

Triple Treat Chocolate Poke Cake

∎ ∎ ∎ ∎ ∎ ∎ ∎ ∎

Vinegar and mayonnaise in a triple chocolate dessert? It does seem impossible, but these are just two of the secret ingredients that deliver more chocolate taste per bite than almost any treat in town! Everyone loves the sweet surprises inside this special cake.   *Serves 12*

1⅓ cups Carnation Nonfat
   Dry Milk Powder ☆
2¼ cups cold water ☆
1 teaspoon white vinegar
1½ cups all-purpose flour
½ cup Sugar Twin or
   Sprinkle Sweet
¼ cup unsweetened cocoa
1 teaspoon baking powder
½ teaspoon baking soda
½ cup Kraft fat-free
   mayonnaise

1 tablespoon vanilla
   extract ☆
¼ cup Nestlé Quik sugar-
   free chocolate mix
½ cup hot water
1 (4-serving) package
   JELL-O sugar-free
   instant chocolate
   pudding mix
½ cup Cool Whip Free

Preheat oven to 350 degrees. Spray a 9-by-13-inch cake pan with butter-flavored cooking spray. In a small bowl, combine ⅔ cup dry milk powder, 1 cup cold water, and vinegar. Set aside. In a large bowl, combine flour, Sugar Twin, cocoa, baking powder, and baking soda. Add mayonnaise, milk mixture, and 2 teaspoons vanilla extract. Mix gently just to combine. Pour batter into prepared cake pan. Bake for 15 minutes or until a toothpick inserted in center comes out clean. Place cake pan on a wire rack and let cool for 5 minutes. Poke top of the warm cake about 20 times with the tines of a fork. In a small bowl, combine dry Nestlé Quik and hot water. Spread chocolate mixture evenly over warm cake. Continue to cool cake completely. In a medium bowl, combine dry pudding mix, remaining ⅔ cup dry milk powder, and remaining 1¼ cups cold water. Mix well using a wire whisk. Blend in Cool Whip Free and remaining 1 teaspoon vanilla extract. Spread pudding mixture evenly over cooled cake. Refrigerate for at least 15 minutes. Cut into 12 servings. Refrigerate leftovers.

Each serving equals:
HE: ⅔ Bread, ⅓ Skim Milk, ¼ Slider, 17 Optional Calories

116 Calories, 0 gm Fat, 5 gm Protein, 24 gm Carbohydrate, 393 mg Sodium, 120 mg Calcium, 1 gm Fiber

DIABETIC: 1½ Starch/Carbohydrate

Pineapple Carrot Cake

▪ ▪ ▪ ▪ ❋ ▪ ▪ ▪ ▪

Here's another American classic with a few new twists! I bet you'll be astonished how sweet and rich this cake tastes, even though I've whisked out most of the fat and added so much extra flavor.

Serves 8

- 1½ cups all-purpose flour
- ½ cup Sugar Twin or Sprinkle Sweet
- 1 (4-serving) package JELL-O sugar-free instant vanilla pudding mix
- 1 teaspoon apple pie spice
- ⅔ cup Carnation Nonfat Dry Milk Powder
- ½ cup water
- 2 teaspoons white vinegar
- 1 cup unsweetened applesauce
- 1 cup (one 8-ounce can) crushed pineapple, packed in fruit juice, undrained
- 1 egg or equivalent in egg substitute
- 1 teaspoon coconut extract
- 2 cups finely grated carrots
- ¼ cup (1 ounce) chopped walnuts
- 2 tablespoons flaked coconut

Preheat oven to 350 degrees. Spray a 9-by-9-inch cake pan with butter-flavored cooking spray. In a large bowl, combine flour, Sugar Twin, dry pudding mix, and apple pie spice. In a small bowl, combine dry milk powder, water, and vinegar. Stir in applesauce, undrained pineapple, egg, and coconut extract. Add milk mixture to flour mixture. Mix gently just to combine. Stir in carrots and walnuts. Spread batter into prepared cake pan. Evenly sprinkle coconut over top. Bake for 45 minutes or until a toothpick inserted in center comes out clean. Place cake pan on a wire rack and allow to cool completely. Cut into 8 servings.

HINT: Good served with 1 tablespoon Cool Whip Lite, but don't forget to count the few additional calories.

Each serving equals:

HE: 1 Bread, ½ Fruit, ½ Vegetable, ¼ Skim Milk, ¼ Fat, ¼ Protein, ¼ Slider, 2 Optional Calories

---

204 Calories, 4 gm Fat, 6 gm Protein, 36 gm Carbohydrate, 218 mg Sodium, 92 mg Calcium, 2 gm Fiber

---

DIABETIC: 1½ Starch/Carbohydrate, ½ Fruit, ½ Fat

Scrumptious Snacktimes

■ ■ ■ ■ ■ ■ ■ ■ ■

*W*e feed dozens of children every day at three local day-care centers, and twice a year we throw parties just for our Healthy Exchanges kids, so we've become experts at knowing just what children love at snacktime! Sure, we could give our toddlers a box of raisins or a small bunch of grapes with a cup of juice, but the delight on those little faces when our catering staff shows up with trays of crunchy cookies or tasty bars, fresh-baked muffins or homemade popsicles in the warmer months tells us that making the time to prepare healthy snacks is time well spent for any parent! I remember one little girl (who'd barely begun to talk) telling me, "Good cookies, good cookies!" How could anyone resist creating goodies for such an appreciative audience!

Nutritionists tell us that snacking is a great way for children to maintain energy and get necessary nutrients, so planning for these snacks is important. This chapter offers lots of healthy and tasty suggestions for these between-meal mini-meals. They look and taste like real treats—just offer your child **Pecan-Toffee Bars** or a **Chocolate Peanut Butter Shake** if you have doubts about competing with store-bought high-fat snacks!

Scrumptious Snacktimes

■ ■ ■ ■ ■ ■ ■ ■ ■

Peanut Butter Sandwich
Snacks

Chunky Carrot Sandwich
Snack

Cinnamon Crisps

Nutcracker Snacks

Applesauce-Oatmeal
Cookies

Peanut Butter Cookies

Peanut Butterscotch Bars

Rocky Road Bars

Pecan-Toffee Bars

Apricot Rocky Road
Clusters

Apple Biscuit Drops

Treasure Chests

Pineapple-Cheese Muffins

Dreamsicles

Frozen Chocolate Banana
Treats

Chocolate Peanut Butter
Shakes

Chocolate Fudge Sodas

Peanut Butter Sandwich Snacks

■ ■ ■ ■ ■ ■ ■ ■

Every child loves peanut butter, but this is a way to serve that old standby that makes it extra-special! What's even better is that every serving provides a full fruit exchange—perfect for getting your picky eaters to gobble down what they need most.

Serves 4

¼ cup Peter Pan reduced-
   fat peanut butter
   (creamy or chunky)
2 tablespoons Cary's
   Sugar Free Maple Syrup

1 cup (1 medium) diced
   banana
¼ cup raisins
8 slices reduced-calorie
   bread

In a medium bowl, combine peanut butter and maple syrup. Stir in banana and raisins. For each sandwich, spread about ¼ cup mixture between two slices of bread. Serve at once or cover and refrigerate until ready to serve.

HINTS:
   1. To prevent banana from turning brown, mix with 1 teaspoon lemon juice or sprinkle with Fruit Fresh.
   2. To plump up raisins without "cooking," place in a glass measuring cup and microwave on HIGH for 15 seconds.

Each serving equals:
HE: 1 Bread, 1 Fat, 1 Protein, 1 Fruit, 5 Optional Calories

242 Calories, 6 gm Fat, 9 gm Protein, 38 gm Carbohydrate, 323 mg Sodium, 42 mg Calcium, 7 gm Fiber

DIABETIC: 1 Starch, 1 Fruit, ½ Meat, ½ Fat

Chunky Carrot Sandwich Snack

∎ ∎ ∎ ∎ ∎ ∎ ∎ ∎

Here's a way to make snacktime an occasion for healthy nutrition! This open-faced sandwich treat provides your children with a little taste of all the important food groups—and a lot of kid-pleasing flavor.

Serves 4

¼ cup Peter Pan reduced-fat chunky peanut butter	½ cup finely shredded carrots
1 tablespoon orange marmalade spreadable fruit spread	2 tablespoons raisins
	4 slices reduced-calorie bread

In a small bowl, combine peanut butter and fruit spread. Add carrots and raisins. Mix well to combine. Spread about 2 full tablespoons of the mixture over each slice of bread. Serve at once or cover and refrigerate until ready to serve.

HINT: To plump up raisins without "cooking," place in a glass measuring cup and microwave on HIGH for 15 seconds.

Each serving equals:
HE: 1 Fat, 1 Protein, ½ Bread, ½ Fruit, ¼ Vegetable

166 Calories, 6 gm Fat, 6 gm Protein, 22 gm Carbohydrate, 195 mg Sodium, 23 mg Calcium, 4 gm Fiber

DIABETIC: 1½ Starch/Carbohydrate, ½ Meat, ½ Fat

Cinnamon Crisps

■ ■ ■ ■ ■ ■ ■

Here's something new to do with that package of tortillas sitting in your fridge. These are crunchy and sweet and go just great with a big glass of milk!   *Serves 6 (4 each)*

½ teaspoon ground   Twin or Sprinkle
   cinnamon   Sweet
2 tablespoons Sugar   6 (6-inch) flour tortillas

Preheat oven to 350 degrees. Spray a cookie sheet with butter-flavored cooking spray. In a small bowl, combine cinnamon and Sugar Twin. Cut each tortilla into 4 pieces. Place tortilla pieces on prepared baking sheet. Lightly spray tops with butter-flavored cooking spray. Evenly sprinkle cinnamon mixture over top. Bake for 10 to 12 minutes or until tortilla pieces are crisp. Serve warm or cold.

Each serving equals:
HE: 1 Bread, 2 Optional Calories

82 Calories, 2 gm Fat, 2 gm Protein, 14 gm Carbohydrate,
155 mg Sodium, 15 mg Calcium, 0 gm Fiber

DIABETIC: 1 Starch/Carbohydrate

Nutcracker Snacks

▪ ▪ ▪ ▪ ▪ ▪ ▪ ▪

The list of ingredients says it all—chocolate and nuts and marshmallows, piled onto a chocolaty cracker! And you get a real-life healthy serving—three of them! *Serves 4 (3 each)*

> 2 tablespoons (½ ounce)
>   mini chocolate chips
> ¼ cup (½ ounce)
>   miniature marshmallows
> 2 teaspoons reduced-
>   calorie margarine

> 2 tablespoons (½ ounce)
>   chopped pecans
> 12 (2½-inch) chocolate
>   graham cracker squares

In a small microwavable bowl, combine chocolate chips, marshmallows, and margarine. Cover and microwave on HIGH (100% power) for 15 seconds. Stir in pecans. Spread about 1 full teaspoon of the mixture over each cracker. Serve at once or refrigerate until ready to serve.

Each serving equals:
HE: 1 Bread, ¾ Fat, ¼ Slider, 5 Optional Calories

105 Calories, 5 gm Fat, 1 gm Protein, 14 gm Carbohydrate, 78 mg Sodium, 3 mg Calcium, 0 gm Fiber

DIABETIC: 1 Starch/Carbohydrate, 1 Fat

Applesauce-Oatmeal Cookies

■ ■ ■ ❋ ■ ■ ■

Marvelously moist, these fruity cookies are beloved classics your family will gobble down. They bake so quickly, you can stir up a batch in no time at all!   *Serves 12 (4 each)*

1 cup unsweetened applesauce	1 teaspoon baking soda
¼ cup vegetable oil	2 teaspoons apple pie spice
¼ cup Sugar Twin or Sprinkle Sweet	½ cup raisins
1 egg or equivalent in egg substitute	¾ cup all-purpose flour
	2 cups (6 ounces) quick oats

Preheat oven to 375 degrees. Spray baking sheets with butter-flavored cooking spray. In a large bowl, combine applesauce, oil, Sugar Twin, and egg. Add baking soda, apple pie spice, raisins, flour, and oats. Mix well to combine. Drop by spoonfuls onto prepared baking sheets to make 48 cookies. Bake for 6 to 8 minutes. Place cookies on a wire rack and allow to cool.

HINT: Don't overbake or cookies will turn out tough.

Each serving equals:
HE: 1 Bread, 1 Fat, ½ Fruit, 7 Optional Calories

158 Calories, 6 gm Fat, 4 gm Protein, 22 gm Carbohydrate, 112 mg Sodium, 14 mg Calcium, 2 gm Fiber

DIABETIC: 1 Starch/Carbohydrate, 1 Fat, ½ Fruit

Peanut Butter Cookies

■ ■ ■ ■ ❋ ■ ■ ■ ■

I bet you thought you'd never find a tasty, healthy peanut butter cookie recipe, but here's what a little Healthy Exchanges magic can do! Be careful not to overbake these, or they'll be too hard. *Serves 16 (3 each)*

1½ cups all-purpose flour
⅓ cup Sugar Twin or Sprinkle Sweet
1½ teaspoons baking powder
2 tablespoons + 2 teaspoons vegetable oil

⅓ cup water
½ cup Peter Pan reduced-fat creamy peanut butter
1 tablespoon vanilla extract
1 egg or equivalent in egg substitute

Preheat oven to 375 degrees. In a medium bowl, combine flour, Sugar Twin, and baking powder. Add oil, water, peanut butter, vanilla extract, and egg. Mix well to combine. Shape into 48 (1-inch) balls. Place balls on ungreased baking sheets and flatten with a fork. Bake for 12 minutes. Place cookies on a wire rack and allow to cool.

Each serving equals:
HE: 1 Fat, ½ Bread, ½ Protein, 6 Optional Calories

109 Calories, 5 gm Fat, 4 gm Protein, 12 gm Carbohydrate, 87 mg Sodium, 28 mg Calcium, 1 gm Fiber

DIABETIC: 1 Fat, 1 Starch/Carbohydrate

Peanut Butterscotch Bars

■ ■ ■ ■ ■ ■ ■ ■ ■

Kids just love these quick bars when the "hungries" strike—
and you can feel good knowing that they're as healthy as they
are tasty. *Serves 8 (2 each)*

¾ *cup all-purpose flour*
½ *cup (1½ ounces) quick*
oats
¼ *teaspoon baking soda*
¼ *cup Brown Sugar Twin*
5 *tablespoons Peter Pan*
reduced-fat peanut
butter

1 *egg or equivalent in egg*
substitute
1 *teaspoon vanilla extract*
2 *tablespoons skim milk*
2 *tablespoons reduced-*
calorie margarine,
melted

Preheat oven to 350 degrees. Spray a 9-by-9-inch cake pan with
butter-flavored cooking spray. In a small bowl, combine flour,
oats, baking soda, and Brown Sugar Twin. In a large bowl,
combine peanut butter, egg, vanilla extract, skim milk, and
margarine. Mix well using a wire whisk. Add flour mixture to
peanut butter mixture. Mix well to combine. Spread mixture
into prepared cake pan. Bake for 15 minutes or until lightly
browned. Place cake pan on a wire rack and allow to cool. Cut
into 16 bars.

Each serving equals:
HE: 1 Fat, ¾ Bread, ¾ Protein, 4 Optional Calories

133 Calories, 5 gm Fat, 5 gm Protein, 17 gm Carbohydrate,
110 mg Sodium, 12 mg Calcium, 1 gm Fiber

DIABETIC: 1 Fat, 1 Starch/Carbohydrate

Rocky Road Bars

■■■ ❋ ■■■

These brownies are nutritious and just crammed with delectable treats! They prove my point, that too much of a good thing can be just wonderful! *Serves 8 (2 each)*

½ cup (1½ ounces) quick oats
6 tablespoons Bisquick Reduced Fat Baking Mix
⅔ cup Carnation Nonfat Dry Milk Powder
⅓ cup Sugar Twin or Sprinkle Sweet
¼ cup unsweetened cocoa
1 teaspoon baking powder

1 cup water
3 tablespoons Peter Pan reduced-fat peanut butter
1 teaspoon vanilla extract
1 cup (2 ounces) miniature marshmallows
¼ cup (1 ounce) chopped walnuts
¼ cup (1 ounce) mini chocolate chips

Preheat oven to 350 degrees. Spray an 11½-by-7½-inch baking pan with butter-flavored cooking spray. In a medium bowl, combine oats, baking mix, dry milk powder, Sugar Twin, cocoa, and baking powder. Add water, peanut butter, and vanilla extract. Mix well to combine. Evenly spread mixture into prepared baking pan. Bake for 8 minutes. Sprinkle marshmallows, walnuts, and chocolate chips evenly over partially baked crust. Return to oven and continue baking for 5 minutes or just until topping starts to melt together. Place baking pan on a wire rack and allow to cool completely. Cut into 16 bars.

Each serving equals:
HE: ⅔ Fat, ½ Bread, ½ Protein, ¼ Skim Milk, ½ Slider, 3 Optional Calories

179 Calories, 7 gm Fat, 6 gm Protein, 23 gm Carbohydrate, 190 mg Sodium, 119 mg Calcium, 2 gm Fiber

DIABETIC: 1½ Starch/Carbohydrate, 1 Fat

Pecan-Toffee Bars

◼ ◼ ◼ ◼ ◼ ◼ ◼ ◼ ◼

I love finding new ways to use familiar products, like the crescent rolls I start with in this recipe. What could be more scrumptious than creamy marshmallow, crunchy toffee, and even a few chopped nuts? Yum. *Serves 8 (4 each)*

1 (8-ounce) can Pillsbury Reduced Fat Crescent Rolls
1 (4-serving) package JELL-O sugar-free chocolate cook-and-serve pudding mix
⅔ cup Carnation Nonfat Dry Milk Powder
1 cup water
½ cup (1 ounce) miniature marshmallows
1 teaspoon vanilla extract
¼ cup Heath Toffee Baking Bits
¼ cup (1 ounce) chopped pecans

Preheat oven to 375 degrees. Spray a rimmed 9-by-13-inch cookie sheet with butter-flavored cooking spray. Unroll crescent rolls and pat into pan, being sure to seal perforations. Bake for 7 to 9 minutes or until light golden brown. Meanwhile, in a medium saucepan, combine dry pudding mix, dry milk powder, and water. Cook over medium heat until mixture thickens and starts to boil, stirring constantly. Remove from heat. Stir in marshmallows and vanilla extract. Spread hot mixture evenly over warm crust. Place cookie sheet on a wire rack. Evenly sprinkle toffee bits and pecans over top. Refrigerate for at least 30 minutes. Cut into 32 bars.

HINT: Do not use inexpensive rolls as they don't cover the pan properly.

Each serving equals:
HE: 1 Bread, ½ Fat, ¼ Skim Milk, ¼ Slider, 18 Optional Calories

171 Calories, 7 gm Fat, 5 gm Protein, 22 gm Carbohydrate, 320 mg Sodium, 70 mg Calcium, 0 gm Fiber

DIABETIC: 1½ Starch/Carbohydrate, 1 Fat

Apricot Rocky Road Clusters

■ ■ ■ ■ ■ ■ ■ ■

These "chunky" treats are absolutely crammed with goodies and couldn't be easier to prepare. Kids think they're fun to eat, too, because each bite offers a great new flavor!

Serves 6 (4 each)

1 (4-serving) package JELL-O sugar-free chocolate cook-and-serve pudding mix
⅔ cup Carnation Nonfat Dry Milk Powder
1 cup water
2 teaspoons reduced-calorie margarine

1 cup (2 ounces) miniature marshmallows
1 cup (4½ ounces) chopped dried apricots
¼ cup (1 ounce) chopped walnuts
½ cup (1½ ounces) quick oats

Line a cookie sheet with waxed paper. In a large saucepan, combine dry pudding mix, dry milk powder, and water. Cook over medium heat until mixture thickens and starts to boil, stirring constantly. Remove from heat. Stir in margarine and marshmallows. Add apricots, walnuts, and oats. Mix well to combine. Drop mixture with a teaspoon onto prepared cookie sheet to form 24 clusters. Refrigerate for at least 1 hour.

Each serving equals:
HE: 1 Fruit, ½ Fat, ⅓ Bread, ⅓ Skim Milk, ¼ Slider, 13 Optional Calories

192 Calories, 4 gm Fat, 6 gm Protein, 33 gm Carbohydrate, 127 mg Sodium, 110 mg Calcium, 4 gm Fiber

DIABETIC: 1 Fruit, 1 Starch/Carbohydrate, ½ Fat

Apple Biscuit Drops

These are wonderfully quick to fix and make a terrific after-school snack. A cozy-warm snack makes family time special and creates a sweet memory with very little effort. *Serves 8*

1½ cups Bisquick Reduced Fat Baking Mix
2 tablespoons Sugar Twin or Sprinkle Sweet
1 teaspoon apple pie spice
¼ cup (1 ounce) chopped pecans
½ cup (1 small) unpeeled and finely chopped cooking apple
½ cup unsweetened apple juice
¼ cup water

Preheat oven to 425 degrees. Spray a baking sheet with butter-flavored cooking spray. In a large bowl, combine baking mix, Sugar Twin, apple pie spice, and pecans. Stir in apple. Add apple juice and water. Mix gently to combine. Drop by spoonful onto prepared baking sheet to form 8 biscuits. Bake for 8 to 12 minutes or until biscuits are browned. Serve at once.

Each serving equals:
HE: 1 Bread, ½ Fat, ¼ Fruit, 1 Optional Calorie

120 Calories, 4 gm Fiber, 2 gm Protein, 19 gm Carbohydrate, 262 mg Sodium, 21 mg Calcium, 1 gm Fiber

DIABETIC: 1 Starch/Carbohydrate, ½ Fat

Treasure Chests

■ ■ ■ ■ ■ ■ ■ ■

Remember that old motto, "It's what's inside that counts"? Well, here it couldn't be more true, when biting into these tasty rounds unearths an explosion of flavor! *Serves 5 (2 each)*

1 (7.5-ounce) can Pillsbury refrigerated buttermilk biscuits
¼ cup (½ ounce) miniature marshmallows

3 tablespoons + 1 teaspoon (⅞ ounce) chopped pecans
2 tablespoons (½ ounce) mini chocolate chips

Preheat oven to 350 degrees. Separate biscuits and place on an ungreased cookie sheet. Flatten each biscuit into a 3-inch circle. Evenly divide marshmallows and place in center of each biscuit. In a small bowl, combine pecans and chocolate chips. Evenly sprinkle mixture over tops. Fold biscuits in half and seal edges with the tines of a fork. Lightly spray tops with butter-flavored cooking spray. Bake for 15 to 20 minutes. Spray tops lightly again with butter-flavored cooking spray. Place cookie sheet on a wire rack and let set at least 5 minutes. Good warm or cold.

Each serving equals:
HE: 1½ Bread, ⅔ Fat, ¼ Slider

170 Calories, 6 gm Fat, 3 gm Protein, 26 gm Carbohydrate, 366 mg Sodium, 3 mg Calcium, 2 gm Fiber

DIABETIC: 1½ Starch/Carbohydrate, 1 Fat

Pineapple-Cheese Muffins

■ ■ ■ ■ ✳ ■ ■ ■ ■

*W*hat a nice after-school snack these cozy muffins provide! Even if you've never considered yourself one of those "moms who bake," you'll win over their taste buds when you bring these to the table! *Serves 8*

1½ cups Bisquick Reduced
  Fat Baking Mix
1 tablespoon Sugar Twin
  or Sprinkle Sweet
Full ½ cup (2¼ ounces)
  shredded Kraft reduced-
  fat Cheddar cheese

1 cup (one 8-ounce can)
  crushed pineapple,
  packed in fruit juice,
  undrained
1 egg or equivalent in egg
  substitute
⅓ cup skim milk

Preheat oven to 400 degrees. Spray 8 wells of a 12-hole muffin pan with butter-flavored cooking spray or line with paper liners. In a large bowl, combine baking mix, Sugar Twin, and Cheddar cheese. Add undrained pineapple, egg, and skim milk. Mix just to combine. Evenly spoon batter into prepared muffin tin, filling wells about ⅔ full. Bake for 15 to 18 minutes or until a toothpick inserted in center comes out clean. Place muffin pan on a wire rack and let set for 5 minutes. Remove muffins from pan and eat warm or continue cooling on wire rack.

HINT: Fill unused muffin wells with water. It protects the muffin tin and ensures even baking.

Each serving equals:
HE: 1 Bread, ½ Protein, ¼ Fruit, 5 Optional Calories

135 Calories, 3 gm Fat, 5 gm Protein, 22 gm Carbohydrate, 340 mg Sodium, 89 mg Calcium, 0 gm Fiber

DIABETIC: 1½ Starch/Carbohydrate, ½ Meat

Dreamsicles

■ ■ ■ ■ ❋ ■ ■ ■ ■

The children who tested these said they were "super-fantastic"! Who wouldn't like creamy orange pops as rich as these are?   *Serves 6*

2 cups unsweetened orange
  juice
⅔ cup Carnation Nonfat
  Dry Milk Powder
½ cup Sugar Twin or
  Sprinkle Sweet
½ cup water

1 tablespoon vanilla
  extract
3 to 4 drops red food
  coloring
2 to 3 drops yellow food
  coloring

In a blender container, combine orange juice, dry milk powder, Sugar Twin, and water. Cover and process on BLEND for 15 seconds. Add vanilla extract and food colorings. Continue processing on BLEND for 5 seconds. Pour mixture evenly into 6 (8-ounce) paper cups. Place a wooden stick or plastic spoon in center of each. Freeze until firm. When serving, tear paper cup away from dreamsicle.

Each serving equals:
HE: ⅔ Fruit, ⅓ Skim Milk, 8 Optional Calories

66 Calories, 0 gm Fat, 3 gm Protein, 12 gm Carbohydrate,
43 mg Sodium, 99 mg Calcium, 1 gm Fiber

DIABETIC: 1 Fruit

Frozen Chocolate Banana Treats

■ ■ ■ ■ ❄ ■ ■ ■ ■

Better than just any old ice cream sandwich, these cool and creamy wonders are a perfect reward for "just being you." Show your family how much you care by treating them to these! *Serves 6 (2 each)*

1 (4-serving) package JELL-O sugar-free instant vanilla pudding mix	½ cup Cool Whip Free
	2 cups (2 medium) diced bananas
⅔ cup Carnation Nonfat Dry Milk Powder	¼ cup (1 ounce) chopped pecans
1 cup water	24 (2½-inch) graham cracker squares

In a medium bowl, combine dry pudding mix, dry milk powder, and water. Mix well using a wire whisk. Blend in Cool Whip Free. Add bananas and pecans. Mix gently to combine. Place about 2 full tablespoons of mixture on 12 of the graham crackers. Top with remaining crackers. Place each in a separate sandwich bag. Freeze.

HINT: To prevent bananas from turning brown, mix with 1 teaspoon lemon juice or sprinkle with Fruit Fresh.

Each serving equals:
HE: 1⅓ Bread, ⅔ Fruit, ⅔ Fat, ⅓ Skim Milk, ¼ Slider, 7 Optional Calories

197 Calories, 5 gm Fat, 4 gm Protein, 34 gm Carbohydrate, 355 mg Sodium, 97 mg Calcium, 2 gm Fiber

DIABETIC: 1 Starch/Carbohydrate, 1 Fruit, 1 Fat

Chocolate Peanut Butter Shakes

■ ■ ■ ■ ■ ■ ■

Homemade milkshakes are always delicious, but because this one is made with skim milk and fat-free yogurt, it's actually good for your kids! It's also oh-so-good!

Serves 4 (scant 1 cup)

1 cup skim milk
¾ cup Yoplait plain fat-free yogurt
¼ cup Peter Pan reduced-fat peanut butter (creamy or chunky)

2 cups Wells' Blue Bunny sugar- and fat-free chocolate ice cream or any sugar- and fat-free ice cream

In a blender container, combine skim milk, yogurt, and peanut butter. Cover and process on BLEND for 10 seconds. Add ice cream. Re-cover and process on BLEND for 20 seconds or until mixture is smooth. Serve at once.

Each serving equals:
HE: 1 Fat, 1 Protein, ½ Skim Milk, ¾ Slider

217 Calories, 5 gm Fat, 12 gm Protein, 31 gm Carbohydrate, 189 mg Sodium, 280 mg Calcium, 1 gm Fiber

DIABETIC: 1½ Starch/Carbohydrate, ½ Fat, ½ Meat, ½ Skim Milk

Chocolate Fudge Sodas

■ ■ ■ ■ ■ ■ ■ ■ ■

You'll be delighted and amazed at how much these taste like the soda fountain kind! Isn't it great to be able to offer your family treats like these at home?   *Serves 2*

¼ cup Nestlé Quik sugar-
free chocolate mix
1 cup carbonated water ☆
1 cup Wells' Blue Bunny

sugar- and fat-free vanilla
ice cream or any sugar-
and fat-free ice cream

In a small bowl, combine dry Nestlé Quik and ½ cup carbonated water. Evenly pour mixture into 2 glasses. Add ½ cup ice cream to each glass and pour another ¼ cup carbonated water over top of each. Stir to blend slightly. Serve at once.

Each serving equals:
HE: 1 Slider, 18 Optional Calories

180 Calories, 0 gm Fat, 4 gm Protein, 41 gm Carbohydrate,
104 mg Sodium, 130 mg Calcium, 1 gm Fiber

DIABETIC: 2½ Starch/Carbohydrate

Special-Occasion Spectaculars

■ ■ ■ ■ ■ ■ ■ ■ ■

One of my daughter, Becky's, most special birthdays was the inspiration for this chapter. When my children were growing up, we didn't let the kids have big birthday parties every year—first of all because we couldn't afford it, but also because we didn't want to make fancy parties something they would take for granted. We decided that in third grade and sixth grade, they could have huge birthday parties and invite all the children in their classes. For Becky's third-grade party, we played host to two dozen excited little girls all dressed up in pretty dresses. Everything we served was pink, the girls all brought their favorite dolls, and I organized it like a little tea party. I even served the punch in the beautiful milk-glass punch bowl that my mother had given me as a wedding gift. The girls just loved all of it, and Becky told me again and again how special it made her feel.

My boys, on the other hand, are more rough and tumble. Tommy was into sports heroes and James was into science when they were growing up. Usually, though, the boys they invited to their parties came to play—softball and football—and I served real "boy food": stuffed loose meat sandwiches, lots of Super Bowl party-type snacks, and of course, a big birthday cake!

To help you plan the menus for your own special occasions, I've suggested recipes that will make any event extra-special! Whether you decide to honor your grandparents with a family dinner and serve a tasty homemade healthy pie, or you promise your teenager a night to hang out with his friends if he makes the honor roll, you'll find delicious dishes like **Three-Cheese Pizza Roll-Ups** and **Luscious Lemon Cheesecake** will make entertaining easier than ever before!

BUT—don't just save these delicious recipes for special times (they're too good to save for only once or twice a year)! Enjoy them often . . . your family will thank you!

Birthday Party Bonanza

Pretty-in-Pink Birthday Party
Magical Kingdom Fluffy Fruit Dip
Fairy-Tale Carrot Salad
Little Princess Chicken Salad Sandwiches
Pretty-in-Pink Birthday Cake
Almost Grown-up Punch

All-American-Boy Birthday Party
Touchdown Dip
Slam-Dunk Coleslaw
Little League Meat and Potatoes
Home Run Chocolate Birthday Cake
Big Boy's Sports Spritzer

Teenagers' Hangout Night
Party Time! Dip
"Cool" Pineapple and Apple Salad
Three-Cheese Pizza Roll-Ups
Peanut Butter Cup Pie
Chill-Out Orange Dew Shakes

Mother's Day Brunch
Mom's Creamy Vegetable Slaw
Frosted Apricot-Pineapple Salad
Jiffy Scalloped Potatoes
Magnificent Baked Chicken
Luscious Lemon Cheesecake

Father's Day Picnic
Dad's Favorite Coleslaw
Baked Scalloped Corn
Classic Picnic Potato Salad
Bacon Cheeseburger Patties
White Cake with Chocolate-Walnut Topping

Grandparents' Appreciation Dinner
Grandma's Perfection Relish Salad
Simmered Carrots
Creamed Peas and Ham on Potato Mounds
Grandpa's Apple Maple Crumb Pie
Lemonade Slush Punch

Pretty-in-Pink Birthday Party

*W*hat little girl wouldn't love to host a festive luncheon for all her best friends? This menu is nutritious, of course, but it's also one of the prettiest I could think of. The chicken salad filling isn't a bit ordinary, the carrot salad features those marshmallows peeking out like flowers, the fruit dip is a perfect pink, the punch tastes like a grown-up treat—and the cake is one any princess would be proud to serve.

Magical Kingdom Fluffy Fruit Dip

Serves 8 (¼ cup)

¾ cup Yoplait plain fat-
free yogurt
⅓ cup Carnation Nonfat
Dry Milk Powder
¾ cup strawberry
spreadable fruit spread

1 cup Cool Whip Free
3 to 4 drops red food
coloring
1 teaspoon coconut extract
2 tablespoons flaked
coconut

In a large bowl, combine yogurt and dry milk powder. Add fruit spread. Mix well to combine. Fold in Cool Whip Free, red food coloring, coconut extract, and coconut. Cover and refrigerate for at least 1 hour. Gently stir again just before serving.

HINT: Wonderful served with fresh strawberries or pineapple.

Each serving equals:
HE: 1½ Fruit, ¼ Skim Milk, 19 Optional Calories

104 Calories, 0 gm Fat, 2 gm Protein, 24 gm Carbohydrate, 39 mg Sodium, 77 mg Calcium, 0 gm Fiber

DIABETIC: 1½ Fruit, ½ Starch/Carbohydrate

Fairy-Tale Carrot Salad

■ ■ ■ ■ ■ ■ ■ ■

Serves 8 (½ cup)

⅔ cup Kraft fat-free
  mayonnaise
1 cup (one 8-ounce can)
  crushed pineapple,
  packed in fruit juice,
  drained, and 2
  tablespoons liquid
  reserved

3½ cups shredded carrots
½ cup finely chopped
  celery
½ cup (1 ounce) miniature
  marshmallows

In a large bowl, combine mayonnaise, pineapple, and reserved pineapple liquid. Add carrots, celery, and marshmallows. Mix well to combine. Cover and refrigerate for at least 30 minutes. Gently stir again just before serving.

Each serving equals:
HE: 1 Vegetable, ¼ Fruit, ¼ Slider

64 Calories, 0 gm Fat, 0 gm Protein, 16 gm Carbohydrate,
197 mg Sodium, 21 mg Calcium, 1 gm Fiber

DIABETIC: 1 Vegetable, ½ Starch/Carbohydrate *or* 1 Starch/
Carbohydrate

Little Princess Chicken Salad Sandwiches

■ ■ ■ ■ ■ ■ ■ ■

Serves 8

2 full cups (12 ounces)
   finely chopped cooked
   chicken breast
¾ cup (3 ounces) shredded
   Kraft reduced-fat
   Cheddar cheese
1 cup finely diced celery
¾ cup Kraft fat-free
   mayonnaise
1 teaspoon dried onion
   flakes

1 teaspoon dried parsley
   flakes
2 teaspoons lemon juice
Sugar substitute to equal 2
   teaspoons sugar
⅛ teaspoon black pepper
8 lettuce leaves
8 reduced-calorie
   hamburger buns

In a large bowl, combine chicken, Cheddar cheese, and celery.
Add mayonnaise, onion flakes, parsley flakes, lemon juice,
sugar substitute, and black pepper. Mix well to combine. For
each sandwich, place a lettuce leaf on bottom half of hamburger
bun, spoon about ⅓ cup chicken mixture over lettuce and
arrange top half of hamburger bun over chicken mixture. Serve
at once or refrigerate until ready to serve.

HINT: If you don't have leftovers, purchase a chunk of cooked
chicken breast from your local deli.

Each serving equals:
HE: 2 Protein, 1 Bread, ¼ Vegetable, 16 Optional Calories

184 Calories, 4 gm Fat, 18 gm Protein, 19 gm Carbohydrate,
498 mg Sodium, 93 mg Calcium, 1 gm Fiber

DIABETIC: 2 Meat, 1 Starch

Pretty-in-Pink Birthday Cake

■ ■ ■ ■ ■ ■ ■ ■

Serves 8

1½ cups all-purpose flour
½ cup Sugar Twin or
   Sprinkle Sweet
1 teaspoon baking powder
½ teaspoon baking soda
½ cup Yoplait plain fat-
   free yogurt
⅓ cup Kraft fat-free
   mayonnaise
1¼ teaspoons almond
   extract ☆

2 cups water ☆
12 to 16 drops red food
   coloring ☆
1 (4-serving) package
   JELL-O sugar-free
   instant vanilla pudding
   mix
⅔ cup Carnation Nonfat
   Dry Milk Powder
1 cup Cool Whip Free

Preheat oven to 350 degrees. Spray a 9-by-9-inch cake pan with butter-flavored cooking spray. In a large bowl, combine flour, Sugar Twin, baking powder, and baking soda. In a medium bowl, combine yogurt, mayonnaise, 1 teaspoon almond extract, 1 cup water, and 10 to 12 drops red food coloring. Add yogurt mixture to flour mixture. Mix gently to combine. Spread batter into prepared cake pan. Bake for 25 to 30 minutes or until a toothpick inserted in center comes out clean. Place cake pan on a wire rack and allow to cool completely. In a large bowl combine dry pudding mix, dry milk powder, and remaining 1 cup water. Mix well using a wire whisk. Spread mixture evenly over cooled cake. Refrigerate while preparing topping. In a small bowl, combine Cool Whip Free, remaining ¼ teaspoon almond extract, and remaining 2 to 4 drops of red food coloring. Evenly spread topping mixture over pudding layer. Cut into 8 servings. Refrigerate leftovers.

HINT: Also good with 2 tablespoons slivered almonds sprinkled evenly over top.

Each serving equals:

HE: 1 Bread, ¼ Skim Milk, ½ Slider, 8 Optional Calories

140 Calories, 0 gm Fat, 5 gm Protein, 30 gm Carbohydrate,
516 mg Sodium, 134 mg Calcium, 1 gm Fiber

DIABETIC: 2 Starch/Carbohydrate

Almost Grown-up Punch

■ ■ ■ ■ ■ ■ ■ ■

Serves 8 (1 cup)

2 cups (two 8-ounce cans)
   crushed pineapple,
   packed in fruit juice,
   undrained
2 cups diet ginger ale

4 cups Ocean Spray
   reduced-calorie
   cranberry juice cocktail
1 cup water

In a blender container, combine undrained pineapple and diet ginger ale. Cover and process on BLEND for 15 seconds or until mixture is smooth. Pour mixture into a large container. Add cranberry juice cocktail and water. Cover and refrigerate for at least 2 hours.

HINT: Double recipe and freeze 2 cups of mixture in a ring mold. Just before serving, place frozen ring and remaining 14 cups punch in a punch bowl.

Each serving equals:
HE: 1 Fruit

64 Calories, 0 gm Fat, 0 gm Protein, 16 gm Carbohydrate, 29 mg Sodium, 9 mg Calcium, 0 gm Fiber

DIABETIC: 1 Fruit

All-American-Boy Birthday Party

○

*C*elebrate your favorite boy's birthday with this wonderful menu of American classics! His friends will enjoy dipping chips (until they drop) into this game-winning dip; they'll appreciate this meaty main dish and crunchy coleslaw; and they're sure to cheer this tasty chocolate cake and slurp down your homemade sports punch!

Touchdown Dip

■ ■ ■ ■ ■ ■ ■ ■ ■

Serves 8 (¼ cup)

1 (8-ounce) package
Philadelphia fat-free
cream cheese
¼ cup Kraft fat-free
mayonnaise
1 cup chunky salsa (mild,
medium, or hot)

¾ cup (3 ounces) shredded
Kraft reduced-fat
Cheddar cheese
2 tablespoons Hormel
Bacon Bits
1 teaspoon dried parsley
flakes

In a large bowl, stir cream cheese with a spoon until soft. Add mayonnaise and salsa. Mix well to combine. Stir in Cheddar cheese, bacon bits, and parsley flakes. Cover and refrigerate for at least 30 minutes. Gently stir again just before serving.

HINT: Wonderful with reduced-fat crackers, potato chips, or corn chips.

Each serving equals:
HE: 1 Protein, ¼ Vegetable, 11 Optional Calories

64 Calories, 2 gm Fat, 8 gm Protein, 4 gm Carbohydrate, 505 mg Sodium, 117 mg Calcium, 0 gm Fiber

DIABETIC: 1 Meat

Slam-Dunk Coleslaw

■ ■ ■ ■ ■ ■ ■ ■

Serves 8 (⅔ cup)

¾ cup Kraft fat-free
  mayonnaise
2 teaspoons dried parsley
  flakes
2 teaspoons dried onion
  flakes
1 tablespoon white vinegar

Sugar substitute to equal 1
  tablespoon sugar
⅛ teaspoon black pepper
6 cups purchased coleslaw
  mix
1 cup finely chopped celery

In a large bowl, combine mayonnaise, parsley flakes, onion flakes, vinegar, sugar substitute, and black pepper. Add coleslaw mix and celery. Mix well to combine. Cover and refrigerate for at least 30 minutes. Gently stir again just before serving.

HINT: 5 cups shredded cabbage and 1 cup shredded carrots may be used in place of purchased coleslaw mix.

Each serving equals:
HE: 1¾ Vegetable, 16 Optional Calories

40 Calories, 0 gm Fat, 1 gm Protein, 9 gm Carbohydrate, 225 mg Sodium, 33 mg Calcium, 2 gm Fiber

DIABETIC: 1 Vegetable

Little League Meat and Potatoes

■ ■ ■ ■ ■ ■ ■ ■

Serves 8

16 ounces ground 90% lean
turkey or beef
1 (10¾-ounce) can
Healthy Request Cream
of Mushroom Soup
1 cup chunky salsa (mild,
medium, or hot)
¼ cup Land O Lakes no-
fat sour cream

1 teaspoon dried parsley
flakes
6 cups (20 ounces)
shredded loose-packed
frozen potatoes
8 (¾-ounce) slices Kraft
reduced-fat American
cheese

Preheat oven to 350 degrees. Spray a 9-by-13-inch baking dish
with butter-flavored cooking spray. In a large skillet sprayed
with butter-flavored cooking spray, brown meat. In a large
bowl, combine mushroom soup, salsa, sour cream, and parsley
flakes. Add potatoes. Mix well to combine. Stir in browned
meat. Spread mixture into prepared baking dish. Evenly arrange American cheese slices over top. Bake for 25 to 30 minutes. Place baking dish on a wire rack and let set for 5 minutes.
Divide into 8 servings.

HINT: Mr. Dell's frozen shredded potatoes are a good choice.

Each serving equals:
HE: 2½ Protein, ¾ Bread, ¼ Vegetable, ¼ Slider, 8 Optional Calories

217 Calories, 9 gm Fat, 15 gm Protein, 19 gm Carbohydrate,
658 mg Sodium, 195 mg Calcium, 1 gm Fiber

DIABETIC: 2 Meat, 1 Starch

Home Run Chocolate Birthday Cake

∎∎∎∎∎ ∎∎∎∎

Serves 8

1½ cups all-purpose flour
¾ cup Sugar Twin or
   Sprinkle Sweet
¼ cup unsweetened cocoa
1 teaspoon baking powder
½ teaspoon baking soda
¼ cup (1 ounce) mini
   chocolate chips
½ cup Yoplait plain fat-
   free yogurt
⅓ cup Kraft fat-free
   mayonnaise

1 teaspoon vanilla extract
2 cups water ☆
1 (4-serving) package
   JELL-O sugar-free
   instant white chocolate
   pudding mix
⅔ cup Carnation Nonfat
   Dry Milk Powder
¾ cup Cool Whip Free
2 (2½-inch) chocolate
   graham cracker squares,
   made into fine crumbs

Preheat oven to 350 degrees. Spray a 9-by-9-inch cake pan with butter-flavored cooking spray. In a large bowl, combine flour, Sugar Twin, cocoa, baking powder, and baking soda. Stir in chocolate chips. In a medium bowl, combine yogurt, mayonnaise, vanilla extract, and 1 cup water. Add yogurt mixture to flour mixture. Mix gently to combine. Spread batter into prepared cake pan. Bake for 25 to 30 minutes or until a toothpick inserted in center comes out clean. Place cake pan on a wire rack and allow to cool completely. In a large bowl, combine dry pudding mix, dry milk powder, and remaining 1 cup water. Mix well to combine. Fold in Cool Whip Free. Spread mixture evenly over cooled cake. Evenly sprinkle cracker crumbs over top. Cut into 8 servings. Refrigerate leftovers.

HINTS:
1. Also good with ¼ cup chopped walnuts stirred into batter.
2. A self-seal sandwich bag works great for crushing graham crackers.

Each serving equals:

HE: 1 Bread, ¼ Skim Milk, 1 Slider, 10 Optional Calories

187 Calories, 3 gm Fat, 6 gm Protein, 34 gm Carbohydrate,
518 mg Sodium, 140 mg Calcium, 2 gm Fiber

DIABETIC: 2 Starch/Carbohydrate

Big Boy's Sports Spritzer

■ ■ ■ ■ ■ ■ ■ ■

Serves 8 (1 cup)

*1 cup (one 8-ounce can)
crushed pineapple,
packed in fruit juice,
undrained*

*4 cups Diet Mountain
Dew ☆
3 cups unsweetened orange
juice*

In a blender container, combine undrained pineapple and 2 cups Diet Mountain Dew. Cover and process on BLEND for 15 to 20 seconds or until mixture is smooth. Pour mixture into a large container. Add remaining 2 cups Diet Mountain Dew and orange juice. Mix well to combine. Refrigerate for at least 30 minutes. Serve over ice.

Each serving equals:
HE: 1 Fruit

56 Calories, 0 gm Fat, 0 gm Protein, 14 gm Carbohydrate, 15 mg Sodium, 12 mg Calcium, 0 gm Fiber

DIABETIC: 1 Fruit

Teenagers' Hangout Night

○

Filled with flavors teens just can't live without—pizza, peanut butter, milkshakes—this is one menu that you'll never have to fix because your teenage kids will say, "Mom, I'd rather do it myself!" And you'll feel even better knowing their teen taste buds will be satisfied with this collection of tasty, healthy recipes!

Party Time! Dip

∎ ∎ ∎ ∎ ∎ ∎ ∎ ∎ ∎

Serves 8 (full ¼ cup)

1 (8-ounce) package
  Philadelphia fat-free
  cream cheese
1 cup Land O Lakes no-fat
  sour cream
1 cup chunky salsa (mild,
  medium, or hot)

1 teaspoon dried parsley
  flakes
1 teaspoon chili seasoning
2 tablespoons Hormel
  Bacon Bits

In a medium bowl, stir cream cheese with a spoon until soft. Add sour cream. Mix gently to combine. Stir in salsa, parsley flakes, chili seasoning, and bacon bits. Cover and refrigerate for at least 30 minutes. Gently stir again just before serving.

HINT: Wonderful with corn chips, crackers, or vegetables.

Each serving equals:
HE: ½ Meat, ¼ Vegetable, ¼ Slider, 16 Optional Calories

52 Calories, 0 gm Fat, 6 gm Protein, 7 gm Carbohydrate, 383 mg Sodium, 73 mg Calcium, 0 gm Fiber

DIABETIC: ½ Starch/Carbohydrate, ½ Meat

"Cool" Pineapple and Apple Salad

░░░░░░░░

Serves 8 (⅔ cup)

1 (4-serving) package
JELL-O sugar-free
instant vanilla pudding
mix
⅔ cup Carnation Nonfat
Dry Milk Powder
1 cup (one 8-ounce can)
crushed pineapple,

packed in fruit juice,
undrained
½ cup water
1 cup Cool Whip Free
3 cups (6 small) cored,
unpeeled, and chopped
Red Delicious apples

In a large bowl, combine dry pudding mix, dry milk powder, undrained pineapple, and water. Mix well using a wire whisk. Blend in Cool Whip Free. Add apples. Mix gently to combine. Cover and refrigerate for at least 30 minutes. Gently stir again just before serving.

Each serving equals:
HE: 1 Fruit, ¼ Skim Milk, ¼ Slider, 8 Optional Calories

92 Calories, 0 gm Fat, 2 gm Protein, 21 gm Carbohydrate,
201 mg Sodium, 76 mg Calcium, 1 gm Fiber

DIABETIC: 1 Fruit, ½ Starch/Carbohydrate

Three-Cheese Pizza Roll-Ups

■ ■ ■ ❋ ■ ■ ■

Serves 8

1 (8-ounce) can Pillsbury
Reduced Fat Crescent
Rolls
1 cup (one 8-ounce can)
Hunt's Tomato Sauce
1 teaspoon dried onion
flakes
1 teaspoon pizza or Italian
seasoning
1 teaspoon Sugar Twin or
Sprinkle Sweet

¼ cup (¾ ounce) grated
Kraft fat-free Parmesan
cheese
Full ½ cup (2¼ ounces)
shredded Kraft reduced-
fat Cheddar cheese
¾ cup (3 ounces) shredded
Kraft reduced-fat
mozzarella cheese

Preheat oven to 375 degrees. Spray a baking sheet with olive oil–flavored cooking spray. Unroll crescent rolls and press perforations together between the triangles to form 4 rectangles. In a medium bowl, combine tomato sauce, onion flakes, pizza seasoning, Sugar Twin, and Parmesan cheese. Add Cheddar cheese and mozzarella cheese. Mix well to combine. Evenly divide mixture among the 4 rectangles, spreading to within 1 inch of edges. Roll each rectangle up jelly-roll fashion, starting with long side. Seal edges. Cut each in half and place seam-side down on prepared baking sheet. Bake for 12 to 15 minutes or until golden brown.

Each serving equals:
HE: 1 Bread, 1 Protein, ½ Vegetable

---

168 Calories, 8 gm Fat, 8 gm Protein, 16 gm Carbohydrate,
633 mg Sodium, 129 mg Calcium, 1 gm Fiber

DIABETIC: 1 Starch, 1 Meat, ½ Vegetable

Peanut Butter Cup Pie

■ ■ ■ ■ ■ ■ ■ ■ ■

Serves 8

1 (4-serving) package
JELL-O sugar-free
instant vanilla pudding
mix
1⅓ cups Carnation Nonfat
Dry Milk Powder ☆
2 cups water ☆
6 tablespoons Peter Pan
reduced-fat creamy
peanut butter

¼ cup Cool Whip Free
1 (6-ounce) Keebler
chocolate piecrust
1 (4-serving) package
JELL-O sugar-free
instant chocolate fudge
pudding mix
1 tablespoon (¼ ounce)
finely chopped dry-
roasted peanuts

In a medium bowl, combine dry vanilla pudding mix, ⅔ cup dry milk powder, and 1 cup water. Mix well using a wire whisk. Blend in peanut butter and Cool Whip Free. Mix well with a wire whisk until smooth. Spread pudding mixture into piecrust. In the same medium bowl, combine dry chocolate fudge pudding mix, remaining ⅔ cup dry milk powder, and remaining 1 cup water. Mix well using a wire whisk. Spread chocolate mixture evenly over peanut butter mixture. Sprinkle chopped peanuts evenly over top. Refrigerate for at least 1 hour. Cut into 8 servings.

Each serving equals:
HE: ¾ Protein, ¾ Fat, ½ Bread, ½ Skim Milk, 1 Slider, 8 Optional Calories

258 Calories, 10 gm Fat, 9 gm Protein, 33 gm Carbohydrate, 550 mg Sodium, 140 mg Calcium, 1 gm Fiber

DIABETIC: 2 Starch/Carbohydrate, 1 Fat, ½ Meat

Chill-Out Orange Dew Shakes

∎ ∎ ∎ ∎ ∎ ∎ ∎ ∎

Serves 8 (full ¾ cup)

2 cups unsweetened orange
   juice
2 cups Diet Mountain
   Dew
1 (4-serving) package

JELL-O sugar-free orange
   gelatin
4 cups Wells' Blue Bunny
   sugar- and fat-free
   vanilla ice cream

In a blender container, combine orange juice, Diet Mountain
Dew, and dry gelatin. Cover and process on BLEND for 10
seconds. Add ice cream. Re-cover and continue to process on
BLEND for 15 to 20 seconds or until mixture is smooth. Pour
into tall glasses and serve at once.

HINT: If you can't find Wells' Blue Bunny, use any sugar- and
fat-free ice cream.

Each serving equals:
HE: ½ Fruit, ¾ Slider, 5 Optional Calories

116 Calories, 0 gm Fat, 5 gm Protein, 24 gm Carbohydrate,
85 mg Sodium, 125 mg Calcium, 0 gm Fiber

DIABETIC: 1 Starch, ½ Fruit

Mother's Day Brunch

For everything she does, and for all the things she is, why not surprise her with this delicious family feast? These recipes are easy enough for Dad and the kids to fix without destroying the kitchen, and Mom is sure to be dazzled by such tasty fare as two colorful salads, irresistible chicken, and scrumptious potatoes, topped off by a cheesecake that's tart and terrific. She'll definitely be touched by your loving efforts!

Mom's Creamy Vegetable Slaw

■ ■ ■ ■ ■ ■ ■

Serves 8 (½ cup)

⅔ cup Kraft fat-free
  mayonnaise
1 teaspoon lemon juice
Sugar substitute to equal 2
  teaspoons sugar
⅛ teaspoon black pepper

3 cups purchased coleslaw
  mix
1½ cups chopped fresh
  broccoli
½ cup finely chopped red
  onion

In a large bowl, combine mayonnaise, lemon juice, sugar substitute, and black pepper. Stir in coleslaw mix, broccoli, and onion. Mix well to combine. Cover and refrigerate for at least 30 minutes. Gently stir again just before serving.

HINT: 2½ cups shredded cabbage and ½ cup shredded carrots may be used in place of purchased coleslaw mix.

Each serving equals:
HE: 1¼ Vegetable, 14 Optional Calories

32 Calories, 0 gm Fat, 1 gm Protein, 7 gm Carbohydrate,
184 mg Sodium, 22 mg Calcium, 1 gm Fiber

DIABETIC: 1 Vegetable

Frosted Apricot-Pineapple Salad

■ ■ ■ ■ ■ ■ ■ ■

Serves 8

1 (4-serving) package
  JELL-O sugar-free
  orange gelatin
1 cup boiling water
2 cups (one 16-ounce can)
  apricot halves packed in
  fruit juice, drained, and
  ½ cup liquid reserved
2 cups (two 8-ounce cans)
  pineapple tidbits,

packed in fruit juice,
  drained, and ½ cup
  liquid reserved ☆
1 cup water
1 (4-serving) package
  JELL-O sugar-free
  vanilla cook-and-serve
  pudding mix
1 cup Cool Whip Free

In a large bowl, combine dry gelatin and boiling water. Mix well to dissolve gelatin. Pour ½ cup apricot juice and ¼ cup pineapple juice into gelatin mixture, stirring well. Reserve remaining juice. Coarsely chop apricots. Fold apricots and pineapple into gelatin mixture. Pour into an 8-by-8-inch dish. Refrigerate for 2 hours or until mixture is firm. In a medium saucepan, combine remaining ¼ cup pineapple juice, water, and dry pudding mix. Cook over medium heat until mixture thickens and starts to boil, stirring constantly. Remove from heat. Cool completely. Blend in Cool Whip Free. Spread mixture evenly over set gelatin. Refrigerate for at least 30 minutes. Cut into 8 servings.

◯ **HINT:** If you can't find tidbits, use chunk pineapple and coarsely chop.

Each serving equals:
HE: 1 Fruit, ¼ Slider, 10 Optional Calories

100 Calories, 0 gm Fat, 1 gm Protein, 24 gm Carbohydrate, 93 mg Sodium, 16 mg Calcium, 1 gm Fiber

DIABETIC: 1 Fruit, ½ Starch/Carbohydrate

Jiffy Scalloped Potatoes

■ ■ ■ ■ ■ ■ ■ ■ ■

Serves 8

6 cups (20 ounces)
    shredded loose-packed
    frozen potatoes
1 tablespoon dried onion
    flakes
¾ cup (3 ounces) shredded
    Kraft reduced-fat
    Cheddar cheese

¼ teaspoon black pepper
1 (10¾-ounce) can
    Healthy Request Cream
    of Celery Soup
½ cup skim milk

Preheat oven to 375 degrees. Spray an 8-by-8-inch baking dish with butter-flavored cooking spray. In a large bowl, combine potatoes, onion flakes, Cheddar cheese, and black pepper. Add celery soup and skim milk. Mix well to combine. Spread mixture into prepared baking dish. Bake for 30 minutes. Place baking dish on a wire rack and let set for 5 minutes. Divide into 8 servings.

HINT: Mr. Dell's frozen shredded potatoes are a good choice.

Each serving equals:
HE: ½ Bread, ½ Protein, ¼ Slider, 6 Optional Calories

111 Calories, 3 gm Fat, 5 gm Protein, 16 gm Carbohydrate,
255 mg Sodium, 122 mg Calcium, 2 gm Fiber

DIABETIC: 1½ Starch/Carbohydrate, ½ Meat

Magnificent Baked Chicken

■ ■ ■ ■ ■ ■ ■ ■

Serves 8

1 cup Kraft fat-free
mayonnaise
¼ cup Dijon mustard
2 teaspoons dried parsley
flakes
¼ cup (¾ ounce) grated
Kraft fat-free Parmesan
cheese

32 ounces skinned and
boned uncooked chicken
breasts, cut into 8 pieces
4 cups (4½ ounces)
crushed cornflakes

Preheat oven to 400 degrees. Spray a 9-by-13-inch baking dish with butter-flavored cooking spray. In a medium bowl, combine mayonnaise, mustard, parsley flakes, and Parmesan cheese. Coat chicken pieces in mayonnaise mixture, then roll in cornflake crumbs. Arrange chicken pieces in prepared baking dish. Bake for 30 minutes. Place baking dish on a wire rack and let set for 5 minutes.

HINT: A self-seal sandwich bag works great for crushing cornflakes.

Each serving equals:
HE: 3 Protein, ¾ Bread, ¼ Slider, 8 Optional Calories

222 Calories, 2 gm Fat, 29 gm Protein, 22 gm Carbohydrate, 574 mg Sodium, 15 mg Calcium, 1 gm Fiber

DIABETIC: 3 Meat, 1½ Starch

Luscious Lemon Cheesecake

■■■■■■■■■

Serves 8

2 (8-ounce) packages
Philadelphia fat-free
cream cheese
1 (4-serving) package
JELL-O sugar-free
instant vanilla pudding
mix
1 (4-serving) package
JELL-O sugar-free
lemon gelatin
⅔ cup Carnation Nonfat
Dry Milk Powder

1 cup Diet Mountain Dew
¾ cup Cool Whip Free ☆
1 (6-ounce) Keebler
graham cracker piecrust
2 tablespoons purchased
graham cracker crumbs
or 2 (2½-inch) graham
cracker squares, made
into crumbs

In a large bowl, stir cream cheese with a spoon until soft. Add dry pudding mix, dry gelatin, dry milk powder, and Diet Mountain Dew. Mix well using a wire whisk. Blend in ¼ cup Cool Whip Free. Spread mixture evenly into piecrust. Evenly sprinkle graham cracker crumbs over top. Refrigerate for at least 1 hour. Cut into 8 servings. When serving, top each piece with 1 tablespoon Cool Whip Free.

ⓗHINT: A self-seal sandwich bag works great for crushing graham crackers.

Each serving equals:
HE: 1 Protein, ½ Bread, ¼ Skim Milk, 1 Slider, 6 Optional Calories

197 Calories, 5 gm Fat, 12 gm Protein, 26 gm Carbohydrate,
706 mg Sodium, 70 mg Calcium, 1 gm Fiber

DIABETIC: 1½ Starch/Carbohydrate, 1 Meat, 1 Fat

Father's Day Picnic

On Dad's special day, there's no more wonderful tribute than a family picnic by his favorite river or lake—and the foods he loves best! Here's a menu that's a true man-pleaser: a classic coleslaw, a scalloped corn dish no man can resist, a perfect potato salad, my version of healthy bacon cheeseburgers, and to remind him just how much you love him, a delicious cake topped with rich chocolate. It's a super way to celebrate the man who's always been there for you!

Dad's Favorite Coleslaw

■ ■ ■ ■ ■ ■ ■ ■ ■

Serves 6 (²⁄₃ cup)

½ cup Kraft fat-free
  mayonnaise
¼ cup Land O Lakes no-
  fat sour cream
2 teaspoons dried onion
  flakes
2 teaspoons dried parsley
  flakes

Sugar substitute to equal 2
  teaspoons sugar
1 tablespoon Dijon
  Country Style mustard
4 cups purchased coleslaw
  mix
½ cup finely diced celery

In a large bowl, combine mayonnaise, sour cream, onion flakes, parsley flakes, sugar substitute, and mustard. Add coleslaw mix and celery. Mix well to combine. Cover and refrigerate for at least 30 minutes. Gently stir again just before serving.

HINT: 3¼ cups shredded cabbage and ¾ cup shredded carrots may be used in place of purchased coleslaw mix.

Each serving equals:
HE: 1½ Vegetable, ¼ Slider, 4 Optional Calories

44 Calories, 0 gm Fat, 2 gm Protein, 9 gm Carbohydrate, 326 mg Sodium, 41 mg Calcium, 1 gm Fiber

DIABETIC: 1 Vegetable, ½ Starch/Carbohydrate

Baked Scalloped Corn

■ ■ ■ ■ ■ ■ ■ ■

Serves 6

2 cups (one 16-ounce can)
 cream-style corn ☆
3 tablespoons all-purpose
 flour ☆
⅓ cup (1½ ounces)
 shredded Kraft reduced-
 fat Cheddar cheese ☆

6 small fat-free saltine
 crackers, crushed ☆
¼ cup (¾ ounce) grated
 Kraft fat-free Parmesan
 cheese ☆
¼ cup skim milk

Preheat oven to 350 degrees. Spread half of corn into an
8-by-8-inch baking dish. Sprinkle half of flour over top. Layer
half of Cheddar cheese over flour. Sprinkle half of cracker
crumbs over cheese. Top with half of Parmesan cheese. Repeat
layers. Evenly pour skim milk over top. Bake for 1 hour. Divide
into 6 servings.

HINT: A self-seal sandwich bag works great for crushing
crackers.

Each serving equals:
HE: 1 Bread, ½ Protein, 4 Optional Calories

130 Calories, 2 gm Fat, 4 gm Protein, 24 gm Carbohydrate,
420 mg Sodium, 64 mg Calcium, 2 gm Fiber

DIABETIC: 1½ Starch/Carbohydrate, ½ Meat

Classic Picnic Potato Salad

■ ■ ■ ■ ■ ■ ■ ■

Serves 6 (⅔ cup)

⅔ cup Kraft fat-free
  mayonnaise
2 teaspoons prepared
  mustard
¼ cup sweet pickle relish
⅛ teaspoon black pepper
3 full cups (16 ounces)

diced cold cooked potatoes
¾ cup diced celery
¼ cup chopped onion
2 hard-boiled eggs,
  coarsely chopped

In a large bowl, combine mayonnaise, mustard, pickle relish, and black pepper. Add potatoes, celery, and onion. Mix well to combine. Fold in eggs. Cover and refrigerate for at least 1 hour. Gently stir again just before serving.

Each serving equals:
HE: ⅔ Bread, ⅓ Vegetable, ⅓ Protein (limited), ¼ Slider, 8 Optional Calories

106 Calories, 2 gm Fat, 3 gm Protein, 19 gm Carbohydrate, 361 mg Sodium, 24 mg Calcium, 1 gm Fiber

DIABETIC: 1 Starch/Carbohydrate

Bacon Cheeseburger Patties

███████████

Serves 6

16 ounces ground 90% lean
    turkey or beef
¼ cup Hormel Bacon Bits
⅓ cup (1½ ounces)
    shredded Kraft reduced-
    fat Cheddar cheese
6 tablespoons (1½ ounces)
    dried fine bread crumbs

2 tablespoons Heinz Light
    Harvest or any reduced-
    sodium ketchup
¼ cup water
6 reduced-calorie
    hamburger buns

In a large bowl, combine meat, bacon bits, Cheddar cheese, bread crumbs, ketchup, and water. Mix well to combine. Using a ⅓-cup measuring cup as a guide, form into 6 patties. Place patties on a grill or a large skillet sprayed with butter-flavored cooking spray. Brown 4 to 5 minutes on each side or until to desired doneness. For each sandwich, place 1 browned patty between a bun.

Each serving equals:
HE: 2⅓ Protein, 1⅓ Bread, ¼ Slider, 2 Optional Calories

232 Calories, 8 gm Fat, 20 gm Protein, 20 gm Carbohydrate, 547 mg Sodium, 61 mg Calcium, 1 gm Fiber

DIABETIC: 2½ Meat, 1 Starch

White Cake with Chocolate-Walnut Topping

■ ■ ■ ■ ■ ■ ■ ■

Serves 8

1½ cups Bisquick Reduced
    Fat Baking Mix
½ cup Sugar Twin or
    Sprinkle Sweet
⅓ cup Carnation Nonfat
    Dry Milk Powder
¾ cup water
2 tablespoons vegetable oil
1 egg or equivalent in egg
    substitute

1 teaspoon vanilla extract
1 (4-serving) package
    JELL-O sugar-free
    instant chocolate
    pudding mix
1½ cups (one 12-fluid-
    ounce can) Carnation
    Evaporated Skim Milk
¼ cup (1 ounce) chopped
    walnuts

Preheat oven to 350 degrees. Spray a 9-by-9-inch cake pan with butter-flavored cooking spray. In a medium bowl, combine baking mix, Sugar Twin, and dry milk powder. In a small bowl, combine water, vegetable oil, egg, and vanilla extract. Add water mixture to baking mix mixture. Mix well to combine. Pour batter into prepared baking dish. Bake for 25 to 30 minutes or until a toothpick inserted in center comes out clean. Place cake pan on a wire rack and allow to cool. In a medium bowl, combine dry pudding mix and evaporated skim milk. Mix well using a wire whisk. Stir in walnuts. Spread mixture evenly over cooled cake. Refrigerate for at least 15 minutes. Cut into 8 servings. Refrigerate leftovers.

Each serving equals:
HE: 1 Bread, 1 Fat, ½ Skim Milk, ¼ Protein, ¼ Slider, 1 Optional Calorie

216 Calories, 8 gm Fat, 8 gm Protein, 28 gm Carbohydrate, 505 mg Sodium, 198 mg Calcium, 0 gm Fiber

DIABETIC: 2 Starch/Carbohydrate, 1 Fat

Grandparents' Appreciation Dinner

Even if you've told them dozens of time how much you're grateful for their love and guidance, why not plan a special dinner to bring the whole family together to say it again? Here's a menu inspired by all those classic comfort foods like Grandma used to make (and Grandpa always loved!): an old-fashioned relish salad made newly healthy, a pretty veggie side dish full of good-for-you taste, a creamy and cozy entree that warms the heart as well as the tummy, a crumb pie that recalls happy childhood times, and a lemonade punch as good as the one you remember sipping on her front porch. Share your joy and a good meal together—what could be better than that?

Grandma's Perfection Relish Salad

■ ■ ■ ■ ■ ■ ■ ■

Serves 8

1 (4-serving) package
  JELL-O sugar-free
  lemon gelatin
1 cup hot water
¾ cup cold water
1½ cups finely chopped
  cabbage
¾ cup shredded carrots
¾ cup finely chopped
  celery

1 teaspoon dried onion
  flakes
1 teaspoon dried parsley
  flakes
⅔ cup Kraft fat-free
  mayonnaise
1 teaspoon lemon juice
Sugar substitute to equal 2
  teaspoons sugar

In a large bowl, combine dry gelatin and hot water. Mix well to
dissolve gelatin. Stir in cold water. Add cabbage, carrots, celery,
onion flakes, and parsley flakes. Mix well to combine. Pour
mixture into an 8-by-8-inch glass dish. Refrigerate until firm,
about 3 hours. Cut into 8 servings. In a small bowl, combine
mayonnaise, lemon juice, and sugar substitute. When serving,
top each piece with a full tablespoon of mayonnaise mixture.

Each serving equals:
HE: ¾ Vegetable, 19 Optional Calories

24 Calories, 0 gm Fat, 1 gm Protein, 5 gm Carbohydrate,
214 mg Sodium, 16 mg Calcium, 1 gm Fiber

DIABETIC: 1 Vegetable

Simmered Carrots

Serves 8 (scant ½ cup)

¼ cup hot water
1 teaspoon lemon pepper
1 teaspoon dried onion
  flakes
1 teaspoon dried parsley
  flakes

4 cups (two 16-ounce cans)
  sliced carrots, rinsed
  and drained

In a medium saucepan, combine water, lemon pepper, onion flakes, and parsley flakes. Stir in carrots. Simmer for 10 minutes or until mixture is heated through and most of liquid is absorbed, stirring occasionally.

Each serving equals:
HE: 1 Vegetable

16 Calories, 0 gm Fat, 0 gm Protein, 4 gm Carbohydrate,
31 mg Sodium, 20 mg Calcium, 1 gm Fiber

DIABETIC: 1 Vegetable

Creamed Peas and Ham
on Potato Mounds

■ ■ ■ ■ ❄ ■ ■ ■ ■

Serves 8

3 cups (two 12-fluid-ounce
  cans) Carnation
  Evaporated Skim Milk
6 tablespoons all-purpose
  flour
1 cup frozen peas, thawed
2 full cups (12 ounces)
  finely diced Dubuque
  97% fat-free ham or any
  extra-lean ham

¼ teaspoon lemon pepper
3½ cups hot water
2⅔ cups (6 ounces) instant
  potato flakes
⅔ cup Carnation Nonfat
  Dry Milk Powder
2 teaspoons dried parsley
  flakes

In a large covered jar, combine evaporated skim milk and flour.
Shake well to blend. Pour into a large skillet sprayed with
butter-flavored cooking spray. Add peas, ham, and lemon pepper. Mix well to combine. Cook over medium heat until mixture starts to thicken, stirring often. Lower heat and simmer.
Meanwhile, in a large saucepan, bring water to a boil. Remove
from heat. Stir in potato flakes, dry milk powder, and parsley
flakes. For each serving, mound about ½ cup potato mixture on
a serving plate and spoon about ¾ cup pea mixture over top.

HINT: Thaw peas by placing in a colander and rinsing under
hot water for one minute.

Each serving equals:
HE: 1½ Bread, 1 Skim Milk, 1 Protein

169 Calories, 1 gm Fat, 14 gm Protein, 26 gm Carbohydrate,
315 mg Sodium, 320 mg Calcium, 2 gm Fiber

DIABETIC: 1½ Starch, 1 Skim Milk, 1 Meat

Grandpa's Apple Maple Crumb Pie

■ ■ ■ ■ ■ ■ ■

Serves 8

1 Pillsbury refrigerated
   unbaked 9-inch piecrust
1 (4-serving) package
   JELL-O sugar-free
   vanilla cook-and-serve
   pudding mix
1 cup unsweetened apple
   juice
1 teaspoon apple pie spice
3 cups (6 small) cored,

unpeeled, and chopped
   cooking apples
¾ cup Bisquick Reduced
   Fat Baking Mix
¼ cup Sugar Twin or
   Sprinkle Sweet
¼ cup (1 ounce) chopped
   walnuts
1 tablespoon Cary's Sugar
   Free Maple Syrup

Preheat oven to 425 degrees. Place piecrust in a deep-dish 9-inch pie plate. Flute edges and prick bottom and sides with the tines of a fork. In a large saucepan, combine dry pudding mix, apple juice, and apple pie spice. Stir in apples. Cook over medium heat until mixture thickens and starts to boil. Spoon hot mixture into prepared piecrust. In a medium bowl, combine baking mix, Sugar Twin, and walnuts. Add maple syrup. Mix gently until crumbly. Evenly sprinkle crumb mixture over apples. Bake for 10 minutes. Reduce heat to 350 degrees and continue baking for 30 minutes. Place pie plate on a wire rack and allow to cool. Cut into 8 servings.

Each serving equals:
HE: 1 Bread, 1 Fruit, ¼ Fat, ¾ Slider, 12 Optional Calories

215 Calories, 9 gm Fat, 2 gm Protein, 34 gm Carbohydrate, 294 mg Sodium, 18 mg Calcium, 1 gm Fiber

DIABETIC: 1 Starch/Carbohydrate, 1 Fat, 1 Fruit

Lemonade Slush Punch

■ ■ ■ ■ ❄ ■ ■ ■ ■

Serves 8 (¾ cup)

**6 cups cold Diet Mountain
  Dew** ☆
**1 tub Crystal Light
  lemonade**

**¼ of lemon, with skin and
  seeds**
2 cups ice cubes
8 maraschino cherries

In a blender container, combine 2 cups Diet Mountain Dew,
dry Crystal Light, and lemon. Cover and process on BLEND
for 60 seconds. Add ice cubes. Re-cover and process on
BLEND until ice is crushed. In a pitcher, combine remaining
Diet Mountain Dew and blended mixture. Mix gently to combine. Pour into glasses and garnish each glass with a maraschino cherry. Serve at once.

Each serving equals:
HE: 10 Optional Calories

---

16 Calories, 0 gm Fat, 0 gm Protein, 4 gm Carbohydrate,
19 mg Sodium, 0 mg Calcium, 0 gm Fiber

DIABETIC: 1 Free Food

The Tiny-Tot Top Ten

■ ■ ■ ■ ■ ■ ■ ■

*E*very recipe in this book was chosen for its appeal to young appetites (though of course many grown-ups never really "grow up" when it comes to favorite foods!). I've decided to feature what I call "The Tiny-Tot Top Ten" in this final section. "Voted" on by the children we feed at the local DeWitt, Iowa, day-care centers as well as young visitors to JO's Kitchen Cafe, these are my award winners—the most popular and welcomed dishes we've served to the younger set!

As you glance through the section, you'll see immediately that our kids love pasta and potatoes in all kinds of sauces. They enjoy finding favorite vegetables like green beans mixed in. And they adore creamy, cheesy, and cozy casseroles that fill their little tummies until they can't eat another bite!

Maybe, after you've been using the recipes in this book for a while, you'll decide to hold your own vote. Whatever the Top Ten in your house turn out to be, the real winners are your children, who are eating healthy—and happy about it!

The Tiny-Tot Top Ten

■ ■ ■ ■ ■ ■ ■ ■

Cowpoke Western Scramble

Zach's Fettuccine and Green Beans

Super Special Chicken

Company's Coming Tetrazzini

Grandma's Special Spaghetti

Junior Pizza Casserole

Kids Business Cavatini

Josh's Potato Ham Bake

Little Ones' Southern Sweet-and-Sour Ham

Ham and Noodles in Cream Sauce

Cowpoke Western Scramble

■ ■ ■ ■ ■ ■ ■ ■ ■

This skillet dish will round 'em up and fill 'em full! It's so easy, even the kids and Dad can stir it up before an early-morning fishing trip. You'll be pleased at how much flavor the lemon pepper adds. *Serves 4*

4 eggs or equivalent in egg substitute
2 tablespoons skim milk
½ teaspoon lemon pepper
2 teaspoons reduced-calorie margarine
½ cup (3 ounces) diced

Dubuque 97% fat-free ham or any extra-lean ham
¾ cup (3 ounces) shredded Kraft reduced-fat Cheddar cheese

In a medium bowl, combine eggs, skim milk, and lemon pepper. In a large skillet sprayed with butter-flavored cooking spray, melt margarine. Stir in ham. Add egg mixture. Mix well to combine. Cook over medium-low heat until eggs are almost set, stirring occasionally. Sprinkle Cheddar cheese over top. Cover and continue cooking for 1 to 2 minutes or until cheese starts to melt. Divide into 4 wedges. Serve at once.

Each serving equals:
HE: 2½ Protein (1 limited), ¼ Fat, 3 Optional Calories

157 Calories, 9 gm Fat, 15 gm Protein, 4 gm Carbohydrate, 434 mg Sodium, 174 mg Calcium, 0 gm Fiber

DIABETIC: 2 Meat

Zach's Fettuccine and Green Beans

■ ■ ■ ❄ ■ ■ ■

This quick-fix pasta dish was inspired by my adorable grand-baby Zach, who is always ready to enjoy one of Granny Jo's creamy noodle concoctions. It's a great choice for a crowd and easily can be doubled or tripled when the soccer team is coming for lunch after practice! *Serves 4 (1 cup)*

⅓ cup Carnation Nonfat
  Dry Milk Powder
1 cup water
1 teaspoon dried parsley
  flakes
2 teaspoons reduced-
  calorie margarine
½ cup (1½ ounces) grated

Kraft fat-free Parmesan
  cheese
2 cups hot cooked
  fettuccine, rinsed and
  drained
1 cup (one 8-ounce can)
  cut green beans, rinsed
  and drained

In a small bowl, combine dry milk powder, water, and parsley flakes. Pour mixture into a large skillet sprayed with butter-flavored cooking spray. Add margarine and Parmesan cheese. Mix well to combine. Stir in fettuccine and green beans. Lower heat and simmer for 5 to 6 minutes or until mixture is heated through, stirring often. Serve at once.

HINT: 1½ cups broken uncooked fettuccine usually cooks to about 2 cups.

Each serving equals:
HE: 1 Bread, ½ Protein, ½ Vegetable, ¼ Skim Milk, ¼ Fat

169 Calories, 1 gm Fat, 7 gm Protein, 33 gm Carbohydrate, 267 mg Sodium, 84 mg Calcium, 3 gm Fiber

DIABETIC: 1½ Starch, ½ Protein, ½ Vegetable

Super Special Chicken

■ ■ ■ ■ ❄ ■ ■ ■ ■

$\mathcal{B}$esides being a top-ten toddler choice, this wonderful dish is a headliner at JO's Kitchen Cafe! I promise that everyone will want to know the ingredients in your "secret sauce"—wait and see! ***Serves 4***

16 ounces skinned and
   boned uncooked chicken
   breasts, cut into 4 pieces
½ cup Kraft Fat Free
   French Dressing
¼ cup Heinz Light
   Harvest Ketchup or any
   reduced-sodium ketchup

1 teaspoon chili seasoning
2 teaspoons dried onion
   flakes
1 teaspoon dried parsley
   flakes

Preheat oven to 350 degrees. Spray an 8-by-8-inch baking dish with butter-flavored cooking spray. Evenly arrange chicken pieces in prepared baking dish. In a small bowl, combine French dressing, ketchup, chili seasoning, onion flakes, and parsley flakes. Evenly spoon dressing mixture over chicken. Cover and bake for 30 minutes. Uncover and continue baking for 15 minutes. When serving, evenly spoon sauce over top.

Each serving equals:
HE: 3 Protein, ¾ Slider, 5 Optional Calories

182 Calories, 2 gm Fat, 26 gm Protein, 15 gm Carbohydrate, 489 mg Sodium, 16 mg Calcium, 0 gm Fiber

DIABETIC: 3 Meat, 1 Starch/Carbohydrate

Company's Coming Tetrazzini

■■■■ ✳ ■■■■

Turkey tetrazzini is a great crowd-pleasing dish for any family occasion, and this variation is especially delectable. Whether you're feeding 20 four-year-olds or inviting your sisters over for Sunday supper, this easy skillet dish is just about perfect!

Serves 4 (1 cup)

½ cup finely chopped onion
1½ cups (8 ounces) diced cooked turkey breast
1 (10¾-ounce) can Healthy Request Cream of Chicken Soup
⅓ cup Carnation Nonfat Dry Milk Powder
⅓ cup water
¾ cup (3 ounces) shredded Kraft reduced-fat Cheddar cheese

¼ cup (one 2-ounce jar) chopped pimiento, drained
1 teaspoon dried parsley flakes
⅛ teaspoon black pepper
2 cups hot cooked spaghetti, rinsed and drained

In a large skillet sprayed with butter-flavored cooking spray, sauté onion and turkey for 5 minutes. In a small bowl, combine chicken soup, dry milk powder, and water. Stir soup mixture into turkey mixture. Add Cheddar cheese, pimiento, parsley flakes, and black pepper. Mix well to combine. Stir in spaghetti. Lower heat and simmer for 10 minutes, stirring occasionally.

HINTS:
1. If you don't have leftovers, purchase a chunk of cooked turkey breast from your local deli.
2. 1½ cups broken uncooked spaghetti usually cooks to about 2 cups.

Grandma's Special Spaghetti

■ ■ ■ ■ ❄ ■ ■ ■ ■

I love cooking for my grandbabies whenever they come to visit, but I don't want to spend all my time in the kitchen when we can be outside walking or working in my garden. This quick-and-cozy dish is a favorite of Zach's and Joshie's; why not try it on your nearest and dearest? *Serves 4 (1 full cup)*

8 ounces ground 90% lean turkey or beef
1¾ cups (one 15-ounce can) Hunt's Chunky Tomato Sauce
1 (10¾-ounce) can Healthy Request Cream of Mushroom Soup
1 teaspoon Italian seasoning
1 tablespoon Sugar Twin or Sprinkle Sweet
⅓ cup Carnation Nonfat Dry Milk Powder
¼ cup (¾ ounce) grated Kraft fat-free Parmesan cheese
2 cups hot cooked spaghetti, rinsed and drained

In a large skillet sprayed with butter-flavored cooking spray, brown meat. In a medium bowl, combine tomato sauce, mushroom soup, Italian seasoning, Sugar Twin, dry milk powder, and Parmesan cheese. Add sauce mixture to browned meat. Mix well to combine. Stir in spaghetti. Lower heat and simmer for 10 minutes, or until mixture is heated through, stirring occasionally.

HINT: 1½ cups broken uncooked spaghetti usually cooks to about 2 cups.

Each serving equals:
HE: 1¾ Protein, 1¾ Vegetable, 1 Bread, ¼ Skim Milk, ½ Slider, 1 Optional Calorie

291 Calories, 7 gm Fat, 18 gm Protein, 39 gm Carbohydrate, 1197 mg Sodium, 124 mg Calcium, 3 gm Fiber

DIABETIC: 2 Meat, 2 Vegetable, 1½ Starch/Carbohydrate

Junior Pizza Casserole

━━ ■ ■ ■ ❋ ■ ■ ■ ━━

$\mathcal{S}$ure, it may be easy to call out for pizza, but why not please your young pizza-lovers with something a little different tonight? This has so many luscious ingredients, it's like a party in a pan! *Serves 6*

8 ounces ground 90% lean
   turkey or beef
¼ cup finely chopped onion
¼ cup finely chopped green
   bell pepper
1¾ cups (one 15-ounce
   can) Hunt's Chunky
   Tomato Sauce
¼ cup (¾ ounce) grated
   Kraft fat-free Parmesan
   cheese

1 teaspoon pizza or Italian
   seasoning
3 cups hot cooked noodles,
   rinsed and drained
1 (3-ounce) package
   Hormel reduced-fat
   sliced pepperoni,
   chopped
⅓ cup (1½ ounces)
   shredded reduced-fat
   mozzarella cheese

Preheat oven to 350 degrees. Spray an 8-by-8-inch baking dish with olive oil–flavored cooking spray. In a large skillet sprayed with olive oil–flavored cooking spray, brown meat, onion, and green pepper. Stir in tomato sauce, Parmesan cheese, and pizza seasoning. Add noodles and pepperoni. Mix well to combine. Spread mixture into prepared baking dish. Bake for 20 minutes. Evenly sprinkle mozzarella cheese over top. Continue baking for 10 minutes. Place baking dish on a wire rack and let set for 5 minutes. Divide into 6 servings.

$\mathcal{H}$INT: 2½ cups uncooked noodles usually cooks to about 3 cups.

Each serving equals:
HE: 2 Protein, 1⅓ Vegetable, 1 Bread

243 Calories, 7 gm Fat, 18 gm Protein, 27 gm Carbohydrate, 904 mg Sodium, 107 mg Calcium, 3 gm Fiber

DIABETIC: 2 Meat, 1 Vegetable, 1 Starch

Kids Business Cavatini

■ ■ ■ ■ ❄ ■ ■ ■

Pasta is a great favorite of the toddlers at Kids Business, one of DeWitt's day-care centers, so we put it on the menu often. They especially love curly rotini, which they call "funny noodles." A few of them do pick out the olive slices, so if your family doesn't love them, leave 'em out.   *Serves 4*

8 ounces ground 90% lean
   turkey or beef
1¾ cups (one 15-ounce
   can) Hunt's Chunky
   Tomato Sauce
2 teaspoons Italian
   seasoning
2 cups hot cooked rotini
   pasta, rinsed and
   drained

¼ cup (1 ounce) sliced ripe
   olives
⅓ cup (1½ ounces)
   shredded Kraft reduced-
   fat Cheddar cheese
⅓ cup (1½ ounces)
   shredded Kraft reduced-
   fat mozzarella cheese

Preheat oven to 350 degrees. Spray an 8-by-8-inch baking dish with olive oil–flavored cooking spray. In a large skillet sprayed with olive oil–flavored cooking spray, brown meat. Stir in tomato sauce and Italian seasoning. Add rotini pasta, olives, and Cheddar cheese. Mix well to combine. Spread mixture into prepared baking dish. Bake for 20 minutes. Evenly sprinkle mozzarella cheese over top. Continue baking for 10 minutes. Place baking dish on a wire rack and let set for 5 minutes. Divide into 4 servings.

HINT: 1½ cups uncooked rotini pasta usually cooks to about 2 cups.

Each serving equals:
HE: 2½ Protein, 1¾ Vegetable, 1 Bread, ¼ Fat

265 Calories, 9 gm Fat, 20 gm Protein, 26 gm Carbohydrate, 983 mg Sodium, 148 mg Calcium, 3 gm Fiber

DIABETIC: 2 Meat, 2 Vegetable, 1 Starch

Josh's Potato Ham Bake

■ ■ ■ ■ ❄ ■ ■ ■ ■

My grandson Josh is passionate about potatoes, whether they're mashed, baked, scalloped, or hash browns! I love to watch him gobble down dishes like this creamy potato casserole because he smiles with every single bite. It's enough to make a grandma get emotional!

Serves 4

1 (10¾-ounce) can
  Healthy Request Cream
  of Mushroom Soup
⅓ cup Carnation Nonfat
  Dry Milk Powder
¼ cup water
1 teaspoon prepared
  mustard
1 teaspoon dried parsley
  flakes

¼ teaspoon black pepper
4½ cups (15 ounces)
  shredded loose-packed
  frozen potatoes
1½ cups (9 ounces) diced
  Dubuque 97% fat-free
  ham or any extra-lean
  ham

Preheat oven to 350 degrees. Spray an 8-by-8-inch baking dish with butter-flavored cooking spray. In a large bowl, combine mushroom soup, dry milk powder, water, mustard, parsley flakes, and black pepper. Add potatoes and ham. Mix well to combine. Spread mixture into prepared baking dish. Cover and bake for 45 minutes. Uncover and continue baking for 15 minutes. Place baking dish on a wire rack and let set for 5 minutes. Divide into 4 servings.

HINT: Mr. Dell's frozen shredded potatoes are a good choice, or raw shredded potatoes may be used in place of frozen potatoes.

Each serving equals:
HE: 1½ Protein, ¾ Bread, ¼ Skim Milk, ½ Slider, 1 Optional Calorie

200 Calories, 4 gm Fat, 13 gm Protein, 28 gm Carbohydrate, 827 mg Sodium, 122 mg Calcium, 2 gm Fiber

DIABETIC: 2 Meat, 1½ Skim Milk/Carbohydrate

Little Ones' Southern Sweet-and-Sour Ham

■ ■ ■ ■ ■ ■ ■ ■

The fruity sauce served with these healthy ham slices is the reason some of our littlest taste testers voted this their absolute favorite! You might want to try this with peach spreadable fruit instead of apricot!

Serves 4

4 (3-ounce) slices
  Dubuque 97% fat-free
  ham or any extra-lean
  ham
2 tablespoons white
  vinegar
¼ cup apricot spreadable
  fruit spread

2 teaspoons prepared
  mustard
1 teaspoon dried onion
  flakes
1 teaspoon dried parsley
  flakes

In a large skillet sprayed with butter-flavored cooking spray, brown ham slices for about 3 minutes on each side. In a medium bowl, combine vinegar, fruit spread, mustard, onion flakes, and parsley flakes. Drizzle mixture evenly over ham slices. Lower heat, cover, and simmer for 3 to 4 minutes. Serve at once.

HINT: A 3-ounce slice of ham is usually ⅓ inch thick.

Each serving equals:
HE: 2 Protein, 1 Fruit

92 Calories, 0 gm Fat, 1 gm Protein, 22 gm Carbohydrate, 37 mg Sodium, 11 mg Calcium, 1 gm Fiber

DIABETIC: 2 Meat, 1 Fat

Ham and Noodles in Cream Sauce

■ ■ ■ ■ ❄ ■ ■ ■ ■

This luscious noodle dish overflows with good-for-you ingredients that children just seem to love. Because the ham and cheese are fat-free and the cream sauce is prepared with skim milk, it tastes decadent—but it's a terrific healthy choice.

Serves 4

1½ cups (one 12-fluid-ounce can) Carnation Evaporated Skim Milk
3 tablespoons all-purpose flour
2 teaspoons prepared mustard
1 teaspoon dried parsley flakes
¼ teaspoon black pepper
1½ cups hot cooked noodles, rinsed and drained

1 cup (one 8-ounce can) sliced green beans, rinsed and drained
1 full cup (6 ounces) diced Dubuque 97% fat-free ham or any extra-lean ham
¼ cup (¾ ounce) grated Kraft fat-free Parmesan cheese

Preheat oven to 350 degrees. Spray an 8-by-8-inch baking dish with butter-flavored cooking spray. In a covered jar, combine evaporated skim milk and flour. Shake well to blend. Pour milk mixture into a large saucepan sprayed with butter-flavored cooking spray. Cook over medium heat until mixture starts to thicken, stirring often. Stir in mustard, parsley flakes, and black pepper. Add noodles, green beans, ham, and Parmesan cheese. Mix well to combine. Spread mixture into prepared baking dish. Bake for 25 to 30 minutes. Place baking dish on a wire rack and let set for 5 minutes. Divide into 4 servings.

HINT: 1¼ cups uncooked noodles usually cooks to about 1½ cups.

Each serving equals:

HE: 1¼ Protein, 1 Bread, ¾ Skim Milk, ½ Vegetable

251 Calories, 3 gm Fat, 19 gm Protein, 37 gm Carbohydrate,
621 mg Sodium, 299 mg Calcium, 2 gm Fiber

DIABETIC: 1½ Meat, 1½ Starch/Carbohydrate, 1 Skim Milk,
½ Vegetable

Making Healthy Exchanges Recipes Work for You

■ ■ ■ ■ ■ ■ ■ ■

You're ready now to begin a wonderful journey to better health. In the preceding pages, you've discovered the remarkable variety of good food available to you when you begin eating the Healthy Exchanges way. You've stocked your pantry and learned many of my food preparation "secrets" that will start you on the way to delicious success.

But before I let you go, I'd like to share a few tips that I've learned while traveling toward healthier eating habits. It took me a long time to learn how to eat *smarter*. In fact, I'm still working on it. But I am getting better. For years, I could *inhale* a five-course meal in five minutes flat—and still make room for a second helping of dessert!

Now I follow certain signposts on the road that help me stay on the right path. I hope these ideas will help point you in the right direction as well.

1. **Eat slowly** so your brain has time to catch up with your tummy. Cut and chew each bite slowly. Try putting your fork down between bites. Stop eating as soon as you feel full. Crumple your napkin and throw it on top of your plate so you don't continue to eat when you are no longer hungry.

2. **Smaller plates** may help you feel more satisfied by your food portions *and* limit the amount you can put on the plate.

3. **Watch portion size.** If you are *truly* hungry, you can always add more food to your plate once you've finished your initial serving. But remember to count the additional food accordingly.

4. **Always eat at your dining room or kitchen table.** You deserve better than nibbling from an open refrigerator or over the sink. Make an attractive place setting, even if you're eating alone. Feed your eyes as well as your stomach. By always eating at a table, you will become much more aware of your true food intake. For some reason, many of us conveniently "forget" the food we swallow while standing over the stove or munching in the car or on the run.

5. **Avoid doing anything else while you are eating.** If you read the paper or watch television while you eat, it's easy to consume too much food without realizing it, because you are concentrating on something else besides what you're eating. Then, when you look down at your plate and see that it's empty, you wonder where all the food went and why you still feel hungry.

Day by day, as you travel the path to good health, it will become easier to make the right choices, to eat *smarter*. But don't ever fool yourself into thinking that you'll be able to put your eating habits on cruise control and forget about them. Making a commitment to eat good healthy food and sticking to it takes some effort. But with all the good-tasting recipes in this Healthy Exchanges cookbook, just think how well you're going to eat—and enjoy it—from now on!

Healthy Lean Bon Appétit!

Index

$\overset{\cdot\overset{\circ}{\smile}\cdot}{I}$ want to hear from you . . .

■ ■ ■ ■ ■ ■ ■ ■

$\mathcal{B}$esides my family, the love of my life is creating "common folk" healthy recipes and solving everyday cooking questions in *The Healthy Exchanges Way*. Everyone who uses my recipes is considered part of the Healthy Exchanges Family, so please write to me if you have any questions, comments, or suggestions. I will do my best to answer. With your support, I'll continue to stir up even more recipes and cooking tips for the Family in the years to come.

Write to: JoAnna M. Lund
c/o Healthy Exchanges, Inc.
P.O. Box 124
DeWitt, IA 52742

If you prefer, you can fax me at 1-319-659-2126 or contact me via E-mail by writing to HealthyJo@aol.com. Or visit my Healthy Exchanges Internet web site at: http://www.neta.com/~healthy

If you're ever in the DeWitt, Iowa, area, stop in and visit me at "The House That Recipes Built" and dine at **JO's Kitchen Cafe**, "Grandma's Comfort Food Made Healthy!"

JO's Kitchen™ Cafe

Grandma's Comfort Food Made Healthy!™

110 Industrial Street • DeWitt, Iowa 52742 • (319) 659-8234

Ever since I began stirring up Healthy Exchanges recipes, I wanted every dish to be rich in flavor and lively in taste. As part of my pursuit of satisfying eating and healthy living for a lifetime, I decided to create my own line of spices.

JO's Spices are salt-, sugar-, wheat-, and MSG-free, and you can substitute them in any of the recipes calling for traditional spice mixes. If you're interested in hearing more about my special blends, please call Healthy Exchanges at 1-319-659-8234 for more information or to order. If you prefer, write to JO's Spices, c/o Healthy Exchanges, P.O. Box 124, DeWitt, IA 52742.

JO'S SPICES . . . A Healthy Way to Spice Up Your Life™